MOBILE AFRICA

AFRICAN DYNAMICS

Volume 1

MOBILE AFRICA

Changing Patterns of Movement in Africa and Beyond

EDITED BY

MIRJAM DE BRUIJN, RIJK VAN DIJK,
& DICK FOEKEN

BRILL
LEIDEN · BOSTON · KÖLN
2001

This book is printed on acid-free paper.

Library of Congress Cataloging-in-Publication Data

Library of Congress Cataloging–in–Publication Data is also available

Die Deutsche Bibliothek – CIP-Einheitsaufnahme

Mobile Africa:
Edited by Mirjam de Bruijn, Rijk van Dijk & Dick Foeken. – Leiden ;
Boston ; Köln : Brill, 2001
(African Dynamics ; Vol. 1)
ISBN 90-04-12072-6

ISSN   1568-1777
ISBN   90 04 12072 6

PRINTED IN THE NETHERLANDS

Contents

Maps

Tables

Preface

This book is the first in a new series by the African Studies Centre (ASC) entitled *African Dynamics*. The history of ASC journals started in January 1961 when the first edition of *Kroniek van Afrika* ('Chronicle of Africa') saw the light of day. It was a simple publication, written in Dutch, that aimed, as was stated on the first page, "to shed more light on the important events in Africa in political, social and cultural areas". From volume 4 onwards, the *Kroniek* became more of a real journal and moved beyond being an information bulletin to contain scientific articles as well. In 1974, the *Kroniek* underwent a complete metamorphosis and became a truly scientific journal that appeared three times a year. It was entirely in English, with each issue devoted to a specific theme. The only thing that remained unaltered was its Dutch title but even this changed two years later into *African Perspectives*. Of the eight issues that appeared between 1976 and 1979, six were in English and two in French.

After a break of 22 years, *African Dynamics* is thus an attempt to give the ASC its own journal again. It was not an easy decision to take. A great deal of work is involved in compiling a journal and there is a myriad of journals on Africa nowadays. In addition, libraries find themselves in a position where they are no longer able to subscribe to all publications. For these reasons, this 'journal' will initially appear as an annual edition. Moreover, in an attempt to increase its appeal, each issue is devoted to a specific theme. In that sense, *African Dynamics* is a true successor to *African Perspectives*.

One of the objectives of the new publication is to present the results of research currently being undertaken at the ASC. It is linked to the seminar programme in the sense that the contents of each volume consist of a selection of papers that were presented at ASC seminars by both ASC staff members and researchers from elsewhere during the preceding year. Additional authors will also be invited to contribute to specific issues to ensure that each theme is comprehensively discussed from different perspectives.

The theme of this first issue of *African Dynamics* is mobility in Sub-Saharan Africa. Again, there is a link with the past as the 1978/1 issue of *African Perspectives* was devoted to migration. Today, more than twenty years later the theme has not lost any of its relevance. Most of the chapters are based on papers that were presented at an ASC seminar entitled 'Moving People: Trends in Population Mobility in Africa', which was held in Leiden on June 22 2000.

We would like to express our gratitude to a number of people. First of all we wish to thank the members of the editorial board Adebayo Olukoshi, Ruth Watson, Paul Mathieu and Piet Konings for their willingness to sit on this committee. Secondly, this volume would not have appeared without the authors who reacted so positively to our invitation to present a paper at the seminar and those who were later on willing to write a chapter for this volume. We appreciate their enthusiasm and constructive criticism.

We are grateful to Ann Reeves for correcting the English text and to Mieke Zwart who did most of the layout work. And finally, our thanks go to Nel de Vink for drawing the maps.

The Editors, July 2001

Mobile Africa: An introduction

Mirjam de Bruijn, Rijk van Dijk & Dick Foeken

Anybody who has ever boarded a city-bound bus in Sub-Saharan Africa will have had the privilege of sharing in part of a typical journey for many Africans. Crammed into an often-ramshackle vehicle is not only half the local community but also chickens, goats, agricultural produce, bicycles, suitcases, trunks, not to mention everything piled on the roof of the bus. A cross-section of the population shares the ride into town and does so for a range of reasons. Some will be trying to sell their produce at the urban market hoping for a profit, others will be visiting hospital, paying relatives a visit, attending a funeral, finding schooling, or are looking to buy goods to sell back home at a price that will cover their bus fare. The bus passes through numerous market places, is swarmed at each stop by vendors trying to sell fruit, drinks and food to the passengers, is checked at police roadblocks and is boarded by Pentecostal preachers who prophesy God's wrath upon the unbeliever. A bus is a microcosm of African life.

This metaphor of a bus ride somewhere on the African continent captures in a nutshell some of the essential ideas this book aims to address. This is not just an everyday story about migration into town but about how mobility is engrained in the history, daily life and experiences of people. In a compressed way, the bus demonstrates how mobility appears to refer to an array of forms of human behaviour, each inspired by different motives, desires, aspirations and obligations. The scope of this phenomenon as well as the enormous variety in expressions and experiences contained in this single example indicate that there is a wide field for academic study to cover if other forms of mobility are also taken into account. Not only are there many ways in which mobility is perceived and experienced by different groups, mobility itself appears in a myriad of forms. Mobility as an umbrella term encompasses all types of movement including travel, exploration, migration, tourism, refugeeism, pastoralism, nomadism, pilgrimage and trade. In these forms, mobility is essential to many, even a means of survival for some, whereas in most African societies it is often a reality that is taken for granted.

This introduction argues that mobility in its ubiquity is fundamental to any understanding of African social life. The astounding degree of mobility in Africa (see Chapter 2) makes one wonder whether it is indeed possible to understand the livelihood of large sections of the African population without taking into account the perspective of movement. To what extent does the African bus metaphor capture the ways in which

African societies survive, maintain social relations, explore opportunities and fulfil hopes and desires?

By exploring mobility on the African continent, this volume aspires to continue a long-running research interest of the African Studies Centre (ASC) marked by the start of a multi-disciplinary research project in the 1970s and that led to a major conference on issues of migration in Africa in 1977. Important insights into processes of migration from the conference were published in a edited volume for the ASC journal at that time, *African Perspectives* (1978, no. 1). Its central focus was migration: the 'geographical displacement of people'. In their introduction the editors critically discussed the then-pervasive approaches to migration; a concept mainly captured in dichotomies such as rural-urban, subsistence economy versus money economy, tradition versus modernity, and so forth. They recorded their unease with this emphasis on dichotomies, stating that: "The dualism pervading most social science approaches to migration in Africa may take too much for granted, distinctions and boundaries (conceptual, structural, political) which the ongoing transformations of Africa may render increasingly irrelevant" (Van Binsbergen & Meilink 1978: 12). It is striking that almost a quarter of a century later this problem is still evident in the way migration is perceived. Despite for instance the convincing argument of Jamal & Weeks (1988) concerning the "vanishing rural-urban gap", a great deal of migration research is even now dominated by the kind of dichotomous interpretations these editors argued against.

Recently it has been more from the side of the Cultural-Studies approach to migration that notions of cultural continuity – for instance through the introduction of concepts like 'travelling culture' or 'diaspora' – have gained headway in understanding mobility in Africa. While this angle inspired ASC research in recent years, no new multi-disciplinary effort had come up with further insights until two seminars were held in June and September 2000. They came to form the basis of this book. The adoption of the term 'mobility' instead of 'migration' in the present volume reflects this change in focus. Moving away from the neo-Marxist perspective of the late 1970s this book reflects on mobility as implying more than just movement from A to B in geographical space alone. As the metaphor of the bus indicates, a cultural perception of mobility implies a close reading of people's own understandings of the spaces and places in which they move and the experiences these movements entail.

Another crucial element of the present approach is how to move away from the interpretation of migration or mobility as a 'rupture' in society, as the result of a social system in disarray. Many forms of mobility are part of life and of making a livelihood. In some societies, *not* being mobile may be the anomaly. The extent to which people themselves perceive travel and movement as forms of breaking away from a social or ecological environment, from family and friends or from a specific cultural domain, needs to be investigated. What we argue is that sedentary, i.e. remaining within set borders or cultural boundaries, might instead be perceived as an act of escaping from social obligations. The whole notion of mobility as presented here turns the supposedly rupturing effect of travelling on its head: through travelling, connections are established, continuity experienced and modernity negotiated.

This perspective does not, however, exclude the fact that there are forms of mobility that do result in ruptures in society, and indeed serious ruptures. Africa has many refugees and their numbers have increased dramatically over the past decades. Dissolving states, interethnic strife, struggles for hegemony and control over natural and mineral resources are causing enormous hardship. This has to be dealt with, not only technically but also as a social issue affecting our own societies. The movement of people within and beyond Africa has become an issue of global concern.

The case studies in this book all critically debate dichotomous interpretations of mobility and reject the idea that migration indicates a breakdown in society. They adopt the approach that sedentary and mobile worlds converge and that mobility is part of the livelihood system of African people. Furthermore, the cases encourage the reader to pose questions about relations between individual, group and larger entities in a much broader geographical perspective. We are challenged to delve into the traveller's mind, as well as those of relatives left behind. People do not think in the bipolar models scientists have developed for them. What they do, are, and want to be unfolds through the decisions they make every day, to move or not to move. Terms like multi-spatial livelihoods, travelling cultures, mobility of forms, ideological representations of mobility, all recur in the case studies. They refer to the fact that interpretations along the lines of dichotomies are no longer our model of analysis and that indeed a new model is emerging.

This book does not try to give a complete overview of mobility in Africa but to show how recent empirical work addresses issues that present themselves in the study of the massive movements of people which are so characteristic of much of Africa. Indeed the insights gained from these empirical studies shed new light on the understanding of mobility in Africa. The different chapters present challenging views on what mobility is in contexts of scale (from the local up to the global), what mobility means for the people involved and what it may mean for our interpretation of historical and current realities. The studies of mobility here deal first of all with many forms of movement of people in geographical space; urban-rural, rural-rural movements, labour migration, nomadism and refugeeism. In addition to geographical interpretations of such forms of movement, socio-cultural interpretations are highlighted. Questions revolve around issues such as how people move within social networks, how forms of mobility go hand in hand with a mobility of social forms, how people become mobile as the result of religious conviction or seek upward social mobility, for instance through labour. Being mobile has many implications for those involved: it influences people's choices, produces specific decision-making processes and leads to the formation of certain social institutions. In short it transforms lives.

How people perceive mobility and the ways in which they give meaning to processes of social change are highlighted in some of the contributions. Several chapters deal with the 'organisation' of mobility (emerging networks, state policies, etc.) and others focus on the various aspects of the flow of mobility (i.e. the statistics and the direction that mobility takes).

The volume opens with an overview paper by *Han van Dijk, Dick Foeken & Kiky van Til* (Chapter 2). After a brief discussion of the definitional and conceptual problems related to migration, an overview of the various flows of mobility in Africa based on the available statistical data is presented. Although migration figures are not always reliable, the authors show a reality that cannot be ignored. It confirms that for millions of Africans, being mobile is part of their daily experience. Some of these modern mobility patterns may be linked to recent developments in the wider world, i.e. the opening up of the international world, but also to such negative processes as the deterioration of the ecological environment. These present-day patterns can be compared to similar processes in Africa's past, such as the slave trade, wars and ecological disasters. Furthermore, labour migration, moving with cattle and seasonal migration are realities of daily life that have specific links to modern times. The authors show that, more than ever before, Africa is indeed a continent 'on the move'.

The following three chapters explore people's own experiences of mobility, the way it is expressed and the way in which these experiences shape people's own worlds. *Todd Sanders* (Chapter 3) offers an insider's view of how one ethnic group, the Ihanzu in Tanzania, are experiencing the slow process of invasion by another group. The Ihanzu articulate their fear of their expanding neighbours in terms of witchcraft; an expression often recounted in dreams that tell of magic buses crossing their land. These buses are hard, if not impossible, to stop but it is the superior knowledge of medicine of the encroaching group that renders the Ihanzu helpless in the face of this invasion. Sanders demonstrates that different rationalities come into play in the perception of mobility and the detrimental consequences it has for a particular society. On the one hand, these rationalities speak of objective economic circumstances and ethnic conflicts, but, on the other hand, do not match with local people's ideas of the causes and consequences of mobility in terms of occult powers.

The contribution by *Marja Spierenburg* (Chapter 4) is another case in point. She deals with the kind of society in which being mobile is institutionalised in the relationships of newcomers with their hosts. In the Dande region of northern Zimbabwe it is a religious form, the territorial cult of the *Mhondoro*, that has always played a crucial role in the regulation of mobility and access to land for newcomers. This *Mhondoro* cult used to provide the ritual means by which newcomers, immigrants and strangers were granted a place in their new environment. As in Sanders's case study, however, important changes in this domain of religion, such as the exclusion of newcomers from certain *Mhondoro* rituals, signal a shift in the perception of newly arrived migrants. They are no longer as welcome as they once were.

Chapter 5 by *Mirjam de Bruijn, Han van Dijk & Rijk van Dijk* deals explicitly with the question of how the concept of mobility can be understood. They indicate firstly that forms of mobility can only be properly understood concomitant with a mobility of forms and the way these influence people's daily lives. The Ghanaian Pentecostal churches that have 'travelled along' with Ghanaian migrants have come to play a crucial role in their communities. The authors apply the term 'travelling culture', as was first introduced by Clifford (1992), to indicate the specific features of situations where forms of mobility (for instance nomadism or intercontinental migration) are combined with a mobility of social forms and institutions. Using the example of the West-African Fulbe, it is argued that some cultures should be seen as being essentially mobile and that these cultures become sedentary only by force of circumstance. A sedentary existence is not taken for granted and this opens new ways of understanding the creation of 'non-sedentary' identities. It challenges the general tendency (in studies of mobility and in policy discourses) to perceive mobility as something anomalous or as carrying a negative connotation.

The next four contributions address changing perspectives in the study of what otherwise is the 'classic' domain of mobility, namely rural-to-urban migration. Jens Andersson and Jonathan Baker each draw attention to the cultural dynamics within these much-studied mobility patterns in Africa. *Jens Andersson* (Chapter 6) shows how Zimbabweans move to town to earn a living and in the process of creating supportive social networks in fact become a travelling culture. The migrants he studied operate within social networks that link villages and cities but do not perceive a geographical space consisting only of two opposite poles: the village versus the city. Instead, the networks the migrants create allow for a continuous movement between various places, making their mobility part of their being. As *Jonathan Baker* (Chapter 7) also demonstrates in his contribution on Ethiopia, people use different spaces to generate a livelihood. Here it becomes difficult to explain the motivations behind being mobile because mobility is part of their cultural repertoire. The accepted idea that migrants leave for negative reasons does not hold in all cases. Although 'negative' push factors are present due to the detrimental economic and ecological situation in Baker's study area, the province of Welo in Ethiopia, many people move out of their own free will in the hope of giving a positive turn to their existence. Their cultural background and their optimistic perception of the outside world encourage them to move.

The contribution by *Dick Foeken & Samuel Owuor* (Chapter 8) also deals with people who have an economic foothold in town as well as in the rural area, a situation termed as multi-spatial livelihoods. They show that the majority of the inhabitants of Nakuru Town in Kenya have access to land in the rural areas, mostly in their 'home area'. However, how and by whom the land is actually used is a different story. Like Andersson, the authors demonstrate the continuity between the various places involved. It appears increasingly difficult to maintain dichotomies like rural versus urban. Moreover, recent research to discover migration flows also shows that the picture of migration and mobility is not linear. There is a whole pattern of rural-urban linkages characterised by, for instance, return migration, circular movements and differentiation within the 'migration flows'. In Chapter 9, *Cecilia Tacoli* describes the recent phenomenon of return migration and how, in various parts of Africa where people are moving out of town in ever greater numbers, this is leading to 'de-urbanisation'. Based on the migration statistics of Tanzania, Nigeria and Mali, she argues that although movement patterns have changed over the last few decades, links between rural and urban areas remain strong. It would be interesting to situate the de-urbanisation discussion in relation to de-agrarianisation, the on-going process of diversification out of agriculture (see e.g. Bryceson 1996). Where do de-agrarianisation and de-urbanisation meet?

The last three chapters deal with yet another dimension of the changing patterns and interpretations of mobility on the African continent. Here the historical and political realities of mobility are considered in addition to the cultural, economic and geographical dimensions discussed earlier in the volume. *Youssouf Diallo* (Chapter 10), dealing with pastoral Fulbe movements in the border region of Burkina Faso, Mali and Côte d'Ivoire, shows that mobility patterns in addition to being very old may also have political consequences. The movements of these nomadic people are constantly changing in reaction to changes in their environment. The author discusses how historically rooted but at the same time adaptive these mobility patterns are. Moving into new territories always leads to new arrangements with other groups and societies, something that can only be interpreted as a political process of the balancing of power and conflict, an idea confirmed by Mirjam de Bruijn, Rijk van Dijk and Han van Dijk in their contribution. As Todd Sanders and Marja Spierenburg both stated, so-called sedentary agricultural people, like those in Diallo's study area, also move in search of good land and/or better watering points. Such mobility patterns can truly be labelled as rural-rural.

Whereas these authors deal with rural-rural mobility patterns at a local level, *Piet Konings* (Chapter 11) highlights the fact that in modern African states such issues can become of national political significance. His contribution on the political developments in western Cameroon illustrates the actual problematic in many African states concerning allochthony versus autochthony. Those who were at first welcomed as labourers on the plantations are today being branded as strangers who should preferably be expelled, by the very same national politicians who once encouraged their participation in the workforce. The same dynamics of national politics are present in the case of Côte d'Ivoire, as described by Diallo, where pastoral people were first welcomed to furnish the booming economy with animal products but today are looked on strangers who do not belong in the country and who have no rights. These people are being sent back to their countries of 'origin'. In some cases the influence of national policies is visible through 'development' projects, as described by Marja Spierenburg in her Zimbabwe case study where rights to resources are no longer defined by the institutions of the people themselves but by outside agencies that privilege those who, in the eyes of the autochthones, are considered outsiders. Such policies thus redefine who the strangers are in a community. Being a 'stranger' is not just a label but is linked to a series of actions sometimes accompanied by violence. The old institutions that formerly integrated strangers are being turned upside down by local or national policies and strongly influence the perception of the people themselves.

The case of the refugees in Rwanda and Burundi described by *Patricia Daley* (Chapter 12) shows the influence of international politics. She describes an extreme case of labelling people as refugees, defining them as an anomaly to be adjusted to the circumstances. People are either forced to return or to become a refugee in a refugee camp. The negative connotations that mobility often carries are highlighted in this chapter. The overall tendency in academia as well as in policy circles of *a priori* assumptions that mobility is problematic in any given society is of particular significance in the refugee situation. Refugees are probably the best example of a form of mobility that is not generally welcomed and that states and policy makers feel needs to be controlled and be re-ordered into a 'decent' sedentary pattern. The dichotomy between sedentarity and mobility frequently recurs in discussions about refugees.

With Daley's article we have come full circle back once more to one of the issues mentioned in Chapter 2, namely moving up from the local to the international in understanding the relevance of the study of African mobility. This mobility has become a pressing international, even intercontinental issue. International migration within the African continent but also to Europe and America is discussed in the chapters by Daley (12), Diallo (10) and De Bruijn, Van Dijk & Van Dijk (3). It appears that land shortages and diminishing economic resources make the mobility of people more problematic today than in the past, a fact that has acquired international ramifications more than ever before. Refugees in many ways have become the vested interest of international involvement with Africa. Their international mobility is the reason why they are recognised as refugees at all, as is shown by Daley's discussion of the situation in central Africa. The case of Pentecostalism in Ghana, described by De Bruijn, Van Dijk & Van Dijk (Chapter 5), shows the concomitant mobility of forms and the way a group of people deals with their (international) mobility and their cultural integrity or identity. In addition to relations of a more material nature (e.g. multi-spatial livelihoods), ideologies may form an important link between the various spaces in which people live and work. Hence, with the term 'mobility' this volume tries to combine insights into the material and immaterial aspects of the movements of people in Africa.

References

Bryceson, D.F. 1996, 'De-agrarianisation and Rural Employment in Sub-Saharan Africa: A Sectoral Perspective', *World Development* 24 (1): 97-111.

Clifford, J. 1992, 'Travelling Cultures', in L. Grossberg, C. Nelson & P.A. Treichler (eds), *Cultural Studies*, New York: Routledge, pp. 96-116.

Jamal, V. & J. Weeks 1988, 'The Vanishing Rural-Urban Gap in Sub-Saharan Africa', *International Labour Review* 127 (3): 271-92.

Van Binsbergen, W.M.J. & H.A. Meilink 1978, 'Migration and the Transformation of Modern African Society: Introduction', *African Perspectives* 1978 (1): 7-20.

2

Population mobility in Africa:
An overview

Han van Dijk, Dick Foeken & Kiky van Til

Although there is an abundant literature on migration in Sub-Saharan Africa and mobility in the continent seems to be increasing, it is remarkably difficult to understand fully the processes underlying the phenomenon. This is partly related to problems with definitions and concepts and partly to a lack of reliable data. This chapter is an attempt to summarise the recent literature and patterns of geographical mobility in Sub-Saharan Africa, dealing with both quantitative and qualitative aspects. By emphasising the complex nature of the phenomenon, it is concluded that systematic quantitative data as well as detailed case studies are needed in order to obtain a clear picture of mobility on the continent.

Introduction

As outlined in the introduction to this volume, the term 'mobility' is preferred to that of 'migration' for two reasons. First, the concept of migration does not cover all types of geographical mobility as is made clear in the section below dealing with mobility as a way of life. Second, mobility is more than the movement of people alone: also non-human and non-material things such as ideas and values can move or adopt specific forms as a result of the movement of people. It should be noted, however, that the overview presented in this chapter is largely based on the recent 'migration' literature concerning Sub-Saharan Africa.

Africans have always been on the move (Amin 1995; Akokpari 1999) but there are indications that mobility is increasing (Akokpari 1999). Moreover, patterns of mobility are changing in the sense that new forms are emerging and old ones are decreasing (Tacoli 1997, this volume). Rural-urban migration seems to be slowing down and in some countries urban-rural migration (return migration) is increasing. Intercontinental migration, particularly to North-West Europe, has started to grow in importance. The number of cross-border labour migrants in Southern Africa has declined substantially (Sachikonye 1998) and finally, and perhaps most strikingly, the number of people in

Africa who can be labelled as 'refugees' or 'internally displaced persons' has grown dramatically.

Some authors use a rough chronology to describe the history of spatial mobility in Africa (e.g. Adepoju 1995; Amin 1995). In pre-colonial times, "population movement aimed at restoring ecological balance and (...) of individuals in search of subsistence food, better shelter and greater security" (Adepoju 1995: 89). The establishment of colonial rule brought an end to this type of movement and migration became largely determined by the labour requirements for plantations, mines, industries and the administrative apparatus. As Amin (1995) said, the movement of peoples during the pre-colonial period gave way to labour migrations in the colonial period. Colonial migration was usually short term and male dominated. Post-colonial mobility has been essentially a continuation of colonial mobility, i.e. directed towards resource-rich areas and urban centres. Female mobility has increased markedly since independence. The present changes in forms of mobility mentioned above do not introduce a new period but should be seen as responses to changing – and usually deteriorating – economic, political and ecological situations.

The chronology seems to suggest that one type of mobility has been replaced by another. However, this is not completely true. Older forms of mobility 'to restore the ecological balance' are now being labelled as rural-rural migration. There are indications that this type of migration is even on the increase under the impact of population growth and periodic drought (see De Bruijn *et al.*, Chapter 5 this volume).

This chapter discusses firstly some definitional problems. The following section deals with the many types of migration that can be distinguished based on a variety of criteria and then, two specific types of migrants are briefly highlighted: those for whom mobility is a way of life, and refugees. An overview of the recent quantitative data on migration in Sub-Saharan Africa is presented and then finally, four important aspects of the study of population mobility are discussed: gender aspects; adaptation and integration of migrants and strangers in the receiving area; the hinterland as an object of study; and relations between migrants and their home areas.

Problems with definitions

Mobility has both a spatial and temporal dimension. Defining mobility (or migration) is not easy because of the many different types. The simplest definition of migration is 'a change of residence' (Bilsborrow & United Nations Secretariat 1993: 1). However, this definition poses two problems. First, 'residence' implies a certain minimum length of stay. How long does a person have to stay in a certain place to be classified as a migrant, a sojourner or a non-migrant? Second, people who move regularly between two or more places may not even have a clearly identifiable 'place of residence'. This refers particularly to those for whom mobility can be considered as a way of life.

Usually, 'migration' is also defined in terms of crossing a political or administrative boundary (Bilsborrow & United Nations Secretariat 1993) but questions arise about the nature of such boundaries. In the case of state boundaries the situation may seem clear, although lack of uniformity among countries in determining who is an international migrant has long been a source of inconsistency in international migration statistics. Nowadays, an 'international migrant' is "a person who changes his or her country of usual residence" (United Nations 1998: 9), i.e. someone who crosses one or more state boundaries to stay in another country for a certain period of time. However, state boundaries and related political jurisdictions are not always static. They change over time and thus introduce confounding effects into the measurement of migration.

At the sub-national level, the situation is even more complex. What is meant by an administrative boundary? Moving from one district to another implies crossing a well-defined administrative boundary. A rural-urban migrant crosses the municipal boundary but what about a person who comes from a rural area and settles just outside the urban boundary or a person who moves from one village to another? Is moving from one province in southern Sudan to another in the north *not* migration whereas crossing the border between Burkina Faso and Ghana means that one does not leave the area inhabited by one's own ethnic group but nevertheless becomes an international migrant? Defining mobility or migration in terms of crossing some kind of administrative boundary is less useful because it excludes certain categories of mobile people. Such an approach to migration neglects other boundaries that, for the migrant, may be more relevant.

Types of migration

The word 'migration' covers a wide range of different types of mobility. When writing on migration, authors usually distinguish various types but these distinctions are seldom based on clearly defined criteria. An attempt is thus made here to identify the large variety of migration forms by using six different criteria: geo-administrative level, area of destination, duration, choice, legality, and migrant's characteristics in relation to motivation.

(1) Based on a *geo-administrative level*, the usual distinction is between international (or inter-state) and intra-national migration. Indeed, for a long time migration was compared with *inter*national migration (emigration), despite the fact that *intra*-national migration is much more common. This is reflected in the fact that statistics on the latter type of migration are still scarce, certainly in Sub-Saharan Africa. Statistics on international migration are much easier to collect, as international migration is subject to state regulation. Foreigners are checked upon entry and are granted permission to stay in a country other than their own only on an exceptional basis (United Nations 1998). *Inter*national migration can be further subdivided into intra-continental and intercontinental. There is quite a difference for a Ghanaian migrant between going to Nigeria and heading for North-West Europe in terms of 'pull' factors as well as the types of problems this migrant will encounter on the way (see de Bruijn *et al.*, Chapter 5 this volume).

(2) Although a wide range of *destination areas* can be distinguished, this criterion is usually, if not always, simplified to the rural-urban dichotomy, resulting in four types of

migration: rural-rural, rural-urban, urban-rural and urban-urban. Of these, rural-urban migration is the one that has received most attention from researchers. African governments tend to concentrate investments in urban centres, thereby attracting people from rural areas who come looking for employment possibilities or educational facilities (pull factors). Rural-urban migration is further influenced by, amongst others, deteriorating economic conditions in the rural (home) area and such social factors as the migrants' perceptions of living conditions in urban areas, the presence of friends and/or relatives in the urban areas, and the expectation of a rise in social prestige associated with migration (Obudho 1998).

Despite the predominant attention that rural-urban migration has received in the literature, in terms of size of flows, rural-rural migration is historically as well as currently probably much more widespread in Sub-Saharan Africa. For centuries, people have moved to areas where there was work in agriculture, a process that became even more important with the widespread introduction of small- and large-scale commercial farming during the colonial period (see Diallo, this volume; Cordell *et al.* 1996). The two other types of migration, urban-urban and urban-rural, have received even less attention. Urban-urban migration is usually considered in terms of gradual migration: migrants from the rural areas move to a small urban centre first, before continuing on to a larger urban area. Urban-rural migration is often equated with return migration, certainly in Sub-Saharan Africa, involving people living in town who go back to their rural home after retirement. 'Retirement migration' usually has an economic base: people can retain or regain land rights and support themselves by farming at home (Peil 1995; Foeken & Owuor, this volume). However, recently, there have been indications that younger urbanites, too, are moving to the rural areas because of the lack of job and income opportunities in town (e.g. Potts 1997; Tacoli, this volume).

(3) As with the previous criterion, a classification based on *duration* of migration can be put into a simple dichotomy: permanent versus temporary. Duration is an essential criterion in establishing whether a person should be classified as a migrant or not. Very few people migrate with the intention of leaving for good but in practice, however, many will never return. Temporary migration is common in Sub-Saharan Africa, mostly in the form of seasonal or circular migration. Seasonal migration is usually connected with the rural-rural type, while circular migration has a rural-urban-rural character. However, the distinction between the two is not always clear, as circular migration can also be seasonal in nature. For instance, the circular movements of an urban woman who spends six or more months a year in the rural 'home' in order to farm there are dictated by the agricultural calendar, particularly in areas like the Sahel (Hampshire & Randall 1999; Cordell *et al.* 1996).

(4) The criterion of *choice* denotes whether migration is forced or voluntary. A voluntary migrant is a person who migrates out of his/her own free will and has the choice to migrate or not. Forced migration, thus, refers to people who have no other option than to migrate. However, the meaning of the word 'forced' can be subjective because while many people consider themselves as forced migrants, often some will stay behind, for whatever reason. Today, millions of Africans can be labelled as forced migrants, either being refugees (international forced migrants) or internally displaced

persons (intra-national forced migrants). The latter group is growing faster than the refugee group (Bascom 1998). Moreover, there are important new dimensions to the present refugee crisis. First, voluntary repatriation (return migration of refugees) has become less common and more difficult. Second, conflicts between incoming refugees and local communities are increasing. And third, environmental resources are being seriously threatened in areas with large concentrations of refugees (Bascom 1998; see also Daley, this volume).

(5) Based on the criterion of *legality*, Ricca (1989) distinguished both 'legal migration' and 'clandestine migration' as forms of labour migration (see below). Each year, hundreds of thousands of individuals cross state borders without going through any formalities. These clandestine migrants usually end up as illegal workers in the informal sector. Legal migration can be further subdivided into 'organised migration' and the 'free movement of persons'. Organised migration refers to "movements of groups of workers, generally low-skilled, who move from one country to another to offset a temporary or long-term labour shortage" (Ricca 1989: 53). Organised migration and the free movement of people are usually sanctioned by a bilateral agreement between the country of departure and the country of destination. There are a few examples of such agreements between African states but their duration was generally short and they covered only a small number of the migration flows.

(6) The final classification criterion concerns the *migrant's characteristics* in relation to motivation: the reasons for migration differ as people differ, in particular in terms of gender, age and education. The literature on labour migration is overwhelming for southern African countries, where large numbers of men from neighbouring countries have migrated to work in mines and plantations in South Africa for contract periods (usually two years at a time) only to return home periodically between contracts, leaving their families in the rural areas (De Vletter 1985). Although men have always migrated to find work, it is only in the last two decades that women have been migrating for work as well, albeit mostly within their country of residence (Vaa *et al.* 1989). The more traditional motive for women migrating was to follow their husband (Cordell *et al.* 1996),[1] often taking their children with them. Children also migrate to go to school (for instance boarding schools in former British colonies but also African students at western universities). As mentioned above, old people may decide to return home after retirement. The third characteristic, education, is highly decisive in relation to migration. For well-educated rural people, there are frequently few jobs in the area of origin. This is also the group for whom international (legal) migration is an option. Low salaries and massive retrenchments have induced many highly skilled people from countries like Ghana, Uganda and Kenya to move to countries in southern Africa and the western world (Adepoju 1991). This 'brain drain' is seen as a substantial loss for the countries of departure.

---

[1] Women migrate in the many patrilineal societies in Africa, as they always move to join their husband's family, mostly in another village, town or even region.

Mobile populations and conceptual problems

Mobility as a way of life

'Migration', as a term, does not cover the whole phenomenon of geographical mobility. Africa is a continent where a considerable part of the population leads a mobile way of life. Nomadic pastoralists, (hunter) gatherers but also healers, Islamic clergymen, students of the Koran, traders, singers, craftsmen and tramps can be found everywhere. In addition, large numbers of people have been uprooted from their place of origin and have become part of a peripatetic category of wandering persons. These people are difficult to classify because they do not fit into perceived notions of what is deemed 'normal' in the administrative and legal logic of the sedentary world.

Historically, mobility has been deeply engrained in African societies. Kopytoff (1987), for example, uses the term 'internal African frontier' to denote the process of expansion of African agricultural societies. Nineteenth-century travel literature abounds with examples of people moving around (Klute 1996). Poor people moved from city to city in search for charity in the West-African savannah states (Iliffe 1987) and pilgrims on their way from West Africa to Mecca were the nuclei of numerous population groups in the British Sudan and Ethiopia (Abu-Manga 1999; Delmet 2000). Oral histories in most African villages start with the dangers encountered by the founders of the village while *en route* to its present location.

For a number of reasons these wandering people cannot be classified as migrants and are conceptually difficult to categorise. In the first place, pastoralists, nomads and peripatetics often move in cycles. Most have some place of attachment, and therefore cannot be classified as migrants as such. Secondly, movement, i.e. being mobile, is not a break with their past or a breakdown of their normal social environment. Instead, these movements are part and parcel of their daily lives. Thirdly, societies of mobile people seem to have a number of distinct characteristics in terms of social organisation and cultural traits.

Though there is an abundant literature on pastoralists in Africa, much less is known about other categories of mobile people, and the organisational and cultural aspects of mobility. The contribution of De Bruijn *et al.* in this volume (Chapter 5) provides some food for thought on this issue.

Refugees and internally displaced persons

A similar conceptual problem is posed by the existence of refugees. Like mobile populations, they cannot simply be classified as migrants. An often-used criterion to distinguish between refugees on the one hand, and migrants and mobile populations on the other, is the question of whether people move voluntarily or not. The most commonly used definition of a refugee is a person who "owing to a well-founded fear of being persecuted for reasons of race, religion, nationality, membership in a particular social group, or political opinion, is outside the country of his nationality, and is unable to or, owing to such fear, is unwilling to avail himself of the protection of that country" (UNHCR 2001). People have to move involuntarily and cross international borders in order to obtain the official status of refugee.

Sub-Saharan Africa has a dismal history of forced (intercontinental) migration. Between 1500 and 1800, some six million Africans were shipped to the New World as slaves, followed by another three million during the nineteenth century (Emmer 1992). Unknown numbers – but there must have been many – have been forced to migrate due to warfare and natural disasters. During the post-colonial period, forced migration has increased again (Bascom 1998). Until the mid-1970s, forced migration increased slowly and was related to the wars of liberation. After that, the number of forced migrants escalated, reaching almost six million during the mid-1990s. The main causes are political and military strife, abuse of human rights by totalitarian regimes, and ecological disasters (Adepoju 1993).

The definition of 'refugee' excludes all those who are or feel forced to leave their homes but remain within national borders. These people are alternatively labelled as 'internally displaced people'. Likewise, people who leave their homes for reasons other than political or military conflict are not able to obtain refugee status. One could, however, question the degree of volition of people leaving their home because of drought, ecological degradation and unremitting deprivation. Some have coined the term 'ecological refugees' for these people (Suhrke 1994; Westing 1994).

An important obstacle preventing accuracy in stating precisely how many refugees there are is that areas where large numbers of refugees are to be found are often chaotic. The acuteness of the problem hampers systematic study in many instances. Furthermore, most people involved with refugees are practitioners rather than academic researchers (Kuhlman 1994; Allen & Morsink 1994; Allen 1996).[2]

A quantitative assessment of migration and population mobility

Most countries in the world – and African countries in particular – lack adequate statistics on migration. Therefore, estimates are calculated, often for five-year periods, based on partial information and projected figures (United Nations 2000: 128). Data on various migratory flows can be obtained from three types of sources: *administrative sources* such as population registers, registers of foreigners, information from applications for visas, residence permits, work permits, etc.; *border statistics* including all data gathered at border controls; and *household-based inquiries* involving censuses and various types of household surveys (United Nations 1997: 5). For international migration, the administrative sources and border statistics are predominantly used, while for intra-national (often called 'internal') migration, household studies are the main sources. Censuses are generally not able to capture temporary migration and tend to miss most return migration. Although surveys are more flexible instruments, they frequently only provide a partial view of the phenomenon, resulting in possible misrepresentations and incomplete data (Bilsborrow & United Nations Secretariat 1993: 2).

---

[2] Nevertheless, a lot of information is available in published and unpublished form. For example an international conference was held in the Netherlands from April 24-27 1999 entitled 'Refugees and the Transformation of Society: Loss and Recovery'. At the University of Oxford the Refugees Studies Centre, http://www.qeh.ox.ac.uk/rsc/, has a documentation centre with over 34,000 bibliographic records.

International migratory flows in Sub-Saharan Africa
Table 2.1 shows the Sub-Saharan African countries with the highest out- and in-migration flows during the 1990s. During the first half of the 1990s, the major 'sending' countries were Malawi, Liberia and Somalia. The major 'receiving' countries were the Democratic Republic of Congo, Mozambique and Tanzania. The picture during the second half of the 1990s was quite different, with Mali and Kenya being the main sending countries and Liberia and Somalia the main receiving countries. The Democratic Republic of Congo had developed from being a receiving country during the first half of the decade to a sending country during the late 1990s.

Table 2.1: Net in- and out-migration, selected countries, 1990-95 and 1995-2000

	absolute per year (x 1,000)	net out-migration rate (%)		absolute per year (x 1,000)	net in-migration rate (%)
Net out-migration 1990-95			*Net in-migration 1990-95*		
Malawi	200	2.10	Dem. Rep. of Congo	227	0.55
Liberia	140	6.00	Mozambique	200	1.16*
Somalia	130	1.63	Tanzania	110	0.37*
Mali	80	0.85	Gambia	n.d.	1.34
Rwanda	350*	5.72	Gabon	8*	0.80
Sierra Leone	41*	0.98			
Eritrea	25*	0.80			
Net out-migration 1995-2000			*Net in-migration 1995-2000*		
Mali	70	0.66	Liberia	140	5.34
Kenya	60	1.99*	Somalia	70	0.77
Dem. Rep. of Congo	284*	0.55	Rwanda	415*	5.39
Burundi	38*	0.56	Eritrea	44*	1.14
			Gambia	n.d.	0.91
			Sierra Leone	43*	0.88

* Calculated with the help of population figures from UNFPA (2000)
Source: United Nations 2000

These figures are all net migration rates. Some countries that were both receiving and sending large numbers of migrants are therefore not included. Burkina Faso and other West-African countries have been and still are major exporters of labour to Côte d'Ivoire (see Cordell *et al.* 1996; World Bank 1990). As a result, almost a quarter of the population of Côte d'Ivoire were born in another country. A large number of Chadians risk being expelled from Libya at present and there is a lively circulation of people across the Niger-Nigeria border, which also does not appear in migration statistics (see World Bank 1990; cf. Rain 1999). And the statistics on refugees in the year 2000, for example, reveal a different picture once again (see Table 2.2).

Moreover, the figures in Table 2.1 only provide information about recent population flows. The World Bank (1990) estimated that, in 1990, 21 million of the 35 million migrants in Africa lived in West Africa. However, none of these countries – except Mali and strife-torn countries such as Liberia and Sierra Leone – figures in Table 2.1. Club du Sahel (1994) estimated that 11% of the population of West Africa lived outside their country of origin. These past population flows also fundamentally altered the population distribution between the coast and the interior: in 1920 half the population were living on the coast but by 1970 the figure had risen to 67%.

Refugee movements

Over the last decade of the twentieth century the largest number of refugees worldwide could be found in Africa,[3] where by the end of 1992 there were about six million refugees (USCR 1991). Whereas in the (recent) past the main causes were struggles for independence and autonomy, nowadays wars, the abuse of human rights and ecological disaster are among the key factors compounding the refugee situation. It should be noted that refugees drawn from the poorest countries in the world seek refuge in equally poor countries (Adepoju 1995: 101).

Table 2.2 presents the numbers of refugees as estimated by the U.S. Committee for Refugees in 1991. The largest group, almost 1.5 million, came from Mozambique as a result of its long civil war. Many of these people found shelter in Malawi, one of the poorest countries in the world but have now been repatriated. Some countries were at the same time a source as well as an asylum country. This applied in particular to the Horn of Africa (Sudan, Ethiopia and Somalia). Parts of West Africa have also become war zones from time to time. For example in 1989, ethnic tensions along the border of Senegal and Mauritania led to the displacement of 70,000 people in both countries and in 1990, the war in Liberia uprooted thousands of people resulting in 125,000 flocking to Sierra Leone and Côte d'Ivoire and 50,000 to Guinée.

According to PIOOM (1998), in the late-1990s there were almost three million refugees and asylum seekers in Sub-Saharan Africa. Of the 15 countries in the world with 100,000 to 500,000 refugees (i.e. the source countries), seven were located in Africa.[4] UNHCR (2001) gives a figure of more than 3.4 million refugees in 2000 with nine source countries with more than 100,000 refugees. What is hidden in these figures is the rapid rate of change in refugee movements. Though the total number of refugees remained fairly constant at the end of the 1990s, UNHCR (2001) recorded more than one-million border crossings by refugees in 2000 (new cases and people who were returning), the net result being an increase of 90,000 more refugees in Africa.

The figures in Tables 2.1 and 2.2 reflect the number of official migrants and recognised refugees. Clandestine migration and unrecorded refugees are not included in these statistics. Refugee movements are in some cases counted as migration. Malawi is a clear example of this as its emigrants were mainly Mozambican refugees (950,000 in 1991) who were repatriated after the end of the civil war in Mozambique. Consequently, by 2000 there were fewer than 100,000 refugees in Malawi. Rwanda experienced a similar pattern. In the 1990-1995 period an enormous emigration flow of 350,000 people per annum was recorded and between 1995 and 2000, 415,000 immigrants per annum were registered as a result of the civil war (Table 2.1). This is not reflected in the number

---

[3] At present with the crisis in Afghanistan, Central Asia may well have become the region with the largest number of refugees worldwide.
[4] Liberia (475,000), Sudan (353,000), Eritrea (323,000), Sierra Leone (297,000), Burundi (248,000), Angola (223,000) and the Democratic Republic of Congo (132,000) (Jongmans & Schmid 1998).

Table 2.2: Major refugee numbers in Sub-Saharan Africa, selected countries, 1991 and 2000
(x 1,000)*

Country of source	number	Country of asylum	number
	1991		
Mozambique	1,483.5	Malawi	950.0
Ethiopia	752.4	Sudan	717.2
Angola	717.6	Guinée	566.0
Liberia	661.7	Ethiopia	534.0
Sudan	443.2	Dem. Rep. of Congo	482.3
Rwanda	208.5	Somalia	350.0
Burundi	203.9	Tanzania	251.1
Somalia	202.5	Côte d'Ivoire	240.4
		Zimbabwe	198.5
		Djibouti	120.0
		Kenya	107.2
		Burundi	107.0
	2000		
Burundi	567.0	Tanzania	680.9
Sudan	485.5	Guinée	433.1
Somalia	441.6	Sudan	401.0
Angola	421.1	Dem. Rep. of Congo	365.0
Sierra Leone	401.8	Zambia	250.9
Eritrea	366.8	Uganda	236.6
Dem. Rep. of Congo	332.4	Kenya	206.1
Liberia	273.2	Ethiopia	198.0
Rwanda	114.1	Congo Brazzaville	123.2
		Côte d'Ivoire	120.7

* Only countries with at least 100,000 refugees.
Sources: USCR (1991) & UNHCR (2001)

of refugees present in the neighbouring countries of Tanzania and the Democratic Republic of Congo (Table 2.2), since these movements took place between1991 and 2000. Surprisingly, conflict-ridden countries like Somalia, the Democratic Republic of Congo and Angola are absent as migration countries in Table 2.1, and do not figure prominently as source countries for refugees. Apparently, refugee flows have come to a standstill but perhaps this is because large numbers of refugees are hosted within the border areas of the countries themselves.

International seasonal migration
Statistics on international seasonal migration are non-existent. Yet, in West Africa this type of migration, popularly called *exode*, is common. It is a temporary, male-dominated form of migration whereby people move out of the Sahel region for a certain period[5] to earn money elsewhere. Men leave after the harvest to come back before the next rainy season begins for cultivation. Wealthy households tend to participate more in this form of migration and gain much from it (Hampshire & Randall 1999).

---

[5] Hampshire & Randall (1999) defined the duration of seasonal economic migration as lasting between one month and two years for their quantitative research, though the time span can be longer.

From the research by Hampshire and Randall, some figures on movements of Fulani in Burkina Faso can be deduced. Of the total sample, 11% had undertaken seasonal labour migration at least once in their lives, while 4.2% had been away the year before. Of the male population between the ages of 18 and 64, 36.6% had been away on seasonal labour migration at least once. The vast majority went to Côte d'Ivoire (mainly to Abidjan) and only a small minority had gone to the two major towns in Burkina Faso.

For some people, their country of usual residence cannot easily be established because by the very nature of their way of life nomads do not have a fixed place of residence. Thus, even if they cross international boundaries, they are often not regarded as moving from their normal country of residence. As a result, this group is excluded from international migration statistics (United Nations 1998).

Intra-national migration
Since statistical evidence on intra-national or internal migration is not readily available, the information presented here is incomplete. Many forms of internal movements exist and some populations are highly mobile. The two best-known forms of intra-national or internal migration are rural-urban migration and forced displacement.

For most African countries, figures on rural-urban migration can only be obtained indirectly from changes in the urbanisation rate, i.e. the growth (or decline) of the percentage of a nation's population living in urban centres. For Africa as a whole, this percentage increased from 18% in 1960 to 34% in 1990 (United Nations 1995). Its urban population increased during that period from 51 to 217 million, a growth of 325% and during the same period, the world urban population increased by 132%. By the year 2000, 37% of the African population was expected to be living in urban areas and in 2025 it is estimated that it will be 54% (UNCHS/Habitat 1996).

Urbanisation rates differ considerably between the various Sub-Saharan African countries. In 1990, the highest levels, i.e. with a rate of 40% or more, were found in the Democratic Republic of Congo, South Africa, Mauritania, Gabon, Zambia, Liberia, Mauritius, Côte d'Ivoire and Cameroon. The least-urbanised countries, with a rate below 20%, were Rwanda, Burundi, Uganda, Ethiopia, Malawi, Niger, Eritrea, Burkina Faso and Lesotho (United Nations 1995).

Kenya is one of the very few countries for which some statistical data on internal migration, based on the 1989 population census, are available. At a provincial level, the numbers of in- and out-migrants have been calculated from the census data. Since the city of Nairobi was a province at the same time, data on in- and out-migration for this city are available. It appears that in 1989, 930,000 Nairobians could be classified as in-migrants, while 157,450 had left the city (Kenya 1996). In general, the Kenyan data show that important movements were from densely populated areas experiencing considerable land shortages to the urban areas of Nairobi and Mombasa for employment reasons and to the Rift Valley in search of arable land. Another type of internal movement concerns 'rotation' within peoples' provinces, indicating that rural-rural migration is important as well.

Conspicuously, rural-urban migration in Ghana is reported to be of minor importance compared to other internal migration flows. According to Sowa & White (1997), less than 10% of all migration in Ghana in 1995 was rural-urban, 25% was urban-urban, 31% urban-rural and 34% rural-rural. In other words, the destinations of more than half of all migrants were rural. This might suggest that perceived opportunities in agriculture were an important driving force behind migration patterns (Sowa & White 1997). However, the authors do not specify 'rural areas'. These could also be small rural towns that were rapidly emerging during the 1990s and attracting many people from the rural hinterlands. Agriculture and also expanding commercial sectors in small rural towns were the driving forces in that case (see, for example, Zondag 2001). Information on other countries also indicates that rural-rural migration makes up a substantial part of total migration in West Africa as a whole (see Mazur 1984; Adepoju 1995; Findley 1997).

Research on 'retirement migration' was done by Peil (1995) who suggested that, in general, Africans prefer to return to their place of origin on or before retirement, rather than settling permanently in the host location. Peil studied senior citizens in five small towns in Nigeria, Sierra Leone and Zimbabwe and concluded that small towns are preferred as a place of retirement because they provide services like health clinics, hospitals and sources of water that are less easily available in villages, and facilitate visits from their children. The retirees can make enough cash for their daily needs from petty trading.

A migration flow of increasing importance is that of elderly women and widows who move to towns and cities to live with a son or daughter. Because nowadays parents increasingly prefer to educate their children in town, it seems more sensible for 'granny' to join the family there, while formerly she would probably have stayed at home and asked for a grandchild to live with her to run errands and keep her company. Older men usually have larger economic, political and social resources at home, control the land and help to run the village so their willingness to move to town is negligible. Instead, a son will move home to run the farm (Masamba ma Mpolo 1984).

Forced displacement is widespread in contemporary Africa. Internally displaced persons include not only those fleeing civil strife but also people displaced because of "oppressive economic conditions" and "sudden natural disasters" (Bascom 1995: 200-201; 1998). Defined that way, the number of involuntary migrants who remained in their own country totalled 16.8 million Africans in the mid-1990s (Hamilton, quoted by Bascom 1995; see Table 2.3). Countries with large numbers of internally displaced people are Sudan, South Africa, Mozambique, Angola and Liberia.[6]

According to Bascom (1995: 200-201), some 600,000 of the almost 17 million internally displaced people could be classified as having fled because of "refugee-like conditions", most of them being environmental migrants. The status of these people and the way in which they are counted (or estimated) remains totally unclear, however. There is little doubt that such a category of people exists but any further information does not go beyond rough guesstimates.

---

[6] Remarkably, UNHCR (2001) gives a figure of approximately 1.1 million internally displaced people in 2000 (e.g. 3,000 in the Democratic Republic of Congo instead of 500,000, Sudan 94,783 instead of 4 million, Angola 257,508 instead of 2 million). The reason for these enormous discrepancies is not known.

Table 2.3: Internally displaced civilians within African countries, 1994

Sudan	4,000,000	Kenya	300,000
South Africa	4,000,000	Rwanda	300,000
Mozambique	2,000,000	Eritrea	200,000
Angola	2,000,000	Togo	150,000
Liberia	1,000,000	Djibouti	140,000
Somalia	700,000	Guinée	80,000
Dem. Rep. of Congo	500,000	Chad	50,000
Burundi	500,000	Mali	40,000
Ethiopia	500,000	Senegal	28,000
Sierra Leone	400,000	Total	16,880,000

Source: Hamilton 1994, in Bascom 1995.

Some aspects of population mobility

A number of subjects have been under-researched in comparison to normal studies of migration. Gradually, research is concentrating more on the processes associated with population mobility and is less preoccupied with a purely statistical approach. Here four of these issues are touched upon.

Gender aspects

Though no less important than male migration, there are several reasons why female migration in Africa has up to now received scant attention. First, women tend to migrate over shorter distances and hence are not always included in migration statistics. Second, women are over-represented in short-term movements such as circular migration. For a long time there has been no consensus on how to define the concept of circular migration, which has made it even more difficult to measure women's participation in this process (Hugo 1998). Third, researchers have tended to focus on economically motivated migration. Women migrating with their husbands or for marriage are often stereotyped as associational migrants (Adepoju 1995; Bilsborrow & United Nations Secretariat 1993).

Despite this, various studies have shown that autonomous female migration is widespread and on the increase. Many women undertake rural-urban movements on their own to attain economic independence through self-employment or wage income (see, for example, Vaa *et al.* 1989; Adepoju 1984, Findley 1987). They take up jobs as varied as public-sector workers, homemakers, prostitutes, and domestic servants.

Adaptation and integration of migrants and strangers

There is a substantial literature on the adaptation and integration of migrants. Population mobility entails also a movement of cultural forms. People not only bring their physical presence but also their food habits, social relations, rituals, religious convictions and ideologies. Given the enormous diversity of cultural forms in Africa and the important role of mobility in social life, it is surprising that the cohabitation of all these people with all its variety has been so peaceful for so much of the time. Apparently there are many ways of regulating relations between groups of people and to manage cultural and social diversity.

The integration and adaptation of people into a host society is a common problem for all moving people, regardless of the reasons why they have moved there. The concept of integration itself is also fraught with difficulties because no good measure can be defined for socio-cultural integration (Kuhlman 1994). It has to be set against the background of the inter-ethnic and social and political relations in the host area as well. Ethnic and socio-economic differences within the host population might be more accentuated than the differences between the host and refugee population.

Another issue to take into account concerns the reasons for moving. So-called ecological refugees drifting slowly southwards from the semi-arid Sahel to more humid areas with what remains of their belongings are obviously in a different position when it comes to integration than the millions of Rwandan refugees who flooded into the eastern part of the Democratic Republic of Congo in 1994. The majority of people labelled as refugees are likely to find themselves in a situation in-between these two examples.

In the literature some attention has been given to the psychological aspects of these processes (Tieleman 1990: 1). This existential aspect of movement may influence the ways in which people experience their lives and consequently act upon in their futures (De Bruijn 1999). This does not only apply to refugees but also to other types of migrants and even to people for whom mobility is a way of life.

The area of origin as an object of study
The mobility of some obviously has important consequences for those who remain where they are. Those who stay behind not only suffer the loss of a member of the family but there are also economic costs incurred. Those who migrate are often the young able-bodied men, and increasingly also women, who would have played a crucial role in the local, mostly rural economy. At the village level, the loss of a substantial number of young people may endanger the viability of a village economy, as the maintenance of all kinds of crucial physical and social infrastructural facilities can no longer be guaranteed. When young families migrate, the care of the weak, infirm and old may be put at risk. Another form of expense incurred by those who stay behind is providing the means for the migrants to make their enterprise successful.

Circular labour migration, for example, is one of the ways of tackling this problem. Young men only migrate during the unproductive season and return before the onset of the rains so that the continuity of the agricultural cycle in their village of origin is ensured. A direct benefit is that there is one less mouth to feed during the more difficult part of the year.

The most immediate problem for people who stay behind is to survive socially and economically until the migrant returns or starts to send home remittances. The migration of males may also have an impact on the position of women at home. Within the nuclear family, they become responsible for all productive activities, which may not just entail difficulties. It may also mean an improvement in their social and economic position since they can liberate themselves from male dominance (Ruthven & David 1995).

Relations between migrants and their home areas

Until recently, relations between migrants and their home areas were almost solely viewed in terms of remittances, i.e. a one-way flow of money and goods from the migrant to the family back home. Indeed, it cannot be denied that the "sending of remittances by migrants is one of the strongest and most pervasive phenomena in Africa's migration systems" (Adepoju 1995: 100). It is characteristic of the fact that migration in Africa is fundamentally a family affair and not an individual activity. In the literature of the 1980s, migration was viewed as part of the livelihood – if not survival – strategy of the rural family.

Meanwhile, structural adjustment and the concomitant increase of prices and reduction in wages and employment in the urban areas have taken their toll in the sense that for many urban dwellers, the social obligation of sending remittances has become compelling as rural links have become "vital safety-valves and welfare options for urban people who are very vulnerable to economic fluctuations" (Potts 1997: 461). Increasingly, urban dwellers have become at least partly dependent on rural sources of food and/or income, causing a reverse flow of goods and perhaps even money from rural to urban areas. Such concepts as 'income diversification' and 'multi-spatial households' should not only be viewed from the rural perspective but also from the urban perspective. The literature on this topic is still sparse (for an overview, see Foeken & Owuor, this volume).

Increased poverty in African countries makes intercontinental migration, in particular to Western Europe, all the more attractive. In a recent study, Arhinful (2001) shows how important assistance from Ghanaian migrants in Amsterdam is for relatives back home in Ghana. It comes in the form of transfers of money and goods (such as clothes, electrical equipment, medicines and even vehicles) to provide material support in times of sickness and old age, and for education and funerals (see Van Dijk 1999). In short, it provides a degree of social security.

Conclusions

This overview of definitions and issues in the study of population mobility in Africa shows that a general theory or approach to population mobility is still a long way off. The complexity of the phenomena observed and the arbitrariness of administrative and conceptual boundaries bedevil any attempt at a systematisation of research or mapping of general trends.

The emphasis in official statistics on national boundaries as the basis for migration figures turns the phenomenon into an administrative problem. Such statistics force an examination of population mobility from the perspective of the state. They do not take into account that many national boundaries have little relevance for the population and are used as opportunities for smuggling or other illicit activities. The fact that very little systematic knowledge is available about *intra*-national movements is telling in this respect. Nevertheless, these movements can be as long and as important in their economic, ecological and political consequences as *inter*national migration and can just as well imply a break with the past because it takes people into unknown territory, socially, ethnically, ecologically and culturally.

For many migrants other variables are much more relevant to their decision to move than the existence of national or administrative boundaries. The presence of economic opportunities in the form of access to natural resources or employment, affiliated ethnic groups and/or kinsmen, people from the same religious denomination, relative safety from prosecution, aid organisations, and the urban character of regions can all be important variables in the decision to move or not to move. In a number of cases adventurism is definitely part of the motivation.

Nevertheless, a number of observations stand out as being of general significance. The first is that refugee movements have and will continue to have an impact on the distribution of the population on the continent. It is unlikely that all refugees will ever return to their home areas. In fact, it seems that large numbers of them integrate in the asylum countries – thus leaving official aid channels – and cease to be refugees. Likewise, large-scale migration from the semi-arid zones towards urban areas and coastal countries will continue unabated. However, current statistical material provides very little insight into the nature and the direction of these movements.

The most valuable information on the processes and factors behind population mobility can be derived from an increasing number of comprehensive case studies trying to grasp the complexity of the process. These studies provide deeper insight into the motivations, desires and ambitions of people's movements than can be achieved from statistical analyses. However, this does not lessen the necessity to have more and better quantitative information. Quantitative data are essential to position the rich variety of case studies and to anticipate the consequences of enormous population movements for the development of infrastructure in cities or the chances for social and political unrest, as seen in Côte d'Ivoire recently. Likewise, insights into the background of population movements are urgently needed. Climate change, the AIDS epidemic and large-scale conflicts as in the Great Lakes Region may fundamentally alter the economies of a number of countries over the coming decades and may incite new population movements. The impact of these events on the economies of African countries and on the lives of mobile and sedentary people may be serious.

References

Abu-Manga, Al-Amin 1999, 'Socio-cultural, Socio-economic and Socio-linguistic Diversity among the Fulbe of the Sudan Republic', in V. Azarya, A. Breedveld, M. de Bruijn & H. van Dijk (eds), *Pastoralists under Pressure? Fulbe Societies Confronting Change in West Africa*, Leiden: Brill, pp. 51-68.

Adepoju, A. 1984, 'Migration and Female Employment in Southwestern Nigeria', *African Urban Studies* 18, Spring.

Adepoju, A. 1991, 'South-North Migration: The African Experience', *International Migration* 29 (2): 205-21.

Adepoju, A. 1993, *The Politics of International Migration in the Post-colonial Period in Africa*, Dakar: IDEP.

Adepoju, A. 1995, 'Migration in Africa: An Overview', in J. Baker & T.A. Aina (eds), *The Migration Experience in Africa*, Uppsala: Nordiska Afrikainstitutet, pp. 87-108.

Akokpari, J.K. 1999, 'The Political Economy of Migration in Sub-Saharan Africa', *African Sociological Review* 3 (1): 75-93.
Allen, T. (ed.) 1996, *In Search of Cool Ground. War Flight and Home-coming in Northeast Africa*, Geneva: UNRISD in cooperation with James Currey, London and Africa World Press, Trenton, pp. 1-23.
Allen, T. & H. Morsink (eds) 1994, *When Refugees Go Home*, Geneva: UNRISD in cooperation with James Currey, London and Africa World Press, Trenton.
Amin, S. 1995, 'Migrations in Contemporary Africa: A Retrospective View', in J. Baker & T.A. Aina (eds), *The Migration Experience in Africa*, Uppsala: Nordiska Afrikainstitutet, pp. 29-40.
Arhinful, D.K. 2001, *"We Think of Them": How Ghanaian Migrants in Amsterdam Assist Relatives at Home*, Leiden: African Studies Centre, Research Report 62.
Bascom, J. 1995, 'The New Nomads: An Overview of Involuntary Migration in Africa', in J. Baker & T.A. Aina (eds), *The Migration Experience in Africa*, Uppsala: Nordiska Afrikainstitutet, pp. 197-219.
Bascom, J. 1998, *Losing Place: Refugee Populations and Rural Transformations in East Africa*, New York/Oxford: Berghahn.
Bilsborrow, R.E. & United Nations Secretariat 1993, 'Internal Female Migration and Development: An Overview', in United Nations, *Internal Migration of Women in Developing Countries*, New York: United Nations, Department for Economic and Social Information and Policy Analysis.
Club du Sahel 1994, *Pour Préparer l'Avenir de l'Afrique de l'Ouest: Une Vision à l'Horizon 2020*, Paris: OCDE/OECD-BAD/ADB-CILSS.
Cordell, D.D., J.W. Gregory & V. Piché 1996, *Hoe and Wage. A Social History of a Circular Migration System in West Africa*, Boulder: Westview Press.
De Bruijn, M. 1999, 'The Pastoral Poor: Hazard, Crisis and Insecurity in Fulbe Society in Central Mali', in V. Azarya, A. Breedveld, M. de Bruijn & H. van Dijk (eds), *Pastoralists under Pressure? Fulbe Societies Confronting Change in West Africa*, Leiden: Brill, pp. 285-312.
De Vletter, F. 1985, *Recent Trends and Prospects of Black Migration in South Africa*, Geneva: ILO, International Migration for Employment Working Paper no. 2.
Delmet, C. 2000, 'Les Peuls Nomades au Soudan', in Y. Diallo & G. Schlee (eds), *L'Ethnicité Peule dans des Contexts Nouveaux*, Paris: Karthala, pp. 191-206.
Emmer, P.C. 1992, 'European Expansion and Migration: The European Colonial Past and Intercontinental Migration: An Overview', in P.C. Emmer & M. Moerner (eds), *European Expansion and Migration: Essays on the Intercontinental Migration from Africa, Asia, and Europe*, New York: Berg, pp. 1-12.
Findley, S. 1987, 'Les Femmes aussi s'en Vont', *Population Sahélienne* 4: 20-22.
Findley, S. 1997, 'Migration and Family Interactions in Africa', in A. Adepoju (ed), *Family, Population and Development in Africa*, London: Zed Books.
Hampshire, K. & S. Randall 1999, 'Seasonal Labour Migration Strategies in the Sahel: Coping with Poverty or Optimising Security?', *International Journal of Population Geography* 5: 367-85.
Hugo, G.J. 1998, 'Migration as a Survival Strategy: The Family Dimension of Migration', in United Nations, *Population, Distribution and Migration*, New York: United Nations, pp. 139-49.
Iliffe, J. 1987, *The African Poor: A History*, Cambridge: Cambridge University Press.
Jongmans, A.J. & A.P. Schmid, 1998, 'Mapping dimensions of contemporary conflicts and human rights violations', text on backside of PIOOM (1998), *World conflicts and human rights map 1998*. Leiden: Leiden University, PIOOM.
Kenya, Republic of 1996, *Kenya Population Census 1989, Analytical Report vVol. 6 – Migration and Urbanisation*, Nairobi, Ministry of Planning and National Development, Central Bureau of Statistics.
Klute, G. 1996, 'The Coming State. Reactions of Nomadic Groups in the Western Sudan to the Expansion of Colonial Powers', *Nomadic Peoples* 38: 49-71.
Kopytoff, I. (ed.) 1987, *The African Frontier: The Reproduction of Traditional African Societies*, Bloomington: Indiana University Press.
Kuhlman, T. 1994, *Asylum or Aid? The Economic Integration of Ethiopian and Eritrean Refugees in the Sudan*, Leiden: African Studies Centre, Research Series vol. 2.
Masamba ma Polo 1984, *Older Persons and Their Families in a Changing Village Society: A Perspective from Zaire*, Washington D.C.: International Federation on Ageing.
Mazur, R.E. 1984, 'Rural Out-Migration and Labor Allocation in Mali', in C. Goldschneider (ed.), *Rural Migration in Developing Countries: Comparative Studies of Korea, Sri Lanka and Mali*, Boulder CO: Westview Press, pp. 209-88.

Obudho, R.A. 1998, 'Population Distribution in Africa: Urbanization under Weak Economic Conditions', in United Nations, *Population Distribution and Migration,* New York: United Nations, pp. 84-101.

Peil, M. 1995, 'The Small Town as a Retirement Setting', in J. Baker & T.A. Aina (eds), *The Migration Experience in Africa*, Uppsala: Nordiska Afrikainstitutet, pp. 149-66.

PIOOM 1998, *World Conflicts and Human Rights Map 1998*, Leiden: Leiden University, PIOOM.

Potts, D. 1997, 'Urban Lives: Adopting New Strategies and Adapting Rural Links', in C. Rakodi (ed.), *The Urban Challenge in Africa: Growth and Management of the Large Cities*, Tokyo/New York: United Nations University Press, pp. 447-94.

Rain, D. 1999, *Eaters of the Dry Season. Circular Labor Migration in the West African Sahel*, Boulder CO: Westview Press.

Ricca, S. 1989, *International Migration in Africa: Legal and Administrative Aspects*, Geneva: International Labour Office.

Ruthven, O. & R. David 1995, 'Benefits and Burdens: Researching the Consequences of Migration in the Sahel', *IDS Bulletin* (26): 1.

Sachikonye, L. 1998, *Labour Markets and Migration Policy in Southern Africa*, Harare: Southern Africa Printing & Publishing House.

Sowa, N.K. & H. White 1997, *An Evaluation of Netherlands Co-financing of World Bank Activities in Ghana 1983-1996*, The Hague: Ministry of Foreign Affairs.

Suhrke, A. 1994, 'Environmental Degradation and Population Flows', *Journal of International Affairs* 47 (2): 473-96.

Tacoli, C. 1997, 'The Changing Scale and Nature of Rural-Urban Interactions: Recent Developments and New Agendas', in UNCHS/Habitat, *Regional Development Planning and Management of Urbanization. Experiences from Developing Countries*, Nairobi: UNCHS/Habitat, pp. 150-61.

Tieleman, H.J. 1990, 'Refugee Problems in the Third World: Some Theoretical Reflections', in H.J. Tieleman & T. Kuhlman (eds), *Enduring Crisis, Refugee Problems in Eastern Sudan.* Leiden: Africa Studies Centre, pp. 1-26.

UNCHS/HABITAT 1996, *An Urbanizing World: Global Report on Human Settlements*, London: Oxford University Press (for United Nations Centre for Human Settlements).

UNFPA 2000, *The State of the World Population 2000*, New York:
    http://www.unfpa.org/swp/2000/english/indicators/indicators2.html

UNHCR 2001, *Provisional Statistics on Refugees and Others of Concern to UNHCR for the Year 2000*, Geneva: UNHCR.
    http://www.unhcr.ch/statist/2000/provisional/main.html

United Nations 1995, *World Urbanization Prospects: The 1994 Revision*, New York: United Nations, Department of Economic and Social Affairs, Population Division.

United Nations 1997, *World Population Monitoring 1997: International Migration and Development*, New York: United Nations, Department of Economic and Social Affairs, Population Division.

United Nations 1998, *Recommendations on Statistics of International Migration,* New York: United Nations, Department of Economic and Social Affairs, Statistics Division.

United Nations 2000, *World Population Prospects: The 1998 Revision: volume III: Analytical Report*, New York: United Nations, Department of Economic and Social Affairs, Population Division.

USCR 1991, *World Refugee Survey: 1989 in Review*, Washington D.C.: U.S. Committee for Refugees.

Vaa, M., S.E. Findley & A. Diallo 1989, 'The Gift Economy: A Study of Women Migrants' Survival Strategies in a Low-income Bamako Neighbourhood', *Labour, Capital and Society* 22: 234-60.

Van Dijk, R. 1999, 'The Pentecostal Gift: Ghanaian Charismatic Churches and the Moral Innocence of the Global Economy', in W. van Binsbergen, R. Fardon & R. van Dijk (eds), *Modernity on a Shoestring. Dimensions of Globalization, Consumption and Development in Africa and Beyond*, London: SOAS/Leiden: ASC.

Westing, A. 1994, 'Population, Desertification, and Migration', *Environmental Conservation* 21 (2): 110-14.

World Bank 1990, *International Migration and Development in Sub-Saharan Africa, 2 Volumes*, Washington D.C.: World Bank, World Bank Discussion Papers 101 & 102 Africa Technical Department Series.

Zondag, R. 2001, *Douentza: A Description of the Dynamics of a Rural Centre in Central Mali*, Leiden: African Studies Centre, ICCD/ASC Working Paper.

3

Territorial and magical migrations in Tanzania

Todd Sanders

This chapter explores culturally specific idioms of movement amongst the Ihanzu and Sukuma of north-central Tanzania. Over the twentieth century, these two neighbouring peoples expanded in all directions in search of more fertile farming and grazing lands. The Sukuma's numerical superiority and their preference for pastoralism have given them a decisive advantage as they increasingly encroach on Ihanzu lands. However, the Ihanzu have been concerned not just with a heightened influx of foreigners onto their soils but, more monumentally, with what they see as an all-out Sukuma witchcraft offensive against them. Migration is, therefore, not simply about moving bodies over physical terrains but is imaginatively crafted through particular cultural lenses. Above all, this chapter compels us to problematise locally-inflected understandings of expansion, migration and mobility and to consider how these interact with well-worn political-economy explanations of such processes.

Introduction

Anthropologists have had an abiding concern with migration, movement and mobility in Africa. Over the years, however, the focus of their attention has changed markedly. Earlier studies considered labour migrations, forced relocations and territorial expansions, and how these short- and long-term movements influenced 'tribal' life (Adam 1963a; Colson 1971; Richards 1973; Schapera 1947). Many such studies shared a concern with the underlying structural and historical forces that gave rise to routine movements from one locale to another, or to more permanent, territorial displacements and expansions. In all cases, mobility *per se* received only scant analytic attention. Mobility was seen rather as the consequence, the inevitable and unavoidable outcome of a host of colonial policies on 'development', migrant labour, taxation and cash cropping among other things.

Today, while anthropologists are still concerned with the structural aspects of mobility, they have come to dwell increasingly on the local *imaginings* of landscapes and people's movements across them. This particular analytic turn comes at a time when anthropologists, like other social scientists, wish to draw attention to local agency and creative potentialities; in other words, to how local actors participate critically in the meaning and making of their own worlds. People are not simply overrun by global structural inevitabilities: instead they resist, creatively accommodate and selectively appropriate symbols and structures in meaningful ways. In Africa as elsewhere, this means that political economies demarcate rather than determine Africans' life-worlds, that structural issues frame people's actions but in no way provide the last word on their meanings. Instead, peoples-on-the-move provide meaning to their own worlds.

In this way, it can be seen how Lesotho migrant labourers working in South Africa frame their social world(s) through the oral poetry of 'word music' (Coplan 1994); how various refugees give meaning to their lives by creatively imagining their history and homeland (Malkki 1995; Wilson 1994); and how certain nomads imagine mobility, not sedentarism, as the state of normality (Turton 1996). Not surprisingly, such culturally specific understandings of mobility are frequently linked to historical consciousness and speak to other facets of social identity as well. Thus, for instance, over the past century the Giriama of Kenya have spread increasingly eastward towards the coast. This territorial expansion they imagine as being not solely about the search for more fertile farmland and waged jobs, which clearly it is, but also as a move between 'past' and 'present', 'tradition' and 'modernity' (Parkin 1991; cf. Cohen & Odhiambo 1989). Similarly, since the early 1900s, the Iraqw of Tanzania have gradually but continually expanded in all directions from their highland homeland in Mama Isara to much of Mbulu District. They, like the Giriama, see this territorial expansion as a move from 'past' to 'present', 'tradition' to 'modernity' (Snyder 1993). One of the principle mechanisms in this expansion, from an Iraqw perspective, is a ritual called *masay*. These rites do many things but one of the most fundamental is to (re)create the boundaries between Iraqw and adjacent territories. Thus, as the Iraqw move into new areas, they use *masay* rites to appropriate these spaces, turning bush and other lands into culturally-meaningful Iraqw landscapes (see Snyder 1997 and 1999; Thornton 1980).

The noteworthy point is that migration, movement and mobility are variously imagined in Africa (and, of course, elsewhere) and that, of late, anthropologists have been keen to detail the myriad ways this is so (Comaroff & Comaroff forthcoming; Masquelier 2000). By imaginings, anthropologists do not mean that such things are culturally-concocted fantasies that can therefore be ignored. On the contrary, many anthropologists today see such imaginings as crucial to understanding migratory processes (Appadurai 1996). This is because people's ideas about movement are not just ways of thinking about the world. They also provide ways to act upon that world. Cultural imaginations, to use Clifford Geertz's terminology, are both models 'of' and models 'for' reality.

This chapter examines one such cultural imagination amongst the Ihanzu of Tanzania to show how they use witchcraft as an idiom of mobility, and as an explanation for Sukuma territorial expansion.[1] The Sukuma, the largest ethnic group in Tanzania, live

[1] This chapter is based on fieldwork carried out in Ibanzu, Tanzania between August 1993 and May 1995 and June – September 1999. The information on the Sukuma derives primarily from my reading of the literature. I thank the UK Economic and Social Research Council, the US National Institute of

immediately to the north and west of Ihanzu. While both the Sukuma and Ihanzu extended their territorial reach during the twentieth century, the Sukuma have proved far more successful on this score. Today, as struggles over farm and grazing lands have become acute, the numerically superior Sukuma continue their expansion into Ihanzu territory virtually unabated.

One of the reasons Sukuma herdsmen have proved so successful, claim the Ihanzu, is due to the new form of witchcraft they bring with them. This witchcraft has allegedly allowed the Sukuma and their cattle to overrun and ruin Ihanzu pastures and farmlands, all the while protecting their own populace and herds against mystical countermeasures. It has also led, so people say, to the 'consumption' or 'disappearance' of many Ihanzu, resulting in the Ihanzu drawing crucial links between witchcraft, ethnicity and mobility.

The first part of the chapter provides background information on some of the political and economic forces that have compelled the Sukuma and Ihanzu to spread across the land, while the second part delves into locally-inflected understandings of these movements. Examining witchcraft as a means of mobility provides an alternative way of thinking about movement in Africa, one that resonates soundly with local concerns.

The Ihanzu in historical perspective

The people who today refer to themselves as the Ihanzu number around 30,000 and are one of the many Bantu-speaking agricultural groups found across Tanzania. They reside in the northernmost part of what is today Iramba District, as they have done since at least the mid-1800s. Over the years, however, the Ihanzu have found it increasingly difficult to survive at home in the villages as formerly productive soils have grown weary. The growing population has put increasing pressure on available food resources. Famines, not unheard of in the past, now appear to be more acute. Colonial and post-colonial administrations have encouraged agricultural intensification (not always to much avail), further straining scarce land resources. For these reasons and others, over the course of the previous century, the Ihanzu have gradually spread from their small, central highland villages onto the lowland plains that surround them in search of more fertile farmlands. This outward expansion continues today.

In the late 1880s, immediately prior to the arrival of German colonial forces, the Ihanzu resided in the small, mountainous area they call 'Ihanzu', an area about one tenth the size of their current territory. The people probably then numbered only a few thousand. Pressures on the land, that was far more productive than today, were few. Even though the area was reportedly densely populated, crop yields were for the most part ample. This is because the soils were reasonably fertile, the population was low and villagers practised intensive agricultural techniques including crop rotation and manuring (*Deutsches Kolonialblatt* 1901: 903; Obst 1912a: 114). Even so, farming was

Health, the Royal Anthropological Institute and the London School of Economics for funding different parts of this research; and the Tanzanian Commission for Science and Technology (COSTECH) for granting me research clearances. I would also like to thank the editors of this volume for their constructive comments.

Map 3.1: Ihanzu- and Sukumaland, Tanzania

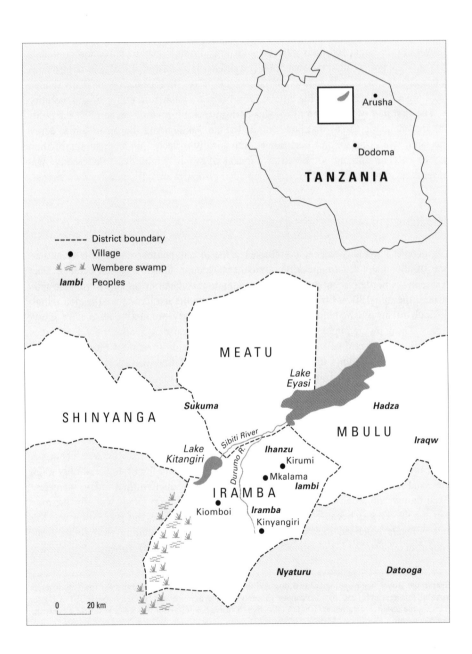

and still is a precarious enterprise in this semi-arid climate, where rainfall averages a meagre 50-75 cm a year.

Staple crops included sorghum and millet that, together with an assortment of wild greens, formed the basis of their diet. Groundnuts, manioc, sweet potatoes, beans and tobacco were also grown. Additionally, some people kept domestic livestock, primarily cattle, sheep, goats and donkeys (*Deutsches Kolonialblatt* 1901: 903; Obst 1923: 218; Reche 1914: 69-70 and 1915: 260; Werther 1894: 238 and 1898: 72).[2]

At the time, each Ihanzu village in this highland homeland was mostly autonomous and male elders informally governed their own internal village affairs. When inter-village feuds developed over murders or adultery, as they sometimes did, fines were negotiated between the parties involved. Movement between villages was sometimes dangerous and required ritual precautions (Adam 1963b: 17; Reche 1914: 85).

Villages and villagers, in spite of tensions between them, were ritually connected in that all recognised the supreme leadership of one clan section called the *Anyampanda wa Kirumi*.[3] In particular, there were two royal leaders of this clan section, one male and one female, known as 'owners of the land' (*akola ihî*). As in other pre-colonial African societies (Feierman 1990; Packard 1981), these leaders served a number of political and ritual functions. These included bringing the rain to Ihanzu each year, presiding over boys' circumcision and girls' initiation rites, and generally ensuring the well-being of Ihanzu and all those who lived there. Together, in short, the owners of the land provided the basis for the pre-colonial Ihanzu political structure as well as a source of collective identity (Adam 1963b; Sanders 1998 and n.d.).[4]

Far from being confined to their mountainous homeland in the pre-colonial era, the Ihanzu (or rather, some Ihanzu men) journeyed widely, maintaining extensive trading networks with most of their neighbours. Ihanzu men regularly bartered with people from the Sukuma, Hadza, Iramba, Nyamwezi and Iraqw areas to acquire such items as glass beads, iron, rhino horns, honey, arrow poison and livestock.[5] In return, Ihanzu traders frequently gave salt gathered at Lake Eyasi or goods made by their own smiths like arrowheads, knives, hoes and axes. The only neighbouring peoples with whom the Ihanzu did not trade or intermarry were the Maasai and Datooga. These pastoral peoples regularly raided Ihanzu for cattle (Adam 1961: 2; Obst 1912a: 112; Reche 1914: 69, 71, 84, 86 and 1915: 261).

The pre-colonial picture of Ihanzu that emerges is one of a small number of decen-tralised and largely autonomous villages clustered around the boulder-strewn centre of the country, each village responsible for its own internal political, legal and economic affairs. People shared some sense of common identity that centred on the two royal

---

[2] Hichens, 1920, 'Mkalama Annual Report 1919/1920 (16 April 1920)', pp. 13-16, Tanzania National Archives (hereafter *TNA*) 1733/1.

[3] Wyatt, n.d., 'Mkalama District Book', p. 9, School of Oriental and African Studies. Adam, V. 1963. 'Draft of Report on Isanzu for Community Development Department of Tanzania', p. 9, Unpublished manuscript at British Library of Political and Economic Science (BLPES).

[4] Hichens, 1920, 'Mkalama Annual Report 1919/1920 (16 April 1920)', p. 7, *TNA* 1733/1. Bagshawe, 1920-1921, 'Kondoa-Irangi Annual Report 1920-1921', pp. 14-15, *TNA* 1733: 5.

[5] On trade with the Nyamwezi see D. Kidamala & E.R. Danielson 1961, 'A Brief History of the Wani-ramba People up to the Time of the German Occupation', *Tanganyika Notes and Records* 56: 67-78.

Anyampanda leaders. Within individual villages, men and women farmed clan lands that appear to have been fertile enough to support those who used them.

When the Germans first arrived in the 1890s, the Ihanzu began gradually to spread from their highland homes to lowland peripheral areas in search of more arable farmlands. This was possible for the first time due to the German suppression of 'tribal' warfare, which coincided with a succession of human and animal plagues across the region (Kjekshus 1977). The German administration's early bush-clearing efforts to allow for the building of roads and to reduce tsetse-fly populations also aided these movements.[6]

Following the First World War, the British administration actively encouraged Ihanzu emigration. As one early and zealous British official noted, the administration's aim was "to continue bush clearing, to reduce flies, [and to] open up cultivation land for natives to increase food supplies".[7] This demanded bush clearing on a massive scale.

From the 1930s onwards, British administrators organised local bush-clearing crews that spiralled out from central Ihanzu in all directions. And as new areas were opened up, the administration encouraged people to farm and live there. Indeed, resettlement was seen as crucial to the success of the anti-tsetse campaign because once people moved to a cleared area they were unlikely to let it return to bush (Johnson 1948: 91).[8]

By the 1940s and 1950s there was a steady out-migration from the central, highland area of Ihanzu onto the surrounding lowland plains. The villages of Ng'wangeza and Ng'wansigwa were established to the east. In the 1950s other Ihanzu moved north onto the plains, while still others established new villages to the north-west, near the border of Sukumaland.

Since independence in 1961, ten new Ihanzu villages have been established on the lowland plains surrounding the central homeland area. All these villages have high proportions of self-identified Ihanzu, and today are also home to many peoples who, in times past, would have lived elsewhere. These include Sukuma, Iramba, Hadza and Datooga.

For the Ihanzu and others, there are – or more correctly, there *were* – significant advantages to farming in these newly opened-up areas. For one, having never been cultivated, the soils were marginally more fertile and thus more productive. Additionally, on the plains, expansive unbroken tracts of land could be cleared and farmed, as opposed to the small, broken parcels typical of the highland area. This meant that ox ploughs and sometimes tractors, rather than hand hoes, could be used to great effect.

For these reasons, particularly in the late 1950s and early 1960s, the colonial (and later post-colonial) administration encouraged plains villagers to grow cash crops. Those villagers who did, most of whom were Christians, grew sunflowers, beans and maize for sale in local and regional markets. One man might cultivate as many as 30 acres of such crops, the wealthiest among them even being able to hire tractors. As one

---

[6] Oberleutnant Ruff, 24 March 1910, in 'Einsiedler Adolf Siedentopf,' *TNA* G55/27; Hichens 1920, 'Mkalama Annual Report 1919/1920 (16 April 1920)', p. 14, *TNA* 1733/1.

[7] Hichens, 'Mkalama Annual Report 1919/1920 (16 April 1920)', p. 14, *TNA* 1733/1.

[8] Letter from D.O., Kisiriri to the Settlement Officer, Kondoa-Irangi dated 6 February 1953, doc. 563 in 'Medical and Sanitation, Mkalama Leper Settlement,' *TNA* 68/37/22.

anthropologist noted in the early 1960s, "there is no scarcity of uncleared land [...] boundary disputes [are] rare".[9]

By the early 1990s the situation in Ihanzu had changed dramatically. Following the tentative cash-cropping boom in the 1960s, there were no longer any local markets for the sale of foodstuffs. All local government agricultural cooperatives had collapsed and the infrastructure, such as it was, was wholly inadequate for farmers to transport their crops to Arusha or Singida. Ihanzu cash cropping, in short, had all but ground to a halt. This was, in part, the result of the 1980s *ujamaa* collectivisation policies gone amiss but can also be attributed to the largely depleted soils on the formerly-fertile plains.

In the outlying plain areas of Ihanzu, pressures on the land have intensified further as soils become less fertile and populations continue to increase. In these areas, there is today little bush left to clear and boundary disputes over carefully demarcated plots have become commonplace. It is against this backdrop of Ihanzu territorial expansion and increasing pressures on the land that the history of Sukuma movements in the area is examined.

The Sukuma in historical perspective

The Sukuma live immediately to the north and west of Ihanzu and form the single largest ethnic group in Tanzania, numbering around four million (Brandström 1990: 1). Sukumaland (*Usukuma*), which covers more than 52,000 square kilometres mainly in Shinyanga and Mwanza Regions, is fairly homogenous savannah with gently undulating hills and expansive plains. In the past, low population densities and high mobility across this vast area made the Sukuma agro-pastoral lifestyle viable and sometimes even prosperous in spite of the often unforgiving climate and poor soils. However, over the twentieth century the Sukuma, like the Ihanzu, had to cope with increasing competition for grazing and farmlands. This has led to a continual expansion in all directions.

'The Sukuma' are a relatively recent innovation. In the pre-colonial era they shared no collective identity, nor did they have any over-arching political or ritual organisation. It was only during the early British colonial period that a distinctive Sukuma identity was forged (Cory 1953: 2; Holmes & Austen 1972; Liebenow 1960: 232).

In the late 1800s, prior to the arrival of German forces, the people today known as Sukuma lived in a number of chiefdom states varying in size from fewer than 2,000 to as many as 90,000 people (Liebenow 1960; Shipton 1984: 120). It never proved possible to amalgamate individual chiefdoms into a larger, more centralised Sukuma state-system. This is because, as Holmes and Austen (1972: 386) noted, "there was almost no ... competition for land, thus little need to centrally regulate its control" (see also Liebenow 1960: 233).

Within individual chiefdoms two social groupings were apparent. On the one hand, there were the 'owners of the land' (*benekile ise*) or chiefs. On the other were the non-chiefly 'builders' (*bazenzi, bazengi*) or 'occupiers' (*banamiko*). The chiefly owners of

---

[9]   Adam, V. 1963, 'Draft of Report on Isanzu for Community Development Department of Tanzania', pp. 157-62, 169, *BLPES*.

the land included the head of the chiefdom – called the *ntemi* – his close relatives and some of his subordinate administrators like headmen. The 'ownership' of *ntemi* amounted, in the main, to his ritual control over the agricultural cycle, rain, hunting and warfare. It was, in fact, his ritual control over these everyday activities that "represented the fundamental source of his authority" (Cory 1951: 74).

An *ntemi* did not act alone. He was assisted in many everyday tasks by sub-chiefs, elders and headmen, many of whom were his relatives and who were also considered 'owners of the land' (see Cory 1954). Headmen, for instance, allocated parcels of arable land to new arrivals to a chiefdom on which people cultivated sorghum, millet and maize. Such lands, usually plentiful, were allocated on a first come, first served basis. There was no absolute upper limit to the size of land holdings. Rather, individual needs were carefully considered in light of family size. Once a parcel was allocated, a family was expected to remain and farm it. Otherwise, expulsion from land was extremely rare (Hartley 1938: 20, 22; Malcolm 1953: 26-27, 51; Tanner 1955).

Practically and symbolically, 'owners of the land' were firmly anchored in their own chiefdoms. For one, chiefly lineages did not fragment as often or widely as did non-chiefly lineages, which meant they remained relatively localised (Shipton 1984: 120). The exception to this was when a contestation occurred over succession to office, at which point an 'owner of the land' might find a new chiefdom elsewhere. Furthermore, since an *ntemi*'s ritual control over the land depended on continual access to his chiefly forebears, owners of the land were buried locally. An *ntemi* and his rainmakers could then visit the chiefly graves for rainmaking and other ancestral veneration (Cory 1951: 49-50; Malcolm 1953: 50). In a number of ways, 'owners of the land' provided relatively permanent reference points on the landscape. This was not so for most Sukuma.

Non-chiefly Sukuma – by far the majority of the Sukuma population – were comparatively mobile both within and between chiefdoms. Their descent groups were shallow and regularly fragmented as conjugal families moved away from their natal homesteads (Hartley 1938: 17; Malcolm 1953: 43). Moreover, commoners did not bury their dead, at least until Christian missionaries arrived, but left them in the bush for wild animals to dispose of (Burton 1860: 25). This was because commoner spirits, unlike chiefly spirits, were not attached to specific parcels of land. Instead, commoners built household spirit shrines (*kigabilo*) to placate their ancestors: "Where the descendants went to live, the ancestors followed" (Shipton 1984: 121; also Tanner 1958: 225). This Sukuma familiarity with mobility greatly facilitated their later territorial expansion.

One of the principle reasons for relocating either temporarily or permanently to another chiefdom was to find new grazing grounds for livestock (Brandström 1985: 30). Although the Sukuma economy was underwritten by cultivation, the Sukuma were also ardent pastoralists. Early explorers were much impressed by the sheer numbers of Sukuma flocks and herds (Broyon-Mirambo 1878: 30; Speke 1864: 286). These beasts, above all cattle, were of ecological, social and symbolic significance (Brandström 1990; Malcolm 1953: 62-82).

Sukuma movements and interactions with others in the pre-colonial past were not confined to Sukumaland alone. By the mid-nineteenth century, some Sukuma were deeply involved in trading and raiding with their close and distant neighbours, linked as they were into the Lake Route that extended from Unyamwezi in the south to Buganda in the far north (Hartwig 1970; Holmes & Austen 1972: 388-96). Closer to home, Ihanzu oral histories, genealogies and early written sources suggest there was at least occasional transit and trade between some eastern Sukuma chiefdoms and Ihanzu.

Sukuma used to (and still do) collect salt on the plains around Lake Eyasi just north of Ihanzu; while sometimes the Ihanzu, who also collected salt from the same lake, would exchange it with Sukuma for iron hoes (Obst 1912a: 112; Reche 1914: 84 and 1915: 261; Senior 1938). Marriage between Ihanzu and Sukuma was not unheard of in the past. During drought and famines the Ihanzu often moved into Sukumaland in search of food; while in the dry season in plentiful years, Ihanzu men used to fish in and gather reeds from the Sibiti River which today forms the boundary between Sukumaland and Ihanzu.[10] Also, in the late 1800s, northern and eastern Sukuma chiefdoms, like Ihanzu, suffered from Maasai and Datooga cattle raids (Ashe 1883 in Millroth 1965: 15; Itandala 1980: 9-13).[11]

On the eve of the colonial encounter, in summary, the Sukuma made up a number of autonomous mini-chiefdoms spread across the land. Each of these chiefdoms was composed of 'owners' and 'builders'. The latter, the vast majority of the Sukuma, could move unproblematically from one chiefdom to another with their livestock. Since land was plentiful and populations generally sparse, they moved whenever they needed grazing grounds. They could also easily gain access to arable land in their new locales. The Sukuma traded with some of their neighbours, including the Ihanzu, but were raided by others like the Maasai and Datooga.

German colonial forces first entered Sukumaland in 1890 and until around 1900 pursued a policy of pacification (see Holmes & Austen 1972: 397). In a number of ways, unbeknown to them at the time, the Germans' entrance and eventual entrenchment served as a catalyst for Sukuma territorial expansion that has continued to the present. Successive colonial and post-colonial regimes provided both the preconditions and the need for such expansion.

German pacification policies were in part responsible for the cessation of conflicts between the Sukuma and their pastoral neighbours, the Maasai and Datooga (Malcolm 1953: 11-12). Fewer raids meant fewer security concerns for the Sukuma. This, in turn, allowed them to relocate easily to distant and isolated locations where better grazing

---

[10] The first German-Ihanzu encounter is similarly telling. C.W. Werther's guide was a Sukuma man who spoke to the Ihanzu men they encountered in the Sukuma language. This seems to have caused no confusion or difficulties. Furthermore, several Ihanzu men managed correctly to identify a particular bull bought by Werther from a Sukuma leader in Meatu, eastern Sukumaland (see Werther 1894).

[11] R.W. Waller (1978) rightly notes that between c. 1820 and c. 1880 Maasai territory extended as far south as modern-day Dodoma District in Tanzania. This aside, his analysis focuses solely on inter-tribal relations between Maa-speakers and *northern* agricultural communities (i.e., Kikuyu, Chagga, etc.) to the exclusion of those in the south (p. 268). His failure to address the southern reaches of Maasai territory led him to overgeneralise, wrongly concluding that '[r]elations with neighbouring agriculturalists, as we shall see, were characterised more by trade than raid' (p. 90). Had Waller paid more attention to the southern Bantu-speaking agriculturalists, the Gogo, Iramba, Ihanzu, Turu and Sukuma, his conclusions might have been less sweeping. Though his data on symbiosis (and conflict) between northern agricultural communities and the Maasai are, as far as they go, convincing, there is no compelling evidence that Maasai relations with those to the south had ever, prior to the colonial period, been anything but hostile.

and farmlands were to be found. Without raiding, the need for chiefly medicinal protection was lessened, if not made superfluous.

Following the First World War, British bush-clearing policies further abetted and indeed demanded territorial expansion. From an early date the British were greatly concerned with eradicating the tsetse fly in Tanganyika, their newly acquired Trust Territory. So detrimental was the tsetse-fly problem in Sukumaland that the British administration chose Shinyanga, in southern Sukumaland and bordering on Ihanzu, as the first large-scale experimental area for bush reclamation and tsetse eradication in the Territory (Brandström 1985: 12). As in Ihanzu, bush-clearing efforts in Sukumaland were massive and continued for many years. The end result was that between 1925 and 1947 the tsetse fly steadily declined on all fronts (Ford 1971: 198-204).

This allowed the Sukuma and their livestock to expand in all directions in search of greener pastures. Well accustomed to moving when conditions so demanded and permitted, it was not only the search for new pastures that propelled the Sukuma and their cattle from central Sukumaland. It was also the need for arable farmland to fuel the colonial enterprise.

The British encouraged cotton cash cropping in Sukumaland and by the early 1930s, cotton production there had reached record highs. Perhaps unsurprisingly, this "severely increased pressures on land..." (Austen 1968: 244). Even so, it was not until after the Second World War that Sukuma cotton production rose dramatically and the pressure on land became acute. This led to yet further territorial expansion (Brandström 1985: 18-19; Shipton 1984: 120). Estimates suggest that between the First World War and the late 1950s the area inhabited by the Sukuma more than tripled in size, from about 10,000 to over 30,000 square kilometres (de Wilde cited in Brandström 1985: 20). This expansion affected all neighbouring districts including Iramba District where the Ihanzu live.

Sukuma territorial expansion has proved even more remarkable in recent years (see also Brandström 1990: 1). The relatively new villages on the Ihanzu plains, especially those in the north and west, all have high proportions of Sukuma living in them, either permanently or on a seasonal basis. In some (originally) Ihanzu villages like Nyaha, located in the far northwestern corner bordering on Shinyanga Region, the Sukuma language and population are now dominant.

In these villages, Sukuma, Ihanzu and others practise a mix of cultivation and herding. On the whole, the Sukuma are more successful pastoralists than the Ihanzu. For an Ihanzu to have twenty head of cattle is to be wealthy, while to own fifty is virtually unheard of. Some Sukuma, on the other hand, although they are themselves reluctant to reveal exact numbers, allegedly own a thousand or more head of cattle.

Many Sukuma are heavily involved in the lucrative cattle trade. They are usually those most involved at local monthly cattle auctions just outside Ibaga village, Ihanzu, often buying what they can at bargain rates. Many Sukuma venture further afield to sell their bovine goods at auctions in Arusha where they fetch top prices. The profits are usually ploughed back into the cattle economy. Such on-going cattle transactions – buying (locally) cheaply and selling (distantly) for high prices – ensure that Sukuma cattle herds thrive, even in difficult years.

For many in northern Tanzania, the year 1999 was perhaps the worst in living memory. The rains and crops failed completely. Famine was widespread. When visiting Ihanzu that year following the (non-)harvest, there was a notable paucity of young and middle-aged men and women, many of whom had not yet returned from migrant labour in other parts of Tanzania. The very young and very old who had remained in the villages were distressingly thin. And for these unfortunate souls, especially for those in Ihanzu's border villages where Sukuma populations are highest, to conjure 'the Sukuma' was akin to speaking a profanity.

Many Ihanzu villagers recounted bitterly how, for the exorbitant price of a cow, wealthy Sukuma cattle owners offered them a kilo or less of grain. Expanding Sukuma herds in search of fresh grazing ground increasingly trespassed on precious but mostly unavailing Ihanzu farmlands. Disputes between Sukuma herders and Ihanzu farmers increased dramatically and some were taken to court. In many of these villages, meeting after meeting was held, both by the government and local vigilante groups (*nkîlî*), to address 'the Sukuma problem'. The common sentiment was that the Sukuma and their cattle were consuming the Ihanzu in their continual territorial expansion.

Witchcraft and migration at the millennium

Many Ihanzu and Sukuma alike have no difficulties understanding or relating the above explanation of territorial expansion. It is they, after all, who have experienced these things first-hand: rising colonial and post-colonial demands for cash cropping and taxation; the sometimes desperate search for fertile pastures and farmlands in a precarious environment; and the more recent invasion of Ihanzu by the highly-mobile Sukuma and their cattle. Yet there are many ways of imagining such movements, not all of them reducible to bottom-line determinants of the regional political economy. The remainder of this chapter turns to alternative Ihanzu imaginings of Sukuma territorial expansion, imaginings that revolve around medicine and witchcraft.

There is perhaps no better way to begin than by discussing some rumours I first heard in the northern villages of Ihanzu in the summer of 1999 immediately following the drought and famine. These were rumours about *gambosh*, a type of witchcraft traditionally associated with the Sukuma not the Ihanzu. Sukuma *gambosh* appear at night in the form of rapidly moving bright lights. They can easily be mistaken for buses. But these are no ordinary buses. While normal buses have a definitive shape and usually travel on well-marked routes, *gambosh* have no definitive characteristics at all apart from their bright lights. They are said to cruise through the bush, often at dangerous speeds. They allegedly collect unsuspecting passengers en route, and transport them to unknown distant locations, perhaps somewhere in Sukumaland. Any hapless man, woman or child who encounters *gambosh* is in danger of disappearing forever.

Most Ihanzu would find this unproblematic were *gambosh* to confine themselves, as they always did in the past, to Shinyanga and Mwanza Regions where most Sukuma live. Regrettably, however, this is no longer the case. In the late 1990s, these Sukuma nocturnal bush-buses were for the first time traversing the borders of Sukumaland into

Ihanzu. And apparently they were doing so in earnest. While people sometimes pointed to specific vanished individuals who had allegedly been abducted by *gambosh*, the tales were often framed more generally and recounted more ominously: *gambosh* are moving into Ihanzu and consuming her people.

It is worth remarking that the presence of witchcraft in Ihanzu today is not in the least unusual. African witchcraft and other traditions have not died as people modernise, as a number of social theorists – Marx, Durkheim and Weber among them – assured us they would. On the contrary, African witchcraft has proved highly flexible, alive to the basic rhythms of our world (Geschiere 1997). Far from withering away, witchcraft has reportedly increased in post-colonial Africa (Colson 2000: 341; Comaroff & Comaroff 1999; Rowlands & Warnier 1988). For this reason and others, anthropologists have sought to problematise Africans' hybrid worlds that contain both tradition and modernity (Lan 1985; Piot 1999; Sanders n.d.).

But what does the recent arrival of Ihanzu *gambosh* reveal about mobility and territorial expansion in Africa? Why should such imaginings be taken seriously? The answer could be that they tell one a great deal about Ihanzu men's and women's sense-of-being in the world, a world that is growing evermore precarious. To see how, Ihanzu notions of medicine and ethnic identity need to be examined.

The meaning of medicine

In the Ihanzu language, the terms for medicines and roots (*makota*; sing. *ikota*) are identical. In Swahili, people use the term *dawa* (pl. *madawa*). Such root medicines are used by diviners, rainmakers and witches, both to heal and allegedly to kill.

Medicine or *dawa*, however, is not confined to the use of roots alone. Hospitals and dispensaries supply *dawa*; dehydrated and compressed foods eaten by soldiers and astronauts are referred to as *dawa*; and drug addicts, too, have their own types of *dawa*.

The term *dawa* (or *ikota*) is itself amoral. It is only when combined with the appropriate know-how and actual use that *dawa* becomes either good or bad. As one local woman rightly noted, "chloroquine given in the correct dose can cure malaria, but too much will kill you". The Ihanzu see all types of medicine with a similar moral ambivalence. The witch and the rainmaker may use the same medicines, the difference being that the former deploys them for evil, the latter for the benefit of all Ihanzu. This said, it is never entirely clear when the use of medicine (potentially good) becomes witchcraft (by definition bad). Thus, for instance, in warfare, people routinely speak of their own use of medicine but the witchcraft (*ûlogi*) of their enemies.

Many consider medicines an essential element of various everyday activities. Ihanzu men and women often use medicines known as *kinga* to protect their plots, homes, livestock and person, or so it is widely believed. *Kinga* consist of ground roots, leaves and other ingredients specially prepared by a seer, which are then strategically placed in one's field, house, cattle pen or worn on one's person, depending on what needs medicinal fortification. These are supposed to protect against medicinal assault on one's property and self. In theory, *kinga* is protective and is therefore morally tenable.

In practice, few admit to using *kinga*, since one man's protective medicine all too easily becomes another man's witchcraft.

Another type of medicine allegedly used on a regular basis is *kisûmba*. This might be called a 'medicine of attraction', since people purportedly use it to attract such things as material wealth, lovers, rain, fish or even a better job. This medicine, called *nsambá* in the Sukuma language, supposedly originated in Sukumaland.

Kisûmba, like *kinga*, is theoretically a good medicine that can be used by anyone without fear of social reprisal. Indeed, many say it would be foolish, perhaps even impossible, to do business without it. Yet only a few admit to doing so, for fear that it might be misconstrued as another form of medicine – witchcraft called *ndagû* – from which one benefits only at the immediate expense of others. Government officials, business persons and the wealthy are often thought to use medicine, good or bad, to acquire their positions and wealth, as well as to keep them once they have done so. The Ihanzu share the nagging suspicion that no one gets something for nothing and that medicines must somehow be involved (Sanders 1999a).

Conflicts, too, are often imagined in medicinal terms (Sanders 1999b). Naturally, conflicts are about this-worldly encounters between adversaries: warriors attack and kill each other, sometimes in violent and unpleasant ways; cattle thieves are occasionally caught and shot with arrows; and neighbours, kin and others have disputes over live-stock and land. Yet at quite another level, such encounters can be and often are also about 'mystical aggression' (Goody 1970). Combatants in large- and small-scale war-fare, especially when victorious, are invariably said to use medicine, both to protect themselves and to overcome their foes. From an Ihanzu perspective, all conflicts poten-tially have a medicinal component to them. Winners, not losers, are presumed to have more powerful medicines, and to have used them.

Finally, for the Ihanzu, medicines and migrations often go hand-in-hand. This is because their ideas about medicinal potency and impotency are often linked to their understandings of ethnic identity.

Medicine and ethnicity

As was alluded to above, ethnic identities are not primordial realities but social con-structions and the products of specific historical circumstances (Beidelman 1978; Ranger 1983). The Sukuma are largely a product of the colonial enterprise. Before the Germans arrived, they did not exist as an imagined collectivity. For the Ihanzu, this is less the case, though of course what is meant by an Ihanzu has changed, and continues to change over the years.

Yet even if ethnic labels are socially and historically malleable, which clearly they are, this should not distract from the fact that they also comprise social realities in their own right. They are highly meaningful at particular moments in time, even if such notions change a great deal in the long run. Somewhat ironically, people the world over see ethnicity in precisely the ways anthropologists tell them they should not: as bounded, atemporal, essentialised, homogenised categories of people. The Ihanzu are no different.

Ethnic identity may be variously conceptualised in terms of culture, clothing, language, subsistence activities, and so forth. The Ihanzu characterise the Sukuma, for instance, in a number of ways according to their distinctive dress and jewellery, their ever-present walking sticks, their language, their large numbers of cattle and the fact that they, unlike the Ihanzu, are not circumcised. Ethnicity is multi-faceted and varies markedly at different times and places, in different historical and social settings. Nevertheless medicinal potency is a primary means by which the Ihanzu define and give meaning to ethnic categories. This includes the Sukuma and others, as well as their own self-defined category, 'the Ihanzu'.

When I first arrived in Ihanzu and told people that I hoped to write a book about them, they often spontaneously launched into stories about former ritual leaders and the royal matriclan, their ancient (and perhaps mythical) journey from Ukerewe Island in Lake Victoria to Ihanzu, and the powerful rain medicine they brought with them (see also Adam 1963b; Kohl-Larsen 1943: 169, 194-95). Until recently, members of neighbouring ethnic groups, the Turu, Iambi, Iramba and Hadza, visited Ihanzu annually so that the rains would be plentiful in their own lands (Adam 1961: 2; Jellicoe 1969: 3). And today, as in the past, the Ihanzu have two ritual leaders whose responsibility it is to bring rain each year.

One of the most profound markers of Ihanzu ethnic identity today is their lengthy history of rainmaking and the connection to potent medicines that such traditions imply. So important were these matters to the men and women of Ihanzu, it turned out, that I abandoned my original research programme and focused instead on rainmaking (see Sanders 1998, 2000, forthcoming and n.d.). In a very real sense, to be 'Ihanzu' today is to situate oneself within this lengthy historical discourse on rainmaking, control over powerful medicines being central to it. If the Nuer picture themselves as 'people of cattle', then the Ihanzu imagine themselves as 'people of powerful medicine'. Of course such medicinal imaginaries, as ethnic glosses, are meaningful only in relational terms, as the following story suggests.

The British District Commissioner (DC) of Iramba once held a contest to discover who amongst the Iramba Native Authority chiefs was the 'real' one. The DC summoned each of the three colonial chiefs separately to the local colonial administrative centre, the former German fortress in Mkalama village, instructing each that he must bring the rain with him when he came. Chief Kingu of Iramba arrived first. He failed to bring rain. The Chief of Iambi followed. He, too, failed to bring rain. Chief Sagilu of Ihanzu kept the DC waiting for some time. Before he left home in Kirumi, a few miles from Mkalama, he and his mother (the then-female ritual leader) agreed that he must arrive with the rain. They prepared their rain medicines in Kirumi, and Sagilu then set off for Mkalama. Slowly, majestically, he walked. And as he did so, the rain followed immediately behind but never touched him, washing away his footprints as he proceeded. When he arrived in Mkalama, the skies suddenly broke. Although it was July and the middle of the dry season, the rain that had followed him from home now poured down, drenching everybody present. It rained continuously for three days. Thoroughly delighted, the DC proclaimed: "You, Sagilu, are the *real* chief!"

This well-known and often-recounted tale is interesting for a number of reasons, not least for what it says about submerged subaltern histories of the colonial enterprise and local notions of power and authority. In Ihanzu eyes, medicinal potency and ethnic identity are linked. In this story, the Ihanzu rain-chief, Sagilu, won because he possessed more powerful medicines than his chiefly Iramba or Iambi counterparts. In fact, 'the Iramba' and 'the Iambi' are always billed by 'the Ihanzu' as medicinally inferior groups. This is similarly the case with the nearby Iraqw and Turu.

Of all their neighbours, only the Sukuma are seen by the Ihanzu as medicinally more powerful than they themselves. It is for this reason that nearly all Ihanzu seers are trained, or claim to have been trained, in Sukumaland. During divination sessions Ihanzu seers often speak to clients in the Sukuma language, entirely or in part, a practice that gives them legitimacy in their clients' eyes: they have learnt from their medicinal masters. Furthermore, some Ihanzu seers, when divining for foreign clients in other parts of Tanzania, invest themselves with some degree of mystical capital by claiming they are themselves Sukuma. If being 'Ihanzu' in many parts of Tanzania carries with it the association of being medicinally capable, then being 'Sukuma' goes that much further.

Like Sukuma seers, Sukuma witches allegedly have access to much stronger medicine than their Ihanzu brethren. Unlike Ihanzu witches, Sukuma witches are allegedly capable of bewitching their intended victims by using the evil eye, or simply by waving to them. It is often feared that the most powerful Ihanzu witches have obtained their medicines in Sukumaland, from where both *ndagû* and *kisûmba* (mentioned above) are said to have originated.

Sukuma medicine is also democratic. Not only Sukuma diviners and witches but also ordinary Sukuma allegedly use medicine liberally to gain and protect their cattle, crops and livelihoods. Common Ihanzu perceptions are that nearly any Sukuma man or woman is, by definition, medicinally better equipped than his or her Ihanzu counterpart. This is what Sukuma do. They make powerful medicine. And they use it.

It is in this context of inter-ethnic imaginings and medicinal potency that the recent arrival of *gambosh* buses is situated. Such understandings account, at least in part, for why the Sukuma have proved so successful in their migratory movements into Ihanzu. They allegedly use powerful medicine (or witchcraft, depending on one's point of view) to overrun Ihanzu farmlands and to protect their own herds. Or so Ihanzu villagers repeatedly claim. Moreover, since the Ihanzu understand Sukuma medicine to be more potent than their own, the outcome is a foregone conclusion. The Sukuma will win. The Ihanzu will lose. The Sukuma are thought capable of consuming the Ihanzu at many levels. The word 'consuming' (*kula*) is used here intentionally, as it is by the Ihanzu, since this is precisely what the Sukuma appear to be doing: consuming in everyday terms Ihanzu's material resources, and in other-worldly witchcraft terms, the Ihanzu themselves. In Ihanzu eyes, this is a multi-fronted migratory offensive. It is about scarce resources, this is true. But more than this, it is also about Ihanzu imaginings of themselves as a people, and their potential consumption by a numerically superior and well-resourced neighbour. Rumours about migrating *gambosh* buses thus express a profoundly pessimistic view of the viability, in the long run, of the Ihanzu as a people.

Conclusions

The relationship between political-economy and witchcraft explanations of Sukuma expansion is a complicated one. Isn't it the case that educated westerners employ materialist explanations while the Ihanzu use witchcraft? And isn't this because we westerners know the former are 'true' while the latter are 'false'? In this sense, because we are correct and the Ihanzu are not, can we not just ignore Ihanzu musings over magical migrations? Not exactly.

While it is probably the case that most westerners would find materialistic, political-economy explanations plausible, this can also be said for most Ihanzu. As noted earlier, the Ihanzu in no way misunderstand the harsh realities – governmental policies, impoverished soils, drought, famine and so on – that compel people to move from one locale to another. It is they, after all, who have lived through such tumultuous times and can thus recall, in uncanny detail, the very real, material reasons for their own and others' movements. Indeed, to be a good farmer or herder, an intimate knowledge of such things is not only possible but absolutely essential. Without such knowledge people's very survival would be called into question.

Given this, it would be unwise to discuss such matters in terms of 'etic' and 'emic' distinctions – that is, *our* migration story is one of political economy while *theirs* is one of witchcraft. For to do so could imply, to the unsympathetic reader, that western and non-western logics and modes of thought are radically different, if not wholly incommensurable. Such unreasonable reasoning borders dangerously close to Lévy-Bruhl's notion of the (non-Western) pre-logical mentality. Moreover, if the Ihanzu themselves have no difficulty understanding or subscribing to a rational political-economy explanation, then surely it makes little sense to see etic perspectives as being held solely by clever outsiders.

Explanations of migration that emphasise either political economy or witchcraft are not so much about western oranges and African apples as they are about additional layers of meaning, and different explanations for different contexts. Through rumours about Ihanzu-eating Sukuma witch-buses, the Ihanzu move well beyond the mere materialities of mobility and address, on a more cosmological level, their location in a rapidly-changing post-colonial world. And it does not stop there: discourses about *gambosh* are not just ways of imagining the world. They are also ways of creatively engaging with it.

The Ihanzu privilege different accounts of Sukuma expansion in different contexts and to different ends. As argued elsewhere (Sanders 1999a), the Ihanzu make a firm conceptual distinction between 'tradition' and 'modernity'. Furthermore, certain things, peoples and acts are said to belong categorically to one or the other. Since this very dichotomy was itself the product of colonialism and its metadiscourse of modernity (Sanders n.d.), it is hardly surprising that vernacular understandings mirror those of dominant European discourses on the matter. For the Ihanzu, all things governmental are said to be 'modern'; while many other things like rainmaking, witchcraft and divination are considered 'traditional'. Naturally, in practice, there is a good deal of slippage between these two ideational categories. But people maintain the distinction all the same.

The important point here is that men and women knowingly situate different discourses about migration and territorial expansion solidly within this overarching tradition-modernity dichotomy. In modern settings, the Ihanzu discuss such movements in terms more material than ethereal, whereas in traditional settings precisely the opposite occurs. Border-village disputes between Sukuma herders and Ihanzu farmers were frequently brought to the government's attention. Many Ihanzu complained bitterly to government officials about the Sukuma and their cattle. In the summer of 1999, government meetings were regularly called to discuss particular and general issues surrounding land usage and conflict. At some of these meetings, government officials attempted to demarcate boundaries around and through villages aimed at keeping Sukuma cattle on one side and Ihanzu farmlands on the other. The discussions observed were always well reasoned and well argued from both sides, for and against such boundaries, and whether such boundaries would work at all. That summer no such measures were ever adopted in any village. What is tellingly, here, is that in such 'modern' settings there was never any mention of Sukuma witchcraft. This topic would wait for late afternoon or evening discussions deemed more 'traditional'.

If Ihanzu villagers were intensely engaged with 'modern' government using 'modern' discourses, they were also visiting diviners and carrying out 'traditional' vigilante meetings in the bush. And at these meetings it was *not* the rather obvious fact that the Sukuma cattle were moving into and eating Ihanzu farmland that most concerned people. It was, instead, the fact that Sukuma were 'consuming' the Ihanzu medicinally with their witchcraft.

The Sukuma are medicinally far superior to the Ihanzu. This everyone knows. And their sheer masses, combined with their undeniable medicinal competence, could imply only one thing: the Ihanzu were doomed. How long this might take was anyone's guess. Understandably, these meetings frequently had an air of despair and resignation about them, as if, faced with such odds, there was little any Ihanzu could do either with or without governmental support. Witchcraft, after all, works invisibly and can cross boundaries like the wind. Sukuma witchcraft, so people suggested, was simply unstoppable.

All told, Ihanzu imaginings of witchcraft are not merely a local lexicon used to conceptualise and contemplate territorial expansions, though this is certainly part of it. This would imply, among other things, that what is *really* at issue in such movements is an everyday struggle over scarce resources, and little more. Rather I would argue that, in Ihanzu eyes, witchcraft is also the very means by which such migrations occur. Thus, witchcraft is both a way to imagine migrations and a way to make them happen. It is a way of conceptualising the world and a way of acting purposively upon it. From an Ihanzu perspective, without powerful witchcraft, Sukuma expansion would hardly have been so successful. What is more, such imaginings – whether ultimately true or false –

have true enough effects in the real world. The fact that the Ihanzu see the world this way, that they see witchcraft and migration as inextricably linked, profoundly affects the form such migratory ventures take. Such imaginings shape the ways the Ihanzu cope with Sukuma inroads into their lands – whether they resist such movements, accept them as inevitable, or do both simultaneously in different contexts. No longer can migrations and territorial expansions be treated as simply the product of broad, structural factors. The real world is far more complicated.

References

Adam, V. 1961, 'Preliminary Report on Fieldwork in Isanzu', Conference Proceedings from the East African Institute of Social Research, Makerere College.

Adam, V. 1963a, 'Migrant Labour from Ihanzu', Conference Proceedings from the East African Institute of Social Research, Makerere College.

Adam, V. 1963b, 'Rain Making Rites in Ihanzu', Conference Proceedings from the East African Institute of Social Research, Makerere College.

Appadurai, A. 1996, *Modernity at Large: Cultural Dimensions of Globalization*, Minneapolis: University of Minnesota Press.

Austen, R. 1968, *Northwest Tanzania under German and British Rule: Colonial Policy and Tribal Politics, 1889-1939*, New Haven: Yale University Press.

Beidelman, T.O. 1978, 'Chiefship in Ukaguru: The Invention of Ethnicity and Tradition in Kaguru Colonial History', *The International Journal of African Historical Studies* 11: 227-46.

Brandström, P. 1985, 'The Agro-pastoral Dilemma: Underutilization or Overexploitation of Land among the Sukuma of Tanzania', African Studies Programme, University of Uppsala, Working Papers in African Studies, 8.

Brandström, P. 1990, 'Boundless Universe: The Cultural Expansion among the Sukuma-Nyamwezi', PhD Thesis, University of Uppsala.

Broyon-Mirambo, P. 1878, 'Description of Unyamwesi, the Territory of King Mirambo, and the Best Route Thither from the East Coast', *Proceedings of the Royal Geographical Society* 22: 28-36.

Burton, R.F. 1860, *The Lake Regions of Central Africa*. Vol. II, London: Longmans.

Cohen, D.W. & E.S.A. Odhiambo 1989, *Siaya: The Historical Anthropology of an African Landscape*, Nairobi: Heinemann Kenya.

Colson, E. 1971, *The Social Consequences of Resettlement: The Impact of the Kariba Resettlement upon the Gwembe Tonga*, Manchester: University Press.

Colson, E. 2000, 'The Father as Witch', *Africa* 70 (3): 333-58.

Comaroff, J. & J.L. Comaroff 1999, 'Occult Economies and the Violence of Abstraction: Notes from the South African Postcolony', *American Ethnologist* 26 (2): 279-303.

Comaroff, J. & J.L. Comaroff forthcoming, 'Alien-Nation: Zombies, Immigrants and Millennial Capitalism', in G. Schwab (ed.), *Forces of Globalization*, New York: Columbia University Press.

Coplan, D.B. 1994, *In the Time of Cannibals: The Word Music of South Africa's Basotho Migrants*, Chicago: University Press.

Cory, H. 1951, *The Ntemi: The Traditional Rites in Connection with the Burial, Election, Enthronement and Magic Powers of a Sukuma Chief*, London: Macmillan and Co.

Cory, H. 1953, *Sukuma Law and Custom*, London: Oxford University Press.

Cory, H. 1954, *The Indigenous Political System of the Sukuma and Proposals for Political Reform*, Nairobi: Eagle Press.

Deutsches Kolonialblatt, 15 December 1901.

Feierman, S. 1990, *Peasant Intellectuals: Anthropology and History in Tanzania*, Madison: University of Wisconsin Press.

Ford, J. 1971, *The Role of Trypanosomiases in African Ecology: A Study of the Tsetse Fly Problem*, Oxford: Clarendon.

Geschiere, P. 1997, *The Modernity of Witchcraft: Politics and the Occult in Postcolonial Africa*, Charlottesville: University Press of Virginia.

Goody, E. 1970, 'Legitimate and Illegitimate Aggression in a West African State', in M. Douglas (ed.), *Witchcraft Confessions and Accusations*, London: Tavistock, pp. 207-44.

Hartley, B.J. 1938, 'Land Tenure in Usukuma', *Tanganyika Notes and Records* 5: 17-24.

Hartwig, G. 1970, 'The Victoria Nyanza as a Trade Route in the Nineteenth Century', *Journal of African History* 11 (4).

Holmes, C.F. & R.A. Austen 1972, 'The Pre-colonial Sukuma', *Journal of World History* 2: 377-405.

Itandala, B. 1980, 'Nilotic Impact on the Babinza of Usukuma', *Transafrican Journal of History* 9 (1 & 2): 1-17.

Jellicoe, M. 1969, 'The Turu Resistance Movement', *Tanganyika Notes and Records* 70: 1-12.

Johnson, V.E. 1948, *Pioneering for Christ in East Africa*, Rock Island: Augustana Book Concern.

Kjekshus, H. 1977, *Ecology Control and Economic Development in East African History*, London: Heinemann.

Kohl-Larsen, L. 1939, *Simbo Janira: kleiner grosser schwarzer mann*, Kassel: Im Erich Röth.

Kohl-Larsen, L. 1943, *Auf den spuren des vormenschen (Deutsche Afrika-Expedition 1934-1936 und 1937-1939)*, Stuttgart: Strecher und Schröder.

Lan, D. 1985, *Guns and Rain: Guerrillas and Spirit Mediums in Zimbabwe*, Berkeley: University of California Press.

Liebenow, J.G. 1960, 'A Tanganyika Federation: The Sukuma', in A. Richards (ed.), *East African Chiefs: A Study of Political Development in Some Uganda and Tanganyika Tribes*, London: Faber & Faber Limited, pp. 229-59.

Malcolm, D.W. 1953, *Sukumaland: An African People and Their Country*, London: Oxford University Press.

Malkki, L. 1995, *Purity in Exile: Violence, Memory and National Cosmology among Hutu Refugees in Tanzania*, Chicago: University Press.

Masquelier, A. 2000, 'Of Headhunters and Cannibals: Migrancy, Labor, and Consumption in the Mawri Imagination', *Cultural Anthropology* 15 (1): 84-126.

Millroth, B. 1965, *Lyuba: Traditional Religion of the Sukuma*, Uppsala: Almqvist & Wiksells Boktryckeri AB.

Obst, E. 1912a, 'Die Landschaften Issansu und Iramba (Deutsch-Ostafrika)', *Mitteilungen der Geographischen Gesellschaft in Hamburg* 26: 108-32.

Obst, E. 1912b, 'Von Mkalama ins land der Wakindiga', *Mitteilungen der Geographischen Gesellschaft in Hamburg* 26: 1-45.

Obst, E. 1923, 'Das abflußlose Rumpfschollenland im nordöstlichen Deutsch-Ostafrika (Teil II)', *Mitteilungen der Geographischen Gesellschaft in Hamburg* 35, 1-330.

Packard, R.M. 1981, *Chiefship and Cosmology: An Historical Study of Political Competition*, Bloomington: Indiana University Press.

Parkin, D. 1991, *Sacred Void: Spatial Images of Work and Ritual among the Giriama of Kenya*, Cambridge: Cambridge University Press.

Piot, C. 1999, *Remotely Global: Village Modernity in West Africa*, Chicago: University of Chicago Press.

Ranger, T. 1983, 'The Invention of Tradition in Colonial Africa', in E. Hobsbawm & T. Ranger (eds), *The Invention of Tradition*, Cambridge: Cambridge University Press, pp. 211-62.

Reche, O. 1914, *Zur Ethnographie des abflußlosen Gebietes Deutsch-Ostafrikas*, Hamburg: L. Friederichsen & Co.

Reche, O. 1915, 'Dr. Obst's ethnographische Sammlung aus dem abflußlosen Rumpfschollenland des nordöstlichen Deutsch-Ostafrika', *Mitteilungen der Geographischen Gesellschaft in Hamburg* 29: 251-65.

Richards, A. (ed.) 1973, *Economic Development and Tribal Change: A Study of Immigrant Labour in Buganda*, Nairobi: Oxford University Press.

Rowlands, M. & J.-P. Warnier 1988, 'Sorcery, Power and the Modern State in Cameroon', *Man* 23: 118-32.

Sanders, T. 1998, 'Making Children, Making Chiefs: Gender, Power and Ritual Legitimacy', *Africa* 68 (2): 238-62.

Sanders, T. 1999a, 'Modernity, Wealth and Witchcraft in Tanzania', *Research in Economic Anthropology* 20: 117-31.

Sanders, T. 1999b, '"They're Eating us!" Medicinal Topologies and the Mystical Over-Determination of Conflict', Sophenberg Castle, Copenhagen.

Sanders, T. 2000, 'Rains Gone Bad, Women Gone Mad: Rethinking Gender Rituals of Rebellion and Patriarchy', *Journal of the Royal Anthropological Institute* 6: 469-86.

Sanders, T. forthcoming, 'Reflections on Two Sticks: Gender, Sexuality and Rainmaking', *Cahiers d'Études Africaines.*

Sanders, T. n.d. 'Disregarding Modernity, Reaffirming Tradition: Bewitching the Rain in Postcolonial Tanzania', Unpublished manuscript.

Schapera, I. 1947, *Migrant Labour and Tribal Life: A Study of Conditions in the Bechuanaland Protectorate*, London: Oxford University Press.

Senior, H.S. 1938, 'Sukuma Salt Caravans to Lake Eyasi', *Tanganyika Notes and Records* 6: 87-90.

Shipton, P. 1984, 'Lineage and Locality as Antithetical Principles in East African Systems of Land Tenure', *Ethnology* 23: 117-32.

Snyder, K. 1993, 'Like Honey and Water: Moral Ideology and the Construction of Community among the Iraqw of Northern Tanzania', PhD Thesis, Yale University.

Snyder, K. 1997, 'Elders' Authority and Women's Protest: the *Masay* Ritual and Social Change among the Iraqw of Tanzania', *Journal of the Royal Anthropological Institute* 3: 561-76.

Snyder, K. 1999, 'Gender Ideology, and the Domestic and Public Domains among the Iraqw', in H.L. Moore, T. Sanders & B. Kaare (eds), *Those Who Play with Fire: Gender, Fertility and Transformation in East and Southern Africa*, London: Athlone, pp. 225-53.

Speke, J.H. 1864, *What Led to the Discovery of the Source of the Nile*, Edinburgh: William Blackwood & Sons.

Tanner, R.E.S. 1955, 'Land Tenure in Northern Sukumaland, Tanganyika', *East African Agricultural Journal* 2: 120-29.

Tanner, R.E.S. 1958, 'Ancestor Propitiation Ceremonies in Sukumaland, Tanganyika', *Africa* 28 (3): 225-31.

Thornton, R.J. 1980, *Space, Time and Culture among the Iraqw of Tanzania*, New York: Academic Press.

Turton, D. 1996, 'Migrants and Refugees: A Mursi Case Study', in T. Allen (ed.), *In Search of Cool Ground: War, Flight and Homecoming in Northeast Africa*, London: James Currey/Trenton N.Y.: Africa World Press, pp. 96-110.

Waller, R. 1978, 'The Lords of East Africa: The Maasai in the Mid-nineteenth Century (c. 1840-1885)', PhD Thesis, Cambridge University.

Werther, C.W. 1894, *Zum Victoria Nyanza: Eine Antisklaverei-Expedition und Forschungsreise*, Berlin: Gergonne Verlag.

Werther, C.W. 1898, *Die Mittleren Hochländer des nördlichen Deutsch-Ost-Afrika.* Berlin: Hermann Paetel.

Wilson, K. 1994, 'Refugees and Returnees as Social Agents: The Case of Jehovah's Witnesses from Milange', in T. Allen & H. Morsink (eds), *When Refugees Go Home*, London: James Currey, pp. 237-250.

Woodburn, J. 1988a, 'African Hunter-Gatherer Social Organisation: Is it Best Understood as a Product of Encapsulation?', in T. Ingold, D. Riches & J. Woodburn (eds), *Hunter and Gatherers: History, Evolution and Social Change*, Oxford: Berg, pp. 31-64.

Woodburn, J. 1988b, 'Hunter-Gatherer "Silent Trade" with Outsiders and the History of Anthropology', Fifth International Conference on Hunting and Gathering Societies, Darwin, Australia.

4

Moving into another spirit province:
Immigrants and the *Mhondoro* cult
in northern Zimbabwe

Marja Spierenburg

Migration has been a continuous factor in the history of Dande, northern Zimbabwe but since the 1980s immigration into Dande has increased considerably. This, in conjunction with a state-induced land reform programme, has placed considerable strain on relations between immigrants and 'autochthons'. A cult of territorial spirits, the Mhondoro, is one of the most important social institutions in the area, fostering the inclusion of 'strangers'. Due to changes in land allocation procedures, however, the opportunities for integration through the Mhondoro cult have diminished. Mounting tensions are affecting the religious domain in such a way that instead of inclusion, witchcraft accusations are on the increase.

Introduction

Migration has been a constant factor of life in Dande in the Zambezi Valley of northern Zimbabwe where the research for this chapter was undertaken[1] and oral history abounds with stories of conquerors and immigrants, people 'coming from elsewhere'. The different groups of people that settled in the area have left their mark on the religious domain, where each is represented by a royal ancestral spirit, a *Mhondoro*. The *Mhondoro* cult in which these spirits are venerated has created 'spirit provinces', areas with well-recognised boundaries controlled by a *Mhondoro* spirit. This may suggest close links between the ancestors and a specific territory, between their descendants and the spirit province to which they seem to belong. Yet, this focus on territoriality has given the cult many possibilities for enhancing the acceptance of immigrants.

---

[1] The fieldwork on which this chapter is based was made possible by the support of the Netherlands Foundation for the Advancement of Tropical Research (WOTRO). I wish to thank the Centre for Applied Social Sciences, University of Zimbabwe, for granting me the status of Research Associate during my stay in Zimbabwe. In the Netherlands I was affiliated to the Amsterdam School of Social Science Research. A draft of this chapter was presented at the seminar 'Of Other Spaces, Mobility and the Religious Domain in Southern Africa' at the African Studies Centre, Leiden, the Netherlands, on 21 September 2000.

Since the mid-1980s, the government of Zimbabwe has tried to limit migration to Dande as well as control local settlement patterns through the Mid-Zambezi Rural Development Project (MZRDP), a project very similar to the ones described by Scott (1998) where states tried to contain and control mobility as well as 'illegal' (at least from the state's point of view) land-use practices. These attempts have not been entirely successful but ideas about migration and movement have changed as a result. This has had repercussions in the religious domain. Although the mediums of the *Mhondoro* cult played an important role in local resistance against the MZRDP, the cult's role in accepting immigrants and transforming them into kinsmen has been considerably reduced. The project has put notions of 'autochthony' and 'stranger' at the forefront again and created conflicts in which official, bureaucratic identities and self-ascribed identities have often clashed. This chapter explores the cult's role in the context of deepening conflicts between local development efforts, immigrant interests and local residents' concerns.

Dande and its migration history

Dande Communal Land is situated in northern Zimbabwe in the Zambezi Valley. To the north Dande borders Zambia and Mozambique, to the south the boundary is formed by the escarpment, to the west by the Angwa River and in the east by the Msengezi River (Map 4.1; see also Lan 1985: 15). Dande falls under the jurisdiction of Guruve (Rural) District.

Climatic conditions for agriculture in Dande are not favourable: summers are hot and rainfall is unreliable. Close to the escarpment the soils are moderately fertile but further to the north soil quality deteriorates (ADF 1986). The majority of residents depend on smallholder agriculture for a living, though often supplemented by income derived from temporary jobs in the major cities of Zimbabwe or on large-scale commercial farms on the Plateau. The most important cash crops grown in Dande are cotton and maize, the latter also being used for household consumption.

Several waves of invaders and immigrants moved into the area in the past. Some groups are still identifiable, each with its own settlement history and founding myths, but not all immigrants have left their mark on oral history (Lan 1985).

One group of people who used to refer to themselves as Tande claim to be descended from the first inhabitants of the area. Sometime in the fifteenth century they are said to have been defeated by a number of lineages emigrating from the south of Zimbabwe (present-day Karanga) (Beach 1980 and 1984). According to Lan (1985: 14), the name 'Korekore' originates from this period. He argues that it was the name given to the conquerors by those whose land they took. Lan interpreted the name as a corruption of *kure kure*, meaning 'far away' or of a word meaning 'locust'.

It is believed that political alliances between the lineages of the invaders formed the basis of the incorporation of Dande's chieftaincies in the Mutapa State (Beach 1980; Lan 1985). The Mutapa State had political authority over a large part of the Plateau and the Zambezi Valley from the fifteenth to the eighteenth century, though its control over its many subject chieftaincies fluctuated. In the eighteenth century, the Mutapa State lost

Map 4.1: Dande Communal Land, Zimbabwe

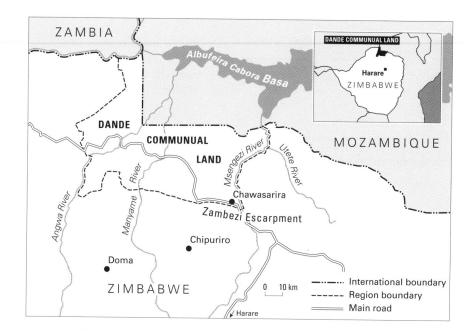

ground to the Rozvi State and as a result, the centre of the Mutapa State moved from the south (near Masvingo) to the Zambezi Valley. It remained there until early in the twentieth century.

During the later Mutapa period, the Dema people appeared in Dande. Their name is interpreted as meaning 'conquerors' but, according to their own mythology, they were defeated and unwillingly incorporated into the Mutapa State. At present, small groups of Dema people live as semi-foragers in the Doma Hills. Possibly due to their prolonged resistance to incorporation within the Mutapa State, they have little access to fertile land (Lan 1985).

Another group of people is made up of descendants of former soldiers in the Portuguese slave armies. Portuguese traders have been present in the Zambezi Valley since the fifteenth century when they traded cloth and beads from India for gold and ivory from Dande. Later, the Portuguese established large farms close to the banks of the Zambezi, which remained in their hands until the early twentieth century. The Portuguese incorporated many of the riverine people living on the north bank of the Zambezi River into their slave armies. The descendants of these people, as well as those of Portuguese landholders, are known today as Chikunda (Lan 1985).

Each of these groups has its own chieftaincies ruled by a lineage that claims to be descended from a founding ancestor, either conqueror or conquered. However, people from all groups live scattered over Dande. Garbett (1967) calculated that only between one quarter and one third of the people living in Dande are members of the chiefly lineage.

In the middle of the nineteenth century, the name Korekore acquired a more general meaning, and from then on was used to refer to all people living in the north and north-west of present-day Zimbabwe (Beach 1980). Not only outsiders (travellers and Portuguese traders) started to use the name in this sense. Even people in Dande who do not have true Korekore ancestors often claim to be Korekore. Lan (1985) suggested that the Korekore had more prestige as conquerors but also that they had a marginally higher economic status. (He offered no explanation as to how the Korekore attained this higher economic status.) Not much is known about how the meaning of the name Korekore changed and finally became the recognised name of a large group of people from different backgrounds.

The guardian spirits of the land: Territoriality and mobility

Mhondoro are the spirits of royal ancestors, the great rulers of the past. All present-day chiefs of Dande claim to be descendants of one of the *Mhondoro*. The spirits are believed to continue looking after the territories they once ruled when they were still alive, by providing rain and fertile soils. In Dande, these areas have well-defined boundaries known to most inhabitants. They were termed 'spirit provinces' by Garbett (1969 and 1977). The land and all other natural resources in a spirit province ultimately belong to the *Mhondoro* of that province.

The *Mhondoro* are thought to communicate with the living through a medium. In theory, a *Mhondoro* medium should not belong to the same clan as the *Mhondoro* spirit that possesses him or her, which means that they are not supposed to belong to the same clan as the chief. They are thus officially classified as 'strangers' or *vatorwa* (see also Lan 1985).[2]

The spirit mediums of the *Mhondoro* can be consulted by individuals in case of sickness or misfortune. More commonly, however, they are consulted by village elders in the event of drought or other natural disasters. In interpreting or explaining climatological or ecological mishaps, the *Mhondoro* mediums also find the moral and political space to voice social comment. Mediums and spirits are believed to be separate entities: a medium cannot be held responsible for what the spirit utters when taking possession of the medium's body, irrespective of the content and meaning of the message. However, there is room for adherents to influence the pronouncements of *Mhondoro* mediums (see Spierenburg 1998 and 2000). Mediums that do not take public opinion into account may subsequently run the risk of being accused of speaking with their own voice instead of the spirit's, and thus might be considered frauds (see also Bourdillon 1979).

The *Mhondoro* cult is mainly concerned with rain and fertility. Each year, two rituals are conducted for the *Mhondoro*. These are *huruva* (or *mbudzirume* or *kamutimuti*) and *tsopero* (or *doro retsepero*).[3] The *huruva* ritual is conducted before the onset of the rainy season to beg the *Mhondoro* for rain and crop protection. After a prosperous harvest, the ritual of *tsopero* is held to thank the *Mhondoro*. Each village or cluster of villages has its own shrine (*dendemaro*) dedicated to the *Mhondoro* of the spirit province where the rituals are conducted. The *Mhondoro* mediums need not be present at all the rituals held in their province as they are conducted by the medium's local assistant (*mutape*, pl. *vatape*). Each village or group of villages with a shrine has a resident ritual assistant, even if the *Mhondoro* of the spirit province has no medium. Unlike this mediumship, the *mutape*-ship is patrilineally inherited. In many cases, the *mutape* is also the village headman or a close relative of his.[4] Apart from organising biannual rituals, the *vatape* also mediate between adherents who wish to consult the *Mhondoro* and the medium.

The concept of spirit provinces seems to emphasise territoriality, a link between ancestors and the land, between their descendants and the area. Indeed, in the struggle for the return of the lands stolen by the white settlers, frequent references are made to ancestral spirits to strengthen claims on certain territories. Yet, the same concept of territoriality allows for mobility, for flexibility in cult membership and for the incorporation of immigrants.

Membership of the *Mhondoro* cult is partly based on lineality. Members of the chiefly clans that claim to be descended from one of the *Mhondoro* spirits can consult their ancestors' mediums regardless of where they are living. For all others, membership is based on territoriality, i.e. all persons living in and, more importantly, cultivating land

---

[2] In practice, however, many mediums (nearly half of all those I have spoken to) actually belong to the same clan as the *Mhondoro* possessing them.

[3] *Mbudzirume* comes from *mwedzi mwembudzi*, the month of the goats, the month during which the ritual is conducted. *Huruva* means dust. The ritual is conducted to calm the winds, to let the dust settle and the rains fall.

[4] But not all village headmen serve as *mutape*.

within a spirit province are supposed to honour the *Mhondoro* in whose province they are living and to recognise their ownership of the land regardless of whether one is a descendant of the *Mhondoro* or not. In other words, strangers living and cultivating in *Mhondoro* territory are more or less automatically included in the cult.

Mobility is reflected in the founding myths in which the *Mhondoro* feature. In Dande it is possible to discern two main lines or lineages of *Mhondoro*: the lineage headed by Bangomwe and representing the autochthonous ancestors, and a lineage representing invaders of Dande from the fifteenth century headed by Mutota. But even the autochthonous *Mhondoro* are believed to come 'from elsewhere'.[5]

The symbolic politics of inclusiveness

When newcomers arrive in the area they not only have to ask permission from the chief and village headman but must also apply to the *Mhondoro* for permission to live in and plough the *Mhondoro*'s territory. A gift must be presented to the *Mhondoro* and the newcomer has to take part in the rituals of the agricultural cycle. By doing so, strangers are accepted as, and are being transformed into, the grandchildren of the *Mhondoro*. In this way, the threat they might pose to the authority of the chiefly, royal lineage is dispelled. The 'strangers who became kinsmen' are defined not in terms of lineage but in terms of territory (Lan 1985) and are included in the *Mhondoro* cult. All adherents have the right to consult Mhondoro mediums.

There can be several reasons for people settling in another chieftaincy: they can either be looking for better land to cultivate or they may have been forced to escape from conflicts with their former chief or village headman. New economic opportunities can also be a pull factor and a lot of myths as well as older people's life histories mention the possibilities of elephant hunting and salt gathering as reasons for moving to Dande.

In the past, the practice of bride service in Dande also contributed to the large numbers of 'strangers' living in the Dande chieftaincies. Since Dande was infested with tsetse fly, it was impossible to keep cattle. Therefore, for those who were not able to acquire prestige goods through participation in trade with the Portuguese, or later earn money in wage labour, it was impossible to pay bride prices. Instead, coming from elsewhere, a groom had to perform agricultural tasks for his in-laws. The period of bride service could last for more than ten years. After its completion, many men decided to stay in the village where they had lived for so long, and would then be allocated their own fields.[6]

Another factor contributing to the presence of 'strangers' in Dande society relates to what are known as *sahwira* relationships. These forms of social relations show not the (re)productive but rather the symbolic importance of the inclusion of migrants for Dande society. When a person dies, the deceased's body cannot be washed or buried by someone from the deceased's family nor even by someone from the same clan. 'Strangers' are needed to bury one's dead and each family has a special agreement with one or more families from a different clan to take care of each other's deceased. The members of these

---

[5] From interviews with the mediums of Bangomwe, Negomo and Nyahuma.
[6] Marriage in Shona-speaking societies is as a rule exogamous.

families refer to one another as *sahwira* (Bourdillon 1987: 61). *Sahwira* relations can be formed between people belonging to different ethnic groups and even a difference in nationality is not seen as an obstacle.[7] In theory, *sahwira* relationships extend to the next generation and are patrilineally inherited. One should never refuse hospitality to one's *sahwira*.

The historical practices of inclusiveness in Dande resulted in complex relationships between clan and territory. Bourdillon (1987: 24) claimed that the word 'clan' might be a misnomer since "it refers to an amorphous and scattered group of people whose only identity as a group is a common clan name". This clan name (*mutupo*) is inherited through the father and the names of clans refer to totem animals or body parts that the members of the clans are forbidden to eat. Clans are subdivided in sub-clans, distinguishable by a praise name added to the clan name (e.g. Nzou Samanyanga means 'elephant'; the name of the clan, 'keeper of the tusk', is the praise name). The sub-clan names are often associated with certain geographical areas, suggesting, according to Bourdillon, that they originated as local pockets of a particular clan. Furthermore, there is a certain association between chiefly clan names and territories but these territories could be extended or lost to conquerors. Nevertheless, many people maintain that the name of a sub-clan (i.e. the name of a clan in combination with a specific praise name) does, in fact, indicate a certain place of origin. Clan membership also facilitates mobility: people who are not related to one another and come from different parts of Zimbabwe (or even Mozambique, provided they belong to a Shona-speaking group) but share the same totem animal are supposed to offer one another hospitality. Such hospitality features in many immigrants' life histories. In theory, clan membership cannot be changed but adopting a new clan name to facilitate settlement in a new area or even 'stealing' a clan name to underpin one's claims to a conquered territory features prominently in the founder myths in Dande. One myth, for instance, recounts how one of Mutota's children stole the elephant tusks that Bangomwe used as headrests. From then on Mutota's descendants claimed to belong to the same clan as Bangomwe: Nzou Samanyanga, elephant, and keeper of the tusks.

Recent immigration into Dande

The latest movement of immigrants to Dande started at the end of the 1960s. It stagnated in the mid-1970s due to fierce fighting in the area between the guerrilla armies of ZANU and ZAPU on one side and the Rhodesian forces on the other. Shortly after independence, however, massive and spontaneous waves of migration into Dande started again (Murphree *et al.* 1989; Spierenburg 1990).

The majority of these recent immigrants mainly spoke Karanga and Zezuru (Shona dialects) and originated from the Communal Lands surrounding Masvingo in the south-southwest of Zimbabwe. A severe shortage of land was the main motive for leaving their home communities, although they were, themselves, not necessarily landless or even from

---

[7] I came across many examples of families who, while they were working on commercial farms on the Plateau of Zimbabwe, initiated *sahwira* relations with families from Zambia and Malawi who belonged to groups that were not Shona-speaking.

the poorest sector of their community. A number of them had regularly managed to produce food crops for marketing and most families had been able to save money from wage labour to invest in agricultural production.

For these immigrants the availability of virgin land in Dande was the area's main attraction. In Dande hardly any land had been appropriated since the Rhodesian government deemed the hot, tsetse-fly and malaria-infested area unsuitable for large-scale commercial farming. The immigrants arrived with the aim of increasing agricultural production for the market. The majority brought in cattle[8] and ploughs from their home area enabling them to cultivate slightly larger tracts of land than the autochthonous inhabitants of Dande (Spierenburg 1990).

A minority of the immigrants were former wage labourers with no ties to land in any of the Communal Areas in Zimbabwe. These immigrants, originally from Mozambique, Zambia and Malawi, came to Dande to find a place to spend their old age. They cultivate only small pockets of land on which they grow maize, often barely (and sometimes not) enough for subsistence (Spierenburg 1990).

The majority of recent immigrants, including those abandoning homes in other Communal Areas, came to Dande via large-scale commercial farms where they met colleagues from Dande. Many had already established *sahwira* relations at the workplace with families from Dande and these relations facilitated their migration. A number of the immigrants who arrived after 1980 were ex-combatants who had fought in Dande during the struggle for liberation and had seen the possibilities the area offered for agriculture.

The immigrants were welcomed by village headmen and chiefs, and in some cases even recruited by the latter. Chiefs and headmen hoped that with more people living in Dande they could put pressure on the new government to improve services and infrastructure in the area. Dande had large wildlife populations that posed a threat to crops and lives, and more inhabitants would mean more land being cleared for agriculture, thus pushing bush and wildlife further away. Immigrants received a lot of support from local communities, including donations of food to bridge the gap until their first harvest. Support continued until the mid-1980s when their numbers increased significantly. By that time, recent immigrants accounted for almost a third of the population of some of the more easily accessible villages along the main roads (Spierenburg 1990; Derman 1993).

As more immigrants arrived, however, the level of hospitality they received began to decrease. They either had to pay autochthons for food or had to buy it in town. But most importantly, they were no longer taken to the spirit mediums to be transformed into grandsons and granddaughters of the soil. Tensions between immigrants and long-term residents increased even further when the Mid-Zambezi Rural Development Project was introduced.

---

[8] After independence, efforts to eradicate the tsetse fly were resumed. The Ministry of Lands, Resettlement and Rural Development claimed that tsetse infestation was controlled by 1985.

Immigrants and the Mid-Zambezi Rural Development Project

The Mid-Zambezi Rural Development Project (MZRDP) was officially introduced in 1987 and covered virtually all of Dande except the area west of the Manyame River. The project's goal was to control spontaneous immigration and rationalise local land-use practices. The project proposed to limit the number of new settlers to 3,000 families, who were to be placed in 130 newly created villages. On the basis of the 1982 national census it was estimated that approximately 4,600 households were already living in the project area prior to implementation. They would have their villages reorganised and their arable fields redistributed (ADF 1986).

The African Development Fund assisted in funding the project although its actual implementation was the responsibility of the Department of Rural Development (DERUDE), a department of the Ministry of Local Government and Rural and Urban Development, and Agritex, the national agricultural extension service.

The MZRDP was one of the pilot projects that introduced internal land reforms the government wished to implement in all Communal Areas of Zimbabwe (see Zimbabwe Government 1985a and 1985b; ADF 1986). The implicit assumption underlying these land reforms was that people in the Communal Areas were using land inefficiently and that improved efficiency and intensification of land use could alleviate the pressures existing in most Communal Areas in Zimbabwe.[9]

All arable land was to be (re)distributed with households receiving twelve acres of arable land and a one-acre residential stand in a reorganised village. Households would not obtain a permanent title deed for the land but would be given temporary user rights. Agritex developed cultivation plans for the twelve-acre units (ADF 1986).

The MZRDP actually managed to create a shortage of land where one had previously not existed. The number of people already living in the project area was greatly underestimated and not enough plots were demarcated to cater for all the inhabitants. About a third of the population present at the time of the introduction of the project would not be able to acquire a registered plot and would become officially landless and illegal squatters.

The MZRDP resulted in conflicts over land at two different levels. One was between the state and the local population (in general). As described elsewhere (Spierenburg 1998 and 2000), the mediums of the *Mhondoro* cult played an important role in conflicts at this level by expressing local grievances, contesting the state's authority over land by claiming that the ultimate owners of the land were the royal *Mhondoro* spirits, and by threatening supernatural punishments if these claims were not recognised. At least in one part of Dande, ancestral threats managed to stall the implementation of the MZRDP indefinitely.

The *Mhondoro* mediums were less influential in the other type of conflict over land, the conflict amongst the local population over who had the rights to plots if the MZRDP could not be stopped. Here, questions of identity played an important role and conflicts arose over the definition of 'immigrants' and 'long-term residents'.

---

[9] Recently, strategies to alleviate land pressure in the Communal Areas in Zimbabwe have changed, though the motives behind these changes can be seriously questioned.

In 1988, the term 'immigrants' was mainly used to indicate the group of newcomers who had arrived since independence, and sometimes applied to those who had arrived in the late 1960s. This group was very heterogeneous and included Shona-speaking people from south-east Zimbabwe (speaking Karanga and Zezuru dialects) and former commercial farm labourers of Malawian, Mozambican and Zambian origin with or without Zimbabwean citizenship. Some of the recent settlers were Mozambicans coming from areas just across the border (sometimes even from the same spirit province since many of these cross the border), who were also referred to as Korekore. Initially they were not considered immigrants but as tensions mounted they became so. With conflicts over land increasing, the definition of 'immigrants' was broadened and people started looking further into the past to find ancestors that were not originally from Dande.

The conflicts amongst the inhabitants of Dande were related to earlier settlement patterns and the way these conflicted with project regulations. Through the MZRDP, the state tried to enforce the official ban on riverine cultivation arguing that it caused erosion and siltation.[10] Most of the villages' early inhabitants, those who considered themselves autochthons (hereafter referred to as 'long-term residents') in Dande had their fields on the banks of the many small rivers running through the area. As immigration continued, it became increasingly difficult for immigrants to get access to riverine fields other than through borrowing or renting. The fields allocated by chiefs and headmen to the more recent newcomers were generally situated further away from the riverbanks, though immigrants were allowed to plant gardens in the riverbeds in winter when the rivers dried up.[11] When existing villages were reorganised, immigrants stood a better chance of obtaining fields, since they were often already farming in the upland areas demarcated by Agritex. Long-term residents had most of their fields near the rivers, and hardly ever had demarcation pegs there. This disadvantageous situation for long-term residents was aggravated by the biases of project personnel who frequently considered the immigrants to be better farmers,[12] i.e. those immigrants who came from other Communal Lands. Retired farm labourers were considered to be the least successful farmers.

Once Agritex had demarcated twelve-acre plots in a certain area, a scramble for land within the new boundaries followed. If a plot had been demarcated within an existing field, it could be officially allocated to the farmer who cultivated the most acres within the plot, provided he had Zimbabwean citizenship and was officially registered at the Rural District Council (this was locally referred to as 'having district citizenship'). These criteria were adopted by project staff under pressure from the Rural District Council and

---

[10] However, Scoones and Cousins (1991) demonstrated that the technical evidence, on which the continuation of the ban was based, contained many inaccuracies and that the practice was far less damaging than often assumed (see also Dambo Research Unit, Loughborough University 1987). When research demonstrated the profitability of maize production on wetlands, this resulted in the legalisation of wetland cultivation in the European areas in the 1960s (see Murombedzi 1991). Farmers in the communal areas, on the other hand, remained bound by the old legislation.

[11] Most rivers in the valley are not perennial and dry up in winter. When the rivers run dry, the moist riverbeds are parcelled out and divided among all villagers for planting vegetable and maize gardens.

[12] Though many long-term residents also consider immigrants (coming from other Communal Lands) to be better farmers, this opinion is not supported by data I gathered concerning the agricultural production of both groups. The advantages that many have in the form of cattle for ploughing is offset by the advantage that the autochthons have of cultivating riverine fields that often yield two harvests a year.

were meant to protect the rights of long-term residents. The desired effect was not always achieved. Many of the recent immigrants had Zimbabwean citizenship and had registered with the Council. Some of the long-term residents, however, had obtained their identity cards outside the district when they were working on commercial farms and in the cities and had never verified the district number on their cards. In order to defend their right to land, long-term residents suddenly claimed large parts of the newly demarcated fields, stating that long ago the chiefs had allocated them land for future use. They transferred all their labour to the new plots, clearing as many acres as possible in order to stand a better chance of being allocated them.

When the project was first introduced, many immigrants welcomed it, thinking it would provide them with more secure rights to land than they felt the chiefs and village headmen could provide, especially since the latter had more or less sabotaged the process of them being transformed into grandchildren of the *Mhondoro*. However, as the project seriously challenged their relations with their hosts, many immigrants changed their minds and supported local resistance to the project. Despite this support, many saw their rights to land in Dande denied.

Violent clashes between immigrants and long-term residents were rare: the killing of one immigrant in a fight over a twelve-acre plot in Karai VIDCO was a sad exception. But tensions mounted and the old mechanisms of inclusion came under pressure. Though in theory *sahwira* relationships cannot be broken, in a number of cases they were no longer respected and hospitality was withheld. Witchcraft accusations were rife, often related to the fact that the most recent immigrants had not been taken through the proper procedures of acceptance by the *Mhondoro* mediums. Many mediums complained that they had not been able to check these immigrants on their tendencies to engage in witchcraft. This did not mean, however, that in conflicts over land it was only the immigrants who suffered from accusations of witchcraft.

The case presented below concerns a conflict over land between two women and shows how identity could become a key issue in claiming land through the MZRDP. It also demonstrates that local labels and official bureaucratic identities do not necessarily coincide. Claims of autochthony were used to appeal for the *Mhondoro* medium's support but this had little effect. Witchcraft accusations then became an important aspect in the conflict, forcing local authorities to take action. However, the MZRDP had taken control over land allocation away from these local authorities.

The conflict between Sylvia and Lucia

The conflict involved two women, Sylvia and Lucia. Lucia was born in the mid-1940s in Dande. Her parents were also born in Dande. Her *mutupo* (clan) was Nzou Samanyanga, which is considered a local clan, the same as that of the *Mhondoro*. When Lucia was about ten or eleven her parents died and she moved with her sister and her sister's husband to the Zimbabwe Plateau where they worked on a white-owned commercial farm. When she was about seventeen she married a Mozambican farm labourer. After her divorce in 1983 she returned to Dande, accompanied by her sister's daughter and two grandsons, all of primary-school age. She did not return to the village where she had been born but instead moved to Chawasarira (see Map 4.1), where her uncle was living. She approached the village headman in Chawasarira to ask for a plot of land and was allocated about four acres. Since the village where she had been born was located in a different spirit province from Chawasarira, she herself insisted on a visit to the *Mhondoro* medium together with the village headman and received his permission to cultivate the land. With the help of the three children, she cultivated maize and cotton. Her neighbour in Chawasarira was Sylvia.

Sylvia arrived in Dande in 1982 when she was in her late thirties. She was born on a white-owned commercial farm, as was her husband. In 1982 the owner of the farm sold it and started a road construction firm. Sylvia's husband then started working as a driver for this firm and lived in town. When the farm was sold, Sylvia and her husband decided it was time for her to secure a home for the family in a rural area. Since she was still capable of working hard, she wanted to make the farm as profitable as possible and planned to grow cotton. She and her husband, however, originally came from one of the Communal Lands close to Masvingo where the Shona dialect of Karanga is spoken and where land was scarce. Her sister, who was married to someone from Dande, told her there was still a lot of land available in Dande. Sylvia and her husband approached the local party secretary and the village headman of Chawasarira and were allocated a six-acre plot. The village headman did not take the husband to see the *Mhondoro* medium but instead clapped his hands[13] to the *Mhondoro* and asked him to protect this 'son of Zimbabwe'. He asked Sylvia's husband to pay him an acceptance fee that he said he would hand over to the *Mhondoro* medium. Sylvia cultivated the six acres, growing maize, cotton and groundnuts with the help of her four youngest children and her mother. Occasionally, she hired labourers from the money her husband sent.

Both Sylvia and Lucia said that prior to the demarcation of the fields they had had good relations with each other. They exchanged groundnuts and vegetables and occasionally helped each other in the fields. Sylvia established a branch of the ZANU (PF) Women's League in Chawasarira, of which Lucia became a member.

In 1988 all the inhabitants of Dande had to register with the Senior Resettlement Officer for resettlement under the MZRDP. Each household head had to show his or her identity card to prove that they had Zimbabwean citizenship. Immigrants also had to show official district administration letters of transfer showing the date of migration. Sylvia and her husband were able to hand over all the required papers and were allocated a plot. This plot included the land Sylvia was already cultivating. Lucia, however, could not prove she was a Zimbabwean citizen. When she had got married, her Mozambican husband had arranged her papers and had registered her as Mozambican. At the time, Lucia did not think there would be any problem, and the village headman had assured her that as a Korekore she had the right to a piece of land in Dande and that she could keep the plot she was allocated by him.

Lucia soon discovered that the four acres she had been allocated by the village headman were within the boundaries of the twelve-acre plot officially allocated to Sylvia and her husband. She asked the resettlement officers where her plot would be, upon which she was told that as a Mozambican she would not be allocated a plot at all. Lucia then went to the

---

[13] Clapping hands is a way of greeting someone and is also a sign of respect.

village headman to complain. Together they approached the Senior Resettlement Officer (SRO) in Mahuwe. The village headman complained that the land he had allocated to a Korekore woman had been given to a Karanga immigrant. The SRO said that there was nothing he could do since he had to follow official procedures. The village headman then accused the SRO, who like the other resettlement officers was not a local man, of tribalism and argued that some of the immigrants who came from other Communal Lands without proper letters of transfer were still allocated a field. The SRO denied these allegations and repeated that he could do nothing for Lucia. (Interviews with immigrants, however, showed that the allegations of the village headman were not completely without reason.)

In Chawasarira many people who considered themselves autochthons complained bitterly that they had either not received any land at all or that it was in a different village. They accused the SRO of favouring immigrants. The week after the village headman and Lucia went to see the SRO, one of the resettlement officers had a car accident. Immediately, rumours spread in Chawasarira that the accident was a sign that the *Mhondoro* did not approve of the demarcation. The fact that one of the DERUDE teams drilling for boreholes in the newly settled areas kept striking rocks was also interpreted as a sign of the *Mhondoro*'s disapproval of the MZRDP.

Lucia went to see Sylvia and demanded that she be allowed to stay on her twelve-acre plot. She argued that she had more rights to the land because she was Korekore than Sylvia who was Karanga. Sylvia refused on the grounds that the government had allocated her the plot, claiming that 'the government' had the ultimate authority to decide how the land should be used. The village headman also put pressure on Sylvia to let Lucia stay. He argued that as a Korekore village headman it was he who had the ultimate right to allocate the land and that he had allocated the twelve-acre plot to Lucia.

Lucia then went with the village headman to see the *Mhondoro* medium to ask for support. When I visited the *Mhondoro* medium and asked him about immigrants and the MZRDP in general he made the following comment:

> Long ago when these people were coming, they first saw the *sabhuku* [village headman]. If the *sabhuku* had land to allocate, he would take the person to the *mutape* [the medium's ritual assistant] and tell him to call *sekuru* [the *Mhondoro*] to inform him about the visitor and the *sekuru* would talk to the visitor because this person might have murdered people where he came from or his ancestors might have bad spirits. (…) The wife of the *mutape* would be asked to grind sorghum and the meal would be given to the *dunzwi* [the medium's messenger]. The *dunzwi* would perform *chiumba* with the meal [i.e. mix it with water, form a sort of ball and place it in the proposed field]. The following morning they would look at the *chiumba* to see whether is had spread [lost its ball-shape form] or not, and if it had spread, they would go back to the spirit to ask the spirit what to do with the person and the spirit would say what was to be done. If the *chiumba* had not spread, the person would be told in which areas he would be allowed to live. (…) But these days these immigrants, we just see them in this area and we do not know where these visitors come from. If the *Mhondoro* asks the chiefs and the *sabhuku* about these immigrants, he is told that this is done by his *muzukuru* [grandson] Mugabe [President of Zimbabwe]. The *Mhondoro* always says that although it is Mugabe who is allowing these people here, why can the [chiefs and *sabhuku*] not inform me about these immigrants? (…) The [Rural District] councillors and the chiefs are the people who are responsible for allocating land to these immigrants. The *Mhondoro* accepts these people but he says we will see what will happen in the future.

The medium blamed the government for denying local authorities control over land and allowing strangers to settle through procedures that it considered legitimate but that locally were not accepted. He said he would back up Lucia's claim but that the resettlement officer had to come and see him, not the other way around. The resettlement officer refused to do so, denying the authority of the *Mhondoro* over land.

A week after Lucia's visit to the medium, Sylvia's mother fell ill, suffering from headaches, stomach pains and fever. Sylvia suspected Lucia of bewitching her mother and when her mother did not recover in spite of taking the malaria tablets she had received at the local clinic, Sylvia went to see Lucia. Outside Lucia's hut, so that anyone passing might hear, she accused Lucia of bewitching her mother.

Two days later, the chairman of the Village Development Committee (VIDCO), the village headman and the local party secretary had a meeting. The village headman supported Lucia, the local party secretary gave his support to Sylvia. The VIDCO chairman, himself an early immigrant who had settled in Dande in 1966, was hesitant about taking sides. After long hours of discussion, a compromise was reached: Sylvia was urged to let Lucia cultivate the four acres till the next harvesting season. The village headman and the VIDCO chairman would accompany Lucia to the District Council in Upper Guruve to support her request for a change of citizenship and Lucia would then be able to register for resettlement in another village in Dande. Sylvia agreed to the solution.

Lucia, however, was unable to raise the money to pay the fees, which had just been considerably increased, to obtain citizenship. She was allocated a field by the village headman in the area designated as a common grazing area by MZRDP staff. She continues to farm there with a number of other villagers who have not received a plot. All are now labelled illegal squatters by the Rural District Council but so far no steps have been taken to evict them.

Concluding remarks

Immigration has always been an important feature of life in Dande. This is reflected in the religious domain where the *Mhondoro* cult almost automatically includes immigrants. Other mechanisms of inclusion, such as the *sahwira* relationship, also hint at the importance of 'strangers' in and for society. However, inclusion means control: to be included in the cult means to accept the authority of the *Mhondoro* over land, and the social and moral rules prescribed by the cult.

Recently, with increasing pressure on land, general acceptance of the latest immigrants has decreased. The procedures for integrating them into the *Mhondoro* cult, and thus acknowledging their right to land, are no longer followed. The Mid-Zambezi Rural Development Project, designed to control settlement patterns and in particular spontaneous migration to the valley, has further increased tensions between recent immigrants and long-term residents. By replacing existing local land allocation procedures, the project has made the application of earlier integration (and control) mechanisms almost impossible. Inclusion and control have been replaced by exclusion and conflict. The shortage of land, created by the project, has resulted in conflicts focused on identity as a means of claiming land. Through bureaucratic rules and regulations it was thought that the rights of 'local' people could be guaranteed. However, in a country where most official papers are registered on an *ad hoc* basis and only for certain purposes, this can create serious problems. Just how complicated the issue of identity is in present-day Zimbabwe was shown in the case described above, where official papers and (self-) ascribed identities seriously conflicted with one another.

Although the *Mhondoro* cult played an important role in resisting the MZRDP, its role in controlling conflicts over land between the inhabitants of the spirit provinces has been reduced. Witchcraft accusations, as in the case study, have become rife but whether they have actually increased as a result of the reduced role of the *Mhondoro* cult remains a suspicion difficult to verify.

References

ADF, African Development Fund 1986, 'Appraisal Report for the Mid-Zambezi Valley Rural Development Project', Agricultural and Rural Development Department.

Beach, D.N. 1980, *The Shona and Zimbabwe, 900-1850*, Gweru: Mambo Press.

Beach, D.N. 1984, *Zimbabwe Before 1900*, Gweru: Mambo Press.

Bourdillon, M.F.C. 1979, 'Religion and Authority in a Korekore Community', *Africa* 49: 172-81.

Bourdillon, M.F.C. 1987, *The Shona Peoples. An Ethnography of the Contemporary Shona, with Special Reference to their Religion*, Revised edition, Gweru: Mambo Press.

Dambo Research Unit, Loughborough University, U.K. 1987, 'Utilisation of Dambos in Rural Development, A Discussion Paper', Unpublished report, University of Zimbabwe.

Derman, W. 1993, 'Recreating Common Property Management: Government Projects and Land Use Policy in the Mid-Zambezi Valley, Zimbabwe', Unpublished paper, University of Zimbabwe, Centre for Applied Social Sciences.

Garbett, K. 1967, 'Prestige, Status and Power in a Modern Valley Korekore Chiefdom, Rhodesia', *Africa* 37: 307-25.

Garbett, K. 1977, 'Disparate Regional Cults and a Unitary Field in Zimbabwe', in R. Werbner (ed.), *Regional Cults*, London: Academic Press, pp. 55-92.

Government of Zimbabwe 1985a, 'Communal Lands Development Plan. A 15-Year Development Strategy. First Draft', Ministry of Land, Resettlement and Rural Development, Harare: Government Printer.

Government of Zimbabwe 1985b, 'Resettlement and Rural Development: Intensive Resettlement Policies and Procedures. Revised Version', Ministry of Land, Resettlement and Rural Development, Harare: Government Printer.

Lan, D. 1985, *Guns and Rain. Guerrillas & Spirit Mediums in Zimbabwe*, Harare: Zimbabwe Publishing House.

Murombedzi, J. 1991, 'Wetlands Conservation under Common Property Management Regimes in Zimbabwe', University of Zimbabwe, Centre for Applied Social Sciences, NRM Occasional Papers.

Murphree, M.W., J. Murombedzi & R. Hawks 1989, 'Survey of In-migration to Portions of the Kariba, Guruve and Kanyati Districts', Unpublished report, University of Zimbabwe, Centre for Applied Social Sciences.

Scoones, I. & B. Cousins 1991, *Contested Terrains: The Struggle For Control over Dambo Resources in Zimbabwe*, London: Drylands Programme, IIED.

Scott, J. 1998, *Seeing Like a State. How Certain Schemes to Improve the Human Condition Have Failed*, New Haven: Yale University Press.

Spierenburg, M. 1990, 'Migrants in Dande Communal Land: A Study of their Origins, their Motives for Migration and their Agricultural Production', Unpublished MA thesis, University of Utrecht.

Spierenburg, M. 1998, 'Healing the Ills of Development: The Role of the *Mhondoro* Cult in the Struggle against an Irrigation Project in Dande', in H. Schmidt & A. Wirz (eds), *Afrika und das Andere, Alteritaet und Innovation*, Hamburg: LIT Verlag.

Spierenburg, M. 2000, 'Social Commentaries and the Influence of the Clientele: The *Mhondoro* Cult in Dande, Zimbabwe', in R. van Dijk, R. Reis & M. Spierenburg (eds), *The Quest for Fruition through Ngoma, Political Aspects of Healing in Southern Africa*, Oxford: James Currey.

5

Cultures of travel:
Fulbe pastoralists in central Mali
and Pentecostalism in Ghana

Mirjam de Bruijn, Han van Dijk & Rijk van Dijk

Population mobility has always been regarded as a special and temporary phenomenon. However, in many instances mobility is the normal state, while sedentarity is the extraordinary situation. This is illustrated with two examples of so-called 'cultures of travel'. The first about the Fulbe in Mali demonstrates the ways in which mobility has historically been embedded in Sahelian cultures under conditions that are marginal from both an eco-logical and an economic point of view. It illustrates how people develop economic and cultural strategies marked by a high degree of opportunism. Their society is, in fact, organised around mobility. The second case, that of Ghanaian Pentecostalism, shows how a specific form of culture acts to bring about a particular form of mobility. Unlike the Fulbe, it is not the whole society that moves but persons who are mobile for individual and personal reasons. It is an example of how people construct and, almost literally, produce cultural forms and means for dealing with everyday problems of mobility, and success and failure in this domain.

Introduction

The study of population mobility in its different forms has started to receive increasing attention. Migration has always been an important topic for geographers, economists of development and development studies but within anthropology the subject used to receive much less attention from anthropologists concentrating on small, territorialised communities. Only fairly recently have scholars such as Appadurai (1991 and 1995), Clifford (1992), Hastrup & Olwig (1997), to name but a few, taken up the challenge of studying the cultural aspects of population mobility. Notions like 'travelling cultures' (Clifford 1992), 'the production of locality' (Appadurai 1995), 'global ethnoscapes' (Appadurai 1991) found their way into the anthropological vocabulary on the wave of the post-modernist shift towards Cultural Studies that took place a decade ago. Large-scale population movements in the form of labour migration, refugee movements, asylum seeking, international and intercontinental travel and tourism have led anthropologists and sociologists into new theoretical and empirical fields.

The exploration of new forms of mobility has encouraged anthropologists to re-examine the foundations of their discipline. According to Hastrup & Olwig (1997: 1), cultures were conceptualised as separate and unique entities corresponding to particular *localities*: "The erection of cultural distinctions and borders is thus closely related to the anthropological practice of understanding culture from an internal *local* point of view" (emphasis added). In his essay on 'travelling cultures', Clifford (1992: 101) proposed an alternative "[...] why not focus on any culture's farthest range of travel while *also* looking at its centres, its villages, its intensive field sites? How do groups negotiate themselves in external relationships, and how is a culture also a site of travel for others? How are spaces traversed from outside? How is one group's core another's periphery?"

Clifford reserved his notion of travel for contemporary forms of travel and excluded involuntary forms of movement like the slave trade and contract labour, modern involuntary travellers like refugees and asylum seekers, and economic travellers like labour migrants. Travel in his view carries with it a special kind of culture, such as that of nineteenth-century British intellectuals and explorers travelling through Europe (especially Italy) and to such remote places as the source of the Nile. In its contemporary form, it seems to refer to movement in a seemingly border-free cosmopolitan world consisting of hotel lounges, airports and the like. This idea of travel applies to those with specific bourgeois class and gender positions and is distinct from other forms of mobility such as labour migration.

This chapter discusses how population mobility in Africa is frequently a cultural phenomenon and is culturally mediated, and how contemporary and past forms of population mobility have given rise to cultural forms and ways of relating to others. The question is not so much whether travelling cultures exist but how they are produced and respond to, mediate and mitigate social, economic, political and ecological conditions in Africa and beyond. Population mobility and the associated travelling culture are decisively influenced by conditions on the ground that force people to move. In Africa some people have developed travel as the very basis of their existence.

The problem with the study of population mobility is that it has always been regarded as a special and temporary phenomenon (Hastrup & Olwig 1997: 6) and that the natural state of people and the world was conceived of in terms of stability and coherence (Davis 1992; Hastrup 1993). Gypsies and nomads, obvious exceptions to this rule, have always been regarded as unruly and undisciplined people. However, today the reality is unprecedented mobility and massive movements of people in Africa and beyond. The various forms of mobility cannot be reduced to abominations of 'normal' patterns of life. In many instances mobility *is* the normal state, while sedentarity is viewed as extraordinary.

This poses some methodological problems. Social science, as a product of our own society, has been marked by strong assumptions of life being organised in bounded geographical spaces of the state, the city or the village. Mobility is assumed to be contained within neatly demarcated territorial boundaries. It is regarded as problematic when it not only overturns our conceptions of culture but also the political, social, ethnic and cultural boundaries that social science supposes to exist. Mobility is often associated with disorder and suffering with poverty, political and military conflicts or ecological disaster frequently the reason for population movements. These subjects have long been neglected in social science (Davis 1992; Hastrup 1993). Our notions of culture and of social order need to be redirected. In this way a new perspective may emerge on mobility in time and space and the processes of de-territorialisation and re-territorialisation, and the disordering and ordering which it involves (cf. Hastrup & Olwig 1997: 7).

The case studies discussed in this chapter deal with various aspects of mobility, showing not only two forms of mobility but also two kinds of mobility of forms. The case of the Fulbe involves the mobility of a whole culture, a specific form from one location to another embedded in a myriad of forms of mobility. It demonstrates the ways in which mobility has historically been embedded in Sahelian cultures. The specificity of the conditions in areas that are marginal from both an ecological and economic point of view means that people develop economic and cultural strategies marked by a high degree of opportunism. The whole society is, in fact, organised around these opportunistic strategies. The second case, that of Ghanaian Pentecostalism, is different. A specific form of culture acts to bring about a particular form of mobility. Moreover, it is not a whole culture or a whole population that is on the move but persons who are mobile for individual and personal reasons. Mobility among Ghanaian Pentecostalists is not yet part and parcel of daily life as it is for the Fulbe but it presents a fascinating example of how people construct and, almost literally, produce cultural forms and means for dealing with everyday problems of mobility, and success and failure in this domain.

In both cases mobility has acquired a momentum in itself, in which something has emerged that may be labelled a culture of travel. A field of practices, institutions, and ideas and reflections related to mobility and travelling, which has acquired a specific dynamism of its own, has arisen out of interaction with conditions 'on the ground'. The most striking aspect of these cultural fields is that they are closely related to others. In the Ghanaian case, the links between mobility and Pentecostal churches, and evangelical Christianity in general, are indispensable for an understanding of particular forms of migration from Ghana. In the case of the Fulbe, the phenomena discussed are part of a larger cultural and historical repertoire that extends back in time and is shared by Fulbe society and most of semi-arid West Africa.

A culture of travel: The Fulbe of Mali, a nomadic cattle-rearing people

Diversity in Fulbe society

The Fulbe are an example of a pre-modern travelling culture. Although questions surround their unity and origins, they have spread over much of Sub-Saharan Africa between Senegal and Ethiopia and the Sahara and the West-African coast, creating an archipelago of "islands of Fulbeness" (Botte & Schmitz 1994). During the eighteenth and nineteenth centuries, their political control extended over pagan populations in Senegal, Mali, Guinea, Burkina Faso, Nigeria and Cameroon. As a result, a string of empires and emirates emerged along the Sahel (Schmitz 1994; Ba & Daget 1984; Robinson 1985; Diallo 1999; Burnham & Last 1994). Other groups of Fulbe who felt uncomfortable within these theocratic states moved north to the northern Sahel to escape political control (Dupire 1962). Fulbe who are descended from pilgrims travelling to Mecca are known as Islamic scholars in Sudan (Abu-Manga 1999; Delmet 2000). They moved into towns in Sierra Leone as traders (Bah 1998).

More recently, other forms of population mobility have emerged. Over the last few decades numerous livestock-keeping Fulbe have moved southward in search of new pastures (Bernardet 1984; Blench 1994; Diallo this volume). This movement accelerated under the impact of drought and economic problems in the Sahel proper, and political problems in Guinea and Mauritania forced some Fulbe to settle as refugees in Senegal (Tanoh 1971; Santoir 1994).

In the literature this mobility has become linked to the fact that they are a cattle-keeping people and therefore moving to feed their livestock. This stereotype is based on the Fulbe's self-image and the ethnic stereotypes held by their neighbours.[1] In reality, this mobility based on a pastoral economy relates to only one of this society's many social groups. However, the cattle-rearing Fulbe have come to represent the Fulbe identity and have found their way as such into coffee-table books produced by Western photographers (Beckwith & van Offelen 1983; Mols 2000) and magazines like *National Geographic*.

It is the mobility and the associated political (and sexual) freedom that attracts these relative outsiders but the role of mobility goes much deeper than this and permeates the ways in which people relate to each other and the shape their social life has taken. Fulbe society is divided into a number of social groups, some of which are sedentary, while others lead a more mobile way of life. The political elite (the chiefly lineages), Islamic clergy, artisans and a group of courtiers have an almost sedentary lifestyle though they have a history of mobility. Mobility is a way of life of a cattle-rearing people that has developed into something else over the course of history. Traditionally the nomadic pastoralists, who form the majority of these people, had a mobile way of life. The keeping of cattle and the cattle themselves symbolise mobility but are not synonymous with it or with Fulbe identity. Other elements of Fulbe identity such as Islam are also related to forms of travel. This case study considers the various aspects of mobility in their contemporary as well as their historical forms.

The Hayre
The Hayre is located in the Sahel, the semi-arid belt extending across Africa from Senegal to the Indian Ocean. The area experiences low annual rainfall (300-600 mm per annum) that is extremely unpredictable in both time and space. This variability accounts for wide variations in the crop and livestock production that forms the basis of the livelihood of the population.

The Hayre ('rock' or 'mountain' in Fulfulde, the Fulbe language) derives its name from the mountains and the plateau that dominate the landscape in the centre of the

---

[1]   See Breedveld (1999) for information on ethnic stereotyping and internal categorisations in relation to the Fulbe.

Niger Bend (see Map 5.1). The region further consists of an area of sandy soils and fixed dunes called Seeno where good pastures can be found, and an area with clayey soils called Ferro that is overgrown with dense forest alternating with strips of bare earth.

The research on which this section is based took place in central Mali in the districts[2] of Douentza and Bandiagara and in south Mali in Koutiala District. It considered the mobility of the Fulbe, how they express mobility in their lives but also in a geographical sense the interactions of the people with their Sahelian ecological environment. Given the climatic conditions, resource availability is extremely varied in time and space. Mobility in a variety of forms is a necessary strategy for dealing with this variability (Gallais 1975). In the past, as well as today, it is not only the climate that has caused mobility but also a variety of social, political and economic factors that are culturally mediated.

The history of population mobility has to be framed within the context of political change in a much larger area. People do not just move due to ecological considerations. They have perceptions of the places they move to or might move to and meanings are attached to these places in cultural ways, acting as coordinates in the process of movement. Outside influences impede or promote movement.

The Fulbe established chiefdoms in the Hayre in the seventeenth century. Before these political entities came into existence, warriors from the Inner Delta (*ardube* or *weheebe*), Fulbe from the Gao area, other Fulbe on the move with their cattle, Sonrai from the north, Bambara from the south and Dogon from the west all moved into the area. Given the insecure political situation, political and military organisation provided protection against outside raiders who regarded this marginal area as a source of booty in the form of livestock and slaves.

With the growth of empires beyond the Hayre, centralised forms of political organisation practised outside the area increasingly influenced the local situation. Initially the Hayre functioned as an independent political entity. However, gradually power was taken over by the Maasina Empire that dominated the Inner Delta of the Niger from 1818-1862. This led to the curtailing of population mobility in the Hayre and the settlement of specific groups within Fulbe society in this area. The political elite along with their entourage consisting of Islamic clergymen, counsellors, craftsmen and slaves to work the fields settled in villages. The basis of the economy changed from almost purely pastoral to a combination of pastoralism and cereal cultivation. The mobile livestock-keeping population that formed the basis of the political power of the chiefs in the past disappeared and lost their control over politics (see De Bruijn & Van Dijk 2001; H. van Dijk 1999).

Political control over movement began to disappear in the second half of the nineteenth century when another Fulbe Empire took over in the larger region, and especially during the colonial period. Moreover, under the French colonial regime, antagonistic relations between various population groups and mutual raiding were suppressed. This led to a pulverisation of the movements of nomadic groups. They were no longer con-

---

[2] In Mali a district is called *cercle*, literally 'circle'.

Map 5.1: The Hayre, central Mali

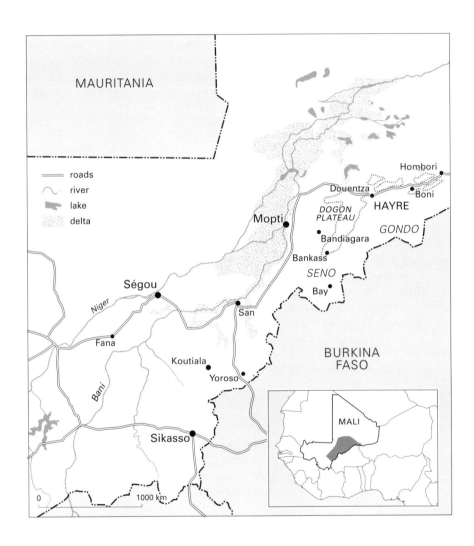

tained in their territories where they maintained some measure of control. At the other end of the spectrum, sedentary groups of cultivators also started to move and occupy large areas of the pasturelands of the mobile livestock-keeping population.

When viewed from afar, the region appears to portray a picture of continuous movement of people and animals and the constant replacement of fields. With increases in political centralisation, the character of movements changed. Some lines moved out of the area, others have come in. Some move faster than others, some lines split up, disperse or even vanish. Others are re-created every year, yet more are created only once, some are circular, others go back and forth to the place of origin.

These lines may involve people moving from one field to another, and people moving with cattle or flocks of small ruminants, sometimes from one village or a camp to another, sometimes just searching for the best pastures while drifting over large areas. One sees the clearing of new fields, the abandonment of old fields and the number of livestock fluctuating. These fluctuations are in turn another source of movement. One sees dispossessed families and individuals move out of an area looking for a better existence elsewhere, and older people moving to large agricultural villages to live off charity. Others stay put and enlarge their fields to create a new existence in cereal cultivation.

Of course the landscape, the background against which these movements take place, is not just a combination of physical objects. It is a deeply humanised landscape providing the people moving in it with the coordinates for orienting their movements. Property relations direct people in a specific direction, for example to reoccupy an old field of their grandfather's somewhere or to water their cattle at their relatives' well. Social and political relations promote and impede travel to specific locations. Hostility prevents people from moving to specific areas and they go to villages where people used to receive them in the past, and with whom they maintain host-stranger relationships (De Bruijn *et al.* 1997). Possibilities for exchanging livestock products such as milk, butter and sour milk for cereals make them reconsider their routes. When a period of drought occurs, all their schemes have to be re-arranged and different vistas have to be explored to escape from the negative effects.

However, ecological conditions are not the only reason for movement. Young boys were and still are sent away with Islamic scholars to study the Koran, surviving by begging in villages or camps. Adolescent boys travel on their own, going from one learned man to another to further their studies. More recently, adolescent boys and young men have started to wander all over West Africa looking for work and adventure and to escape from the harsh reality of existence in the Hayre. Those who stay behind have to cope without their contribution to the family's existence (De Bruijn 2001).

Perceptions of mobility
Reflections on these movements of the people indicate that all have different reasons for being mobile but for most, movement is the natural thing to do. It is embedded in their social organisation and forms part of their Sahelian identity. Historical accounts, songs and oral histories are all imbued with mobility. The main Fulbe narrator living in the Hayre started his introduction to the history of his people with a story about migration.

The very first chiefs of the Fulbe in this area came from elsewhere as hunters with their horses and dogs. They settled, but never permanently, and became leaders of a group of wandering nomads in the region. They assured their survival and hegemony by raiding other wandering groups such as the Tuareg but probably also other Fulbe groups.

This narrative about the origin of Fulbe society in this area stresses that these people are not from one place and their strength is their geographical mobility that ensures their subsistence. At the same time, the existence of this narrative gives the people a feeling of belonging, of being of the same stock, of having created a society. Today this feeling of belonging reaches far into Burkina Faso and into the south of Mali where the Hayre is still recognised as the point of origin by many and everyone sharing this feeling is part of their group. The mobility in the narrative supplements the movement of 'them' as a people.

The story explains why some groups are more mobile than others. The cattle-rearing groups are most mobile because of the wishes and needs of the cattle. Herders have to be mobile to explore the best pastures, to gain access to water in the dry season, and also to reach markets. Other social groups like the political and religious elite and former slaves are less mobile and administer the country and provide religious services. The slaves are put to work on the land to produce the cereals that serve as the basic food of the noblemen. Differences in mobility are thus based on a political and historical division of labour but there is also a strong cultural dimension. Manual labour is regarded as degrading by the noblemen and herdsmen (see De Bruijn & Van Dijk 1994).

Narrative additionally depicts other ethnic groups in the region, like the Dogon, as being more sedentary. However, a closer look at their strategy shows they are also mobile and move within the year from inner to outer fields, and over the years over large distances from their cultivation hamlets. They are also experts in seasonal migration. Nevertheless, they consider themselves different to the herding groups, as sedentary and having less of an ideology of movement than the elite and former slaves of the Fulbe.

From past to contemporary forms of mobility
Over the course of the twentieth century, Dogon from the Bandiagara Plateau and villages on the escarpment migrated to the Seeno Plain, occupying large areas of the pastures used by the Fulbe herdsmen (Gallais 1975; Martinelli 1995). Some, in their turn, moved onto the Bandiagara Plateau and established villages and camps there (H. van Dijk 2001). Many Fulbe and Dogon moved out of the area to look for a better life elsewhere. After major periods of drought at the beginning of the twentieth century, rainfall was more abundant in the 1950s and 1960s. People moved less and were able to live relatively prosperous lives for some decades.

The situation changed dramatically with the droughts of the 1970s and 1980s, which led to a profound crisis for the inhabitants of the Hayre, as existing production systems were not able to absorb these climate changes. The droughts of the 1980s in particular gave rise to new forms of mobility in all groups of Fulbe society as large numbers of Fulbe lost the livestock that served as the basis for their livelihood. Some families split up, while others were able to maintain some form of internal cohesion and carve out a new existence. The stories of a couple of Fulbe families who ventured into new areas to look for fresh opportunities to herd the few remaining livestock or to find employment in livestock keeping, trade or other economic activities illustrate some of the responses to the crisis.

Research carried out all over Mali, on the Bandiagara Plateau, along the border with Burkina Faso and in the cotton-growing area around Koutiala, showed that there were Fulbe families camping outside the official villages in the bush, sometimes just one or two families per village territory, at other times a whole camp was established in the bush. At one site, representatives from other status groups in Fulbe society could be found (artisans and former slaves) performing the same tasks as in their area of origin (see Van Steenbrugge 2001).

Moving along one of the lines representing mobility to the south of the Seeno is the Forest of Bay, south of Bankass and Koro in the border area between Mali and Burkina Faso. It consists partly of a flood plain and each year, if the rains are good, it is flooded by the Volta River. Fulbe have been using the Forest of Bay as a dry-season grazing reserve for a long time and have even settled permanently in villages there. Other population groups, mainly Samo and some Dogon, also live in the surrounding areas.

The line connecting the Hayre and the Forest of Bay reappears each year but it has not yet become as important as after the drought of the 1980s. The line is not straight and the people moving along it do not all belong to one group. They come from different camps and families and move at different times in various years. When they arrive in Bay, they do not camp at the same place nor do they stay in one place for a long time. They know and have contact with each other and sometimes set up camp together. Their stories differ in the reasons for mobility, in their wandering history and in their wealth. When considering each individual migration history, the general picture crumbles and becomes a very fine net of lines between the Hayre and Bay.

The first story is of two brothers from Yirma. They left Yirma accompanied by two other brothers and their father when they only had two cows left. Their father, with their older brother, camped somewhere on the Seeno, north of Bay, the youngest brother lived somewhere else. All herd cattle belonging to the sedentary cultivating population.

Initially they took refuge in Burkina Faso but had to leave because of Burkina government tax demands. They settled temporarily on the Seeno where the older of the two brothers said he had been on his way home even though he had a problem with his knee and foot, both of which were so swollen that he could not walk. They have many goats and a few cows. But will they ever return? He did not plan to travel any further back to Yirma. He does not know if it is possible to have a reasonable life there and he appears disinterested because ultimately he will just continue wandering.

The other brother and his wife have more contact with the people in Yirma. They do not consider returning because in Bay there is more space and they seem to be doing pretty well. They offered us visitors sugar and tea and they were all well fed. This no-man's land also gave them the opportunity to escape all kind of rules imposed upon them by a government they do not consider their own.

In the third hut lived an old woman. She followed her son who has been wandering for years because his future near Booni was not promising. His elderly mother had no one other than her son to take care of her so she travelled with him. Her presence is a burden for her son, making him immobile, so he said.

In the evening many other Fulbe appear from an apparently empty land to greet the white visitors coming from their 'home' area and to hear the latest news. They arrived from across the border or from the Forest of Bay. All these people are migrants from the Hayre, the Seeno or further north. They reported that many of the people who had come with them had moved on to the south. Bay was becoming overcrowded, as we discovered ourselves the next day when we continued our journey. The road was full of cattle and pastures were being heavily exploited.

The people travelling still further to the south do not go in a straight line either. They travel from place to place, sometimes visiting acquaintances but in most cases creating acquaintances by inviting themselves or by creating ties with a family residing in the place where they hope to settle. All the people we interviewed knew people, sometimes close family, who had moved with them and who had gone further. They were looking for better pastures, for a herd to watch, or for adventure. Virtually no one went back to where they had come from, though the majority are still in contact with those who stayed behind, but to varying degrees. After the drought of the 1980s a new network of Fulbe developed extending far into south Mali and over the border into Burkina Faso and Côte d'Ivoire, a web of people.

Most of these people disappear administratively. They are invisible for the Malian government and do not appear in statistics. If they cross the border they are immigrants at best tolerated. They do not reside in villages but camp in the bush. They are not invisible to themselves. They live their lives on the margins of society in a nation-state that is not theirs, creating their own web of people with its own rules, its own sense of law and order, in short, its own mobile, travelling culture.

Mobility and identity

Taking the perspective of mobility in this area of central Mali leads one along different tracks away from villages and towns to people who are not directly visible, who do not live in 'localities'. It illustrates another aspect of their lives and of the lives of the presumed sedentary people: they live in and with their mobility. Daily talk is about being mobile, and relations with others are all placed in the perspective of mobility. In fact we have a mobile culture, a travelling culture. Their hotel lounges and airports, to paraphrase Clifford, are local and regional markets or watering points for the livestock. They do not communicate by mobile phone or e-mail but through an immense network of kinsmen, acquaintances, hosts and traders who transmit messages in code.

This is clear among the cattle-keeping Fulbe but also other Sahelian people seem to be adopting a mobile lifestyle, a mobility which is central to their lives. The basis of this lifestyle is '*la condition sahélienne*' as Gallais (1975) put it, the innate necessity to move in an environment so unreliable and patchy in resources as the Sahel. However, in the course of history it is not only adaptation to a climate or a certain geography, it has become more to include other domains such as religion, trade and youth culture. It has indeed become a pre-modern, non-cosmopolitan, non-bourgeois, non-consumerist travelling culture with its own narratives, ideology, and social organisation.

This mobility is definitively not only a coping strategy to deal with the diminishing or increasing availability of natural resources, as an answer to the insecurities of the dry-land environment in terms of rainfall and biomass production. It is also a socially and culturally constructed phenomenon with its own *raison d'être*. Some people do migrate; others stay around the whole year. The question has to be raised as to why some migrate while others do not. Is this again only an adaptation to the same environmental and contextual factors or are there cultural and social or even political reasons for doing so?

A consequence of their mobility is that they are regarded everywhere as 'the other' or 'the stranger'. They are always the people who come from far away. Also in areas where they have been politically dominant, their hegemony has been relatively short, as is stressed in oral traditions. There too, they are regarded as the 'strangers' in relation to the original population that they ruled. In the Hayre, they were the last to arrive. In disputes over land that are increasingly taking place, they are often on the losing end nowadays because they cannot claim the right of first occupancy. In areas where they were the first they often have problems maintaining control over land because of the low intensity of the use of the land, their mobile way of life and the associated flexible rights that they define over land and pastures.

As a consequence, the Fulbe do not relate their identity to a specific territory in the same way their sedentary cultivating neighbours do. They define themselves by referring to a common ideology in which livestock, Islam and their way of life are the main components. Depending on the context, they may stress different aspects of their identity. The Fulbe who move to the south are politically marginal in the eyes of the others, of the sedentary townspeople, also in terms of development interventions or national politics.

However, marginality is also a group survival strategy. By remaining marginal, they are able to claim a specific position wherever they happen to be. As marginal people, as strangers, they do not form a threat to the existing order. They use their marginality and their illegality to live as the people they want to be, to formulate a counter discourse. As Agrawal (1998: 167) formulated for the Raikas in India: "[a mobile lifestyle] allows them to construct an ideology and practice of difference that other village castes might find more difficult. Their fragmented agency finds birth in precisely those practices that in their minds are differently constituted from those of their [sedentary] neighbors".

These features of a mobile culture – specifically including the people's own daily discourse about being mobile, about moving somewhere and about how and when to do so – question sedentarity. This Fulbe nomadism is a form of mobility that does not take it for granted that culture necessarily has to relate to a sedentarised life as if their culture can only exist when attached to locality. In fact their *form of mobility* also implies a *mobility of form* by which it is meant that forms of social interaction, exchange, rituals and family structures travel along on the pathways they take, and are attuned to this mobile way of life. By exploring this mobility of forms, *a priori* assumptions about sedentarity can be questioned. The following case study aims to demonstrate just that. Here, in the spread of specific Ghanaian religious forms outside Ghana, other elements call a sedentary perspective into question. The issue is that although in Ghana and elsewhere 'citizenship' presupposes an attachment to a place and to a state, religious forms may crosscut that and create a kind of moral domain in which people move about. In this culture, spirits, gods and deities and their forms of worship are considered unhampered by states and localities and attempts to bind people to certain places. This specifically applies to the spread of a new form of Christianity, Pentecostalism, and the way it has come to appeal to Ghanaian migrants worldwide.

From migration to multi-locality:
The Ghanaian Pentecostal diaspora and its subject

In Ghana, on the road leading from the coast to Kumasi, the age-old capital of the Asante Empire, is what superficially looks like any other remote rural village. On both sides of the tarmac road are huts, some in much better shape than others, and people seem to be busy with their daily chores. This image of a mundane, quiet and rural life is, however, deceptive. The first indication of something special about this place is a small building bearing a sign saying 'Reception'. Adjacent to it there is another small building with a sign that reads 'International Calls'. The more perceptive may even have noticed that the place has a peculiar name, 'Adomfa', a 'Blessing Taken', a locality where powers of supernatural origin are at work.

It is the Adomfa Residential Prayer Camp belonging to the largest of the Pentecostal churches in Ghana, the Church of Pentecost. It is led by the 75-year-old prophetess and deaconess, Grace Mensah Adu and is the oldest of all the prayer camps in the country. Since its inception in the early 1960s it has attracted thousands of visitors. The prophetess's prayers are considered so powerful that they help to resolve a wide range of illnesses, problems, conflicts and misfortune. Many people come to consult the prophetess and attend her prayer-healing sessions. In November 1997, the registration books of the camp showed that over 70,000 people had visited over the previous years. Some just stay for one day, feeling assured that the prayer-healing sessions have alleviated their problems, while others stay in one of the many houses for weeks or months before they are certain that the heavenly powers have worked to their advantage and have resolved their problems spiritually.

What does the existence of these prayer camps have to do with mobility and migration? The fact is that many people visiting camps such as the one at Adomfa perceive mobility and migration as a spiritual problem (R. van Dijk 1997). Or perhaps better, there is a profound and popular conception within Ghana that there are barriers to overcome which prevent ordinary people from travelling abroad, from partaking in the massive intercontinental migration to the West in which so many West Africans seem to participate. Peil (1995) estimated that by the mid-1980s more than 15% of Ghana's population were living abroad, a figure that by now probably is a conservative estimate. Many want to travel, a desire largely inspired by the global spread of images of the West, its wealth and its luxuries, but find serious obstacles in their way such as the inability to raise enough money to buy air tickets, passports and a visa from the dealers in Accra, the so-called connection boys (De Thouars 1999).

This inability is first and foremost conceived of as a spiritual blockage, something that occult forces have concocted and for which somebody else must be responsible. So, Prophetess Grace Mensah organises prayer sessions over passports, visas and air tickets and urges those that come for 'travel problems' to engage in dry-fasting, i.e. no food and water for the maximum number of days a human body is able to sustain such a practice. This is all meant to strengthen a person's own spiritual powers, to have visitations in the night by spirits that come to inform about good and bad so that the powers of the prophetess will hit hard and provoke a 'breakthrough' (*ogyee*) against those forces that block progress and prosperity. During the day the Pentecostal prophetess organises ecstatic prayer meetings where people scream and shout, experience possession by the Holy Spirit, fall down and roll on the ground, showing in their bodily gestures the serious fights that are going on inside them with the evil forces that control their lives. Special times are reserved for 'travel problems' when people facing such problems are requested to step forward so as to receive special blessings. Those who are not yet in possession of a passport and visa, and who want to ensure their travels to Europe are successful, put documents at the feet of the prophetess who engages in loud ecstatic prayers to 'bind the powers' that may concoct something bad for the person to whom these documents belong.

The transnational dimensions of the prayer camp are striking. A Ghanaian, let's call him David, who had come from Amsterdam to spend a couple of weeks at the camp demonstrated how these camps create their own international domain. Prayers and fasting at another camp had provided him with a 'breakthrough' a couple of years ago allowing him to travel successfully to Amsterdam using a false passport and by overstaying the tourist visa that he had obtained through bribery.

Before then, he had held some powers in his family that were responsible for him being unsuccessful in emigrating. Those prayers of some years ago had effectively dealt with the powers although when he arrived in Amsterdam, he was not entirely sure whether all these occult powers that came from within his family had been broken (*obubu*) effectively as he experienced difficulties in finding work and earning a living. He decided to join one of the satellite groups in the Netherlands that had emerged from these Pentecostal prayer camps. They have been developing as independent Ghanaian Pentecostal churches in such places as Amsterdam, the Hague, Hamburg and London.

The prayers helped for a while and he was not visited at night by visions of the occult, he got a couple of odd jobs and even began a relationship with a Dutch girl. But then his troubles returned and he felt forces from his family mounting against him. His illegal stay in Amsterdam began to become troublesome, his partner walked out on him and he felt a serious threat of spiritual weakening which ultimately would jeopardise his entire position in the Netherlands. If the Dutch police arrested him and forcibly repatriated him to Ghana, he would face serious social disgrace. It would demonstrate that he had not 'made it' or lived up to the expectations of the family to provide for them in a material sense. In addition, however, it would also show a failure to keep afflicting forces under control, powers that in the spiritual realm cause misfortune and mishap. David therefore decided that it was time to seek spiritual help at a prayer camp where the right kind of charismatic powers were available, and for that he needed to return to Ghana.

Upon arrival he went straight to Adomfa and felt that through prayers and fasting another breaking of those powers that were 'pulling him down' would soon be effectuated. His mother had also visited a prayer camp on several occasions since her son had not been able to remit money to her. She had been praying for a 'financial breakthrough' on his and her behalf while he was still in the Netherlands. "Perhaps I will need two more weeks of fasting to get back to Amsterdam," he said.

Mobility and identity in ideological spaces
What can be seen from examples like this is that migration and mobility are deeply cultural and secondly that geographical spaces are just one of many that can be conceived of as spaces in which people move about. Pentecostalism, an immensely popular form of Christianity, appears to create its own specific ideological space, very transnational and at the same time very multi-local. Multi-local here means that the creation of the Pentecostal ideological space is produced not only in Ghana but also at many other locations around the world at the same time.

Building on the experiences of the prayer camps, a more modern form of Pentecostalism has emerged in Ghana in recent years, characterised by the establishment of hundreds of churches particularly in the urban areas (Gifford 1998; Meyer 1998; R. van Dijk 1997 and 1999). Many young, upwardly mobile urbanites and those of the emerging urban middle classes are attracted to these new churches, some of which have in the meantime grown into mega-churches with many thousands of members. Their moral views have become highly influential in the public domain, mainly because of their access to the modern media. They are considered a political force of tremendous importance.

All of these churches have in common a zest for establishing branches in as many places outside Ghana as possible (R. van Dijk 2001a): By adding words such as 'international', 'global' and 'world' to their names they indicate to everybody their presence in the field of transnational relations and intercontinental migration. Nearly 40 of these Pentecostal churches have emerged in the Ghanaian migrant community in the Netherlands, particularly in Amsterdam, the Hague and Rotterdam where a total of 30,000-40,000 Ghanaian migrants live (Ter Haar 1998; R. van Dijk 2001a and forthcoming). One of the striking facts is that these are not only satellite churches from Ghana but that a number of them are Ghanaian Pentecostal churches that have emerged on Dutch soil and are spreading from the Netherlands to Ghana and other parts of the world.

In other words, there is a multi-local production of Ghanaian Pentecostalism worldwide, albeit not in a singular, uniform format. There are important differences in the way for instance the prayer camps operate in Ghana as compared to these newer Pentecostal churches in the Diaspora (R. van Dijk 1997). Each of these forms appears to contribute in its own way to the notion of a worldwide Pentecostal ideological space which the Ghanaian migrants can easily tap into at the many places they tend to travel to.[3] For many migrants the notion of spiritual coverage – a spiritual blanket – is considered crucial, as the case of David shows. Any member of a Pentecostal church, whether in Ghana or in the West, is at the same time a member of a larger transnational community. At the prayer camps, the ritual practice the aspiring migrants go through prepares them spiritually for detachment from their families and their wider social environment. The practices of deliverance and fasting are meant to break the spiritual ties connected to the family in the first place, ties that when they take the form of occult powers obstruct the person from migrating to the West. As these practices foster the experience of 'de-localising' the person, detaching him or her from local cultural bondage, Pentecostalism appeals to many as it helps to restructure kinship relations and obligations, specifically 'at home'. Pentecostal prayers and fasting are meant to keep the powers from the family at bay, and thus create a spiritual opportunity for bringing kinship obligations under the control of its individual members. Pentecostal ideology rejects the power of the ancestors and tends to confront family authority head-on as part of creating a modern identity and a sense of modern 'individuality'.

In addition, and most appealingly to migrants, Pentecostalism actively reformulates the compulsory gift-giving system, which in Ghana is considered crucial to the maintenance of kinship relations (R. van Dijk 1999). Gifts (remittances) to the family are proclaimed by the Pentecostal leaders to be spiritually endangering and therefore in need of thorough moral supervision. This is of particular significance in the Diaspora where many migrants are faced with the obligation to send money to relatives living at home and elsewhere. In restructuring such obligations the churches can often seen to be taking on 'surrogate' family responsibilities thereby communicating the message that religious and moral control of such relations are at stake. Often the church leaders re-direct the flow of gifts away from the family into their own rituals of exchange (in the context for instance of funerals, marriages and birthing ceremonies they organise) or perform 'consecration' of the gifts that are sent to or received from the family. In this way they hope to be able to disentangle their members from this reciprocity and the way in which family members can be suspected of sending, along with the gifts, occult and binding forces to these migrants.

In breaking with the spiritual ties with the family, in critiquing cultural practices in Ghana and in developing its own distinctive gift-economy, Pentecostal groups appear to be engaged in specific identity work. Appadurai (1995), Rouse (1991 and 1995), Basch *et al.* (1994) and others explore situations in which identities emerge that can no longer be indicated by referring to localities and communities that have a firm geographical anchorage. Particularly through the global spread of ideas, images and ideologies that crosscut national or cultural borders in both Africa and the West, the migrant, the refugee, the tourist and the traveller form de-territorialised categories and localities. Pentecostalism is one such newly emerging 'locality' that has developed in the process of Ghanaian intercontinental migration and is based on an ideological 'footing' in the first place. It is on the basis of adhering to that ideology and by following its often rigid,

---

[3]   The case of Ghanaian Pentecostalism is not exceptional. Similar trends in the transnational success of Pentecostal groups have also been reported from other countries (see for instance Marshall 1998; Corten & Marshall-Fratani 2001; Poewe 1994).

moral creeds (no alcohol, no smoking or drugs, no ancestral veneration etc.) that a person may gain access to all it can offer in practical terms of help and support.

Whereas in prayer camps in Ghana, such as the one described above, people go through a ritual process with the intention of cutting away ties and bonds with the family and the control that is exerted over them through the ancestral domain, the Ghanaian Pentecostal groups in the Netherlands ensure the person is not 'localised'. Integration in Dutch society is not their hallmark. The creation of images of 'Dutch citizenship' to be followed by all is not the intention of their rituals or proclamations. Furthermore, church leadership often holds highly critical views of public morality in the Netherlands and tends to declare the country a wild place with omnipresent dangers. In a specific way, therefore, this mobility of form establishes a 'de-local' identity: an identity whereby the meaning of being a Ghanaian Pentecostal is to create a certain distance from Dutch society while at the same being able to hold Ghanaian cultural traditions (for instance relating to ancestral worship) at bay as well. In other words, by becoming Pentecostal and by joining a Pentecostal community in the places where one has migrated to, such as the Netherlands, one remains neither 'fully' Ghanaian nor becomes totally Dutch.

Ghanaian Pentecostal groups have been established in many parts of the world, from England to Germany, the Netherlands, Italy, the United States, Israel and even Japan. There is much interchange between these groups in terms of travelling preachers and musical performers, trade in specific cloths and clothes, intermarriage and support in times of difficulty (funerals for example). The continuous contact and exchange from place to place between the Ghanaian Pentecostal churches also creates a high level of uniformity in the ways meetings and rituals are conducted, the content of the messages preached to audiences and the format of the various organisations within these communities. This enables migrants to travel from place to place and church to church without difficulty in joining in and relating to what may be going on locally.

Discussion of the 'identity work' of these Pentecostal groups has left one question unanswered. To what extent is mobility, in this case a mobility of a form i.e. that of Ghanaian Pentecostalism, to be regarded as exceptional? Is it something that from the perspective of a sedentary type of life appears as out-of-the-ordinary, as a reaction or a form of adaptation available to migrants who have arrived in an estranging environment? Or is it to be regarded as something that is representing certain cultural forms that, like Fulbe nomadism, are characterised and determined by mobility?

Mobility of form versus sedentarity

In Ghana there is a saying that if a bird sits on a branch of a tree for too long it can expect a stone to be thrown at its head, meaning that if a person does not look for opportunities elsewhere, his or her environment will hit hard. Mobility is on everybody's mind and one of society's ideals is to become a 'bin-to', that is somebody who has been to Europe and has come back with something worthwhile for the family as a whole. Many families aspire to having relatives abroad and many often have family members residing in a number of countries outside Africa. For important events in life, ranging from sending children to school, the organisation of the customary and costly funeral or wedding ceremonies or the care of the elderly, families have become increasingly dependent on organising, in fluid and mouldable ways, their relations with those living *aburokyire* (beyond the horizon or literally 'beyond the maize'). This 'multi-spatial livelihood' (see Foeken & Owuor, this volume) has not only become transnational but intercontinental. The intercontinental movement of people, particularly to the West, follows, to a greater extent, earlier forms of massive movement both within and beyond Ghana's present-day borders. It is not difficult to point to a range of religious and cosmological notions and repertoires that have played a role in the historical track record in Ghana of mobile socio-cultural forms of life. In fact, there is a striking relationship between religion and mobility in Ghana that can be related to these developments of mobility in colonial and post-colonial times.

From the early eighteenth century onwards, the Asante kings established a highly centralised rule by conquering neighbouring groups and subverting them under their hierarchy of power (McCaskie 1995; Chazan 1988). Even before the colonial era, politics had become a well-defined and distinct domain of thought and action, separate from other sectors of public life. The epithet of power was the golden stool of the Asantehene, a stool symbolising the religiously sanctified power of the king given to him by the High God of *Onyame*. Within this centralised Akan polity, ideas of 'citizenship' and 'strangerhood' emerged which identified a circumscribed space for the traveller and sojourner. Special arrangements were made for travel within its boundaries, which in a cosmological sense would not endanger or annoy the local gods or the High God. The Akan polity in particular is known to have had a network of royal roads, travel shrines, professional travellers, a logic of time-reckoning based on the covering of specified distances to and from Kumasi, and an articulated mode of distance trading, upon which a specific cosmology was grounded (Perbi 1991; Wilks 1992). This operated separately from the religious domain that was and still is closely related to the family (*abusua*), its elders and its ancestral veneration. Each family would have its own house (*fie*) with a shrine, often located at a significant place (for example near rivers), where the offerings to the ancestral deities (*abosom*) would be made to ask for their protection and benevolence towards family members. While this religious form was political in that it sanctified the belonging to a particular family, the authority of the elders and at a higher level the citizenship to the wider polity, its exclusivism denied a place to strangers. The regionalised cosmologies pertaining to travel shrines and the like, however, provided a sacred crossing for strangers and included the notion that within these cosmologies the stranger was allowed a circumscribed space for protection, ancestral veneration and safe travel.

These notions not only played a role in how conquered neighbouring groups were perceived and how these interlinked with the making of slaves and slavery on the Atlantic coast but also with the place of mobility as a whole in society. Within the dominant polity, various notions of strangerhood were held, varying from the *ohoho*, that is the internal stranger, i.e. an Ashanti or Akan from another chiefdom, to outsiders considered to be real strangers who were excluded from any right of ownership and investment in Asante or Akan. The most despised were the *odonko*, the slaves brought in from the northern peoples, employed to perform the most menial tasks in the Asante-

Akan polity (see Fortes 1975; Rosenthal 1997).[4] Under the rule of the Asantihene, cities and towns in pre-colonial and colonial times were ruled by policies regulating the flow of people and determining who was a stranger and who had the right to call himself a citizen. Special areas were designated for strangers in the so-called *zongo*, a practice, perhaps not exclusive to the Akan polity in West Africa, which persisted throughout colonial times.

Authors such as Schildkrout (1979), McLeod (1975) and Peil (1979) have pointed out that one of the most dominant streams of migration emerged in the late-nineteenth and early-twentieth centuries. At this time, a massive labour migration from the northern Sahelian areas to the south began to take place. Most of the northerners settled in the *zongo* areas. This southbound migration was related to the fact that, in the fertile southern areas, cocoa production had increased under the influence of expanding colonial trade. More labour was needed for gold mining and in the urbanising areas along the coast where trade and commerce were becoming increasingly important. Under the influence of this migration, the former *zongo* were growing steadily and the nature of the relationship with strangers and their concomitant religiously protected crossing changed.

Werbner (1989) highlighted the remarkable interrelationship between the various forms of strangerhood and the rise of the *zongo* on the one hand and the influx of specific personal security cults and a variety of shrines that became part of the southbound traffic of people into the Asante and Akan rural and urban areas on the other. These cults accompanied and guided the traveller by providing ritually protected corridors and a cosmology that incorporated the local and the ancestral into the regional. Along with the import of people and labour from the north into Asante came shrines, *materia sacra*, substances, cultural codes and ritual activities. Certain cults, with shrines in the north such as the Talis' Boghar Cult or the Tigare anti-witchcraft cult from Wa, established satellite shrines in the south or developed travelling shrines to speak to the migration movement.

While these types of cults developed and safeguarded the crossing of strangers into other cultural domains, the Ashanti and Akan fascination with powerful protection originating from elsewhere had a tremendous influence on the shrines within their domain. Although the strangers of the *zongo* were perceived in terms of great social distance, their religious expansion, their cosmological powers of the travelling shrines and their ability to venture into the bush and travel safely resonated deeply in Asante life. Asante shrines began to cross to other cultural areas replacing, as Werbner showed (1989: 238), those of the northerners. Hence, the possibilities for religiously protected travelling and trading also expanded for the southern groups and covered a region far greater than ever before.

A second development that enhanced the notion of a wider world of travel and opportunity reaching the heartland of Asante was the arrival of Christianity. As with the northern personal security cults, strangers brought this religious form to Asante. Wide-

---

[4] These northern groups included the Dagomba, the Mamprusi, the Tallensi or Frafra and the Dagati, while groups originating from surrounding countries were also included such as the Mossi, Haussa, Yoruba and Zabarama (see Schildkrout 1979: 186).

spread fascination started to emerge with a new window out onto a larger world. Missionary education, health care and the possession of all sorts of Western objects not only produced awe and respect but also a desire to become part of that world (Goody 1975; Meyer 1995 and 1999). As Hefner (1993) pointed out, conversion also meant a cultural conversion into a different world. The strong western 'missionisation' after the late 1880s by the established Christian churches (Roman Catholic, Basel Mission, and Methodists, but also missionary Pentecostal churches from England and the United States) brought new vistas of modernity, of an enticing world where new skills could be acquired and fortunes made. As early as 1900, these religions facilitated access to a wider world for increasing numbers of Ghanaians and encouraged many to migrate to the United States and the UK, often in search of education.

Local appropriations of Christianity took the form of independent prophetic-healing churches, which began to appear in large numbers in the 1930s and 1940s (see Wyllie 1980; Meyer 1995). Hundreds of churches emerged, often combining syncretically elements from Christianity with local cosmological notions and practices especially those concerning healing. These churches spread rapidly through the activities of itinerant prophets and healers, and seemed to cater to the needs of the rural-to-urban migrant. Many settled in the fast-developing cities of Kumasi, Accra and Cape Coast. In a deeper sense, these prophet-healing churches formed a continuation and transformation of the personal security cults mentioned above. Through the use of water, concoctions, herbs, candles, rings and statues they could offer healing and ritual protection in a wide variety of places to ever-increasing numbers of migrants. In so doing, they embodied a critique on the missionary churches that perceived issues of spiritual healing and protection as mere superstition. At the same time they rendered services, like the personality cults did, at a regional level and demonstrated the deep-seated fascination for the kind of religious powers that originate from elsewhere (namely Christianity) and the way in which they could be incorporated.

The rise of charismatic Pentecostalism highlights yet another development in the relationship between religion and mobility. This form of Pentecostalism did not develop so much in the context of regional mobility and the growth of cities, but emerged at a time when transnational travel and migration were becoming significant in the post-colonial years. Around independence in 1958, Ghana became part of cross-border flows of labour migration in and out of the country. Due to increasing cocoa production, mining and trading, large groups of migrants from neighbouring countries, such as the Yoruba from Nigeria, arrived in Ghana. As Peil (1979) and Sudarkasa (1979) showed, the word 'alien' was not in common usage in Ghana until the proclamation of the Compliance Order in November 1969. In the face of a declining economy, it set in motion a massive expulsion of aliens, many of Nigerian origin, from post-colonial Ghanaian society.

Ghana's economy started to decline rapidly in the 1970s causing Ghanaians, and Ashanti in particular, to migrate in ever-greater numbers to neighbouring countries, specifically Nigeria. In their turn, these Ghanaian migrants soon found themselves harassed and expelled in large numbers from Nigeria in 1983. Aggravated by this expulsion of more than a million Ghanaian labour migrants from Nigeria, many young men saw very limited chances of finding paid employment in Ghana's urban centres. The rural sectors had equally lost their appeal as well as their absorption power due to sharp declines in world-market export commodity prices (especially that of cocoa). A steep increase in intercontinental migration occurred. There are, for example, many Ghanaian migrants who arrived in the Netherlands after 1983, after having tried their luck in Nigeria before deciding to leave for Europe.

Thus, the rise of Pentecostalism from this time onward comes as no surprise. Its prosperity gospel promised access to opportunities, to wealth and God's benevolence for the true believer. With an emphasis on style, clothes, religious entrepreneurship, money donations and the like, many hundreds of churches not only focused on rising consumerism in Ghanaian society but also on some deeper cultural notions of what can be expected of religious forms. Extending to new areas, holding 'crusades' in villages and even jumping on the bandwagon of globalisation meant that this religious form signalled a message of being able to open up profitable opportunities to all those who were willing to follow its creed. Some Pentecostal churches in Ghana resulted directly from the return migration from Nigeria as they appear to have Nigerian origins and in some cases even Nigerian leadership (for instance the well-known Deeper Life Ministries). Many churches established 'deliverance ministries' focusing on restoring prosperity through spiritual means for those who felt their success in life blocked by forces beyond their control. In the context of the Pentecostal prayer camps described above, international travel and the crossing of state borders became a matter of spiritual protection as well.

The point made in this overview is, first of all, that since pre-colonial times an intimate relationship has existed between mobility and religious forms. Secondly, this relationship is still present in Pentecostalism today despite the transformations that have taken place in religious forms since the occurrence of personal security cults, and despite the differences in geographical scale that have emerged in the domain of mobility. The third point is that these forms of religion have always appeared to be able to crosscut political boundaries and identity formations. Ranging from the erstwhile security cults of travelling shrines that crossed the boundaries set by the Akan centralised polity to the new transnational Pentecostal churches, all these cases show a dialectic relationship existing with 'citizenship' in political terms. These religious forms appear to bear an element of strangerhood – as exemplified in the travel shrines of the security cults, the itinerant prophets of the healing churches and the transnational orientation of the Pentecostal churches – that creates a distanced if not tense relationship with political power. Much of the political power of chieftaincy, of the colonial rulers or the post-colonial state was focused on regulating flows of people and of creating a citizenship that could be known and controlled, such as the mass expulsion of 'aliens' demonstrated.

It must be emphasised that in the post-colonial situation the new Pentecostal churches were not particularly concerned with contributing to citizenship in a political sense. Theirs was not a discourse of belonging to a certain place or a certain country. Instead, a problematic and ambiguous relationship frequently developed with political authorities whereby during the Rawlings regime some churches came closer to his power while others preferred to develop a position of being critical moral watchdogs.[5] They stressed the need to christianise the nation and make it part of a larger modern world in which the nation-state would become disentangled from its cultural roots and all the ancestral powers that dominated it. When it comes to traditional keepers of power, especially the chiefs, it is important to note that this duality of religiously inspired mobility and politically maintained sedentarity applies again. Chiefs do not and cannot become members of Pentecostal churches as they are seen to embody ancestral powers that, in the eyes of the Pentecostalists, are demonic and tie people to certain places and shrines where veneration takes place. The opportunities and vistas the Pentecostal churches offer in their ritual practices are not available to chiefs as the custodians of 'local custom', unless they become deeply delivered from whatever may tie them to their traditions. Even violent conflicts have resulted from this disparity in the acknowledgement of the chiefs' authority. This has been the case, for instance, with the traditional authorities of the ethnic unit of Gas in Accra who invaded some of the Pentecostal churches in an attempt to enforce their rulings (R. van Dijk 2001b).

In the Diaspora as well the Ghanaian Pentecostal community, churches cannot be perceived to be interested in promoting Dutch citizenship or in establishing fixed identities within stable communities. Instead, interest lies with the individual, with personal moral life and with the saving of the personal soul unto the believer. The concept of soul (*(o)kra*) is considered of great importance by the leaders of the Pentecostal groups in the Netherlands. A frequently heard expression in these groups is *Okra ye ohoho* (the soul is the stranger), a well-known Ashanti saying (Bempong 1992). It indicates a specific quality of every individual that instead of signalling ancestral relations with the family represents detachment and strangerhood. Both modalities are generally perceived to be present in each and every person: each person is expected to have an *okra* in addition to family spirits, and thus an element of strangerhood. Upon death, the *kra* will leave the body and return to God, *Onyame*, from where it came. In the context of the Diaspora churches, it is an expression meant to indicate that the political field, in this case the Dutch authorities, will never be able to capture fully the Ghanaian Pentecostal identity. This ideology perceives religious mobility and political sedentarity as a duality that runs through the body personal and the body social at the same time. This thinking is not without significance in a context where the Dutch government has increased its efforts to curb migration from Africa and has put in place a range of measures to check identities and record them in every possible detail.

So, whereas things religious and relating to 'soul' have all the characteristics of crosscutting boundaries, of guiding travel to other places and gaining access to resources elsewhere, the political field of authority is seen to control and fixate identities. In other words, these religious forms, in their mobility, provided and in the case of Pentecostalism still provide notions of opportunity and prosperity elsewhere, in other places or spiritual spaces. Religion in these forms and varieties in an important way is perceived by many of its adherents as a kind of port of entry, as a doorway leading to

---

[5] Mensa Otabil, founder and leader of the influential International Central Gospel Church in Accra became particularly well known for this.

these opportunities elsewhere, beyond the boundaries often set by the polity that, for instance, Ghanaian Pentecostalism now encounters in the Dutch state.

To conclude this section, the Fulbe case demonstrated that sedentarity and locality cannot *a priori* be assumed to be the paradigmatic point of departure for exploring mobility. This section has aimed to show that mobility must be explored on its own terms. A change of perspective may apply to an entire culture such as the Fulbe but may also be fruitfully applied to the exploration of an *aspect* of a culture; in this case not an entire culture but elements of a culture, namely certain highly mobile religious forms, have been explored in their mobile characteristics. In so far as these can be distinguished from other aspects of culture (an epistemological point that is left untouched in the context of this contribution), the analytical point here is that a perspective that assumes and operates from sedentary notions will not ensure a total understanding of Ghanaian Pentecostalism. It is not about creating locality, settlement, citizenship or anything else to which other forms of power in Ghanaian society cater. Pentecostalism is about mobility, of being 'moved by the Spirit' in ecstasy, of creating 'breakthroughs' so that successful travelling can commence for its followers and so on. In this perspective another saying by which Pentecostals refer to their churches is apt: *asore ye kra* which means 'the church is soul, but a wandering soul altogether'.

Concluding remarks

These two case studies show the importance of mobility and the complexity of related phenomena. Population movements have always been and are still important vehicles for self-promotion, survival and, in case of the Fulbe, part of their self-definition. As the Ghanaian case shows, people sometimes create ideological spaces to constitute some form of identity that produces and allows for mobility. Even though in both cases these aspects of identity do not directly enhance their situation in material terms, they nevertheless provide people with a social network, a sense of belonging, which indeed may act as a social and ideological environment of a 'normal' sedentary form.

So far, the inherent socio-cultural features of these kinds of 'societies' have often escaped social scientists. Anthropologists have typically frozen their objects of study in villages, tribes, territories, reproducing the paradigm of the North-Atlantic mode of organisation so closely intertwined with the hegemonic colonial and post-colonial state. Geographers have been much more sensitive to geographical mobility but have mostly dealt with its economic and spatial aspects and not with its social and cultural forms.

The two example cases presented here stimulate new ways of thinking about mobility leading back to the central concern set out at the beginning of the chapter about how to develop new ways towards a cultural understanding of moving people. This is also a plea for empirical research. As the case studies have shown, it is only through the richness of ethnographic detail derived from research in multi-sited settings that the real dynamics of mobile cultures and people are revealed. Some have said that to look for data is also to look for oneself. While that may be true, it is even more relevant in the sense that the issue of mobility has become so intimately integrated in our own way of life that looking for another while moving may offer new insights and new ways of looking at ourselves.

In addition, perhaps an even more pressing issue is at stake. Moving people have indeed become a problem in the sense that refugee movements in Africa – because of dissolving states, interethnic strife, struggles for hegemony, and control over natural and mineral resources – are causing enormous hardship. This has become an unsettling predicament that must be dealt with, not only technically but also as a social issue affecting our own societies. The movement of people within and outside Africa has become an issue of global concern to many other nation-states, international organisations, local NGOs and the like. Often *a priori* mobility is constructed as problematic, irrespective of the extent to which mobility is experienced as unsettling by people themselves or by the societies concerned. Regardless of local forms of mobility that may have been in existence long before considerations of international intervention of any sort were at stake, the problematic nature of mobility is defined for them but often without them and without a close reading of how problems are being experienced and expressed.

Both cases show the consistent failure of the North-Atlantic mode of organisation to contain people within the established boundaries set for them. Little is known about the economic, social and cultural dynamics of these transnational and trans-African 'societies'. How do people remain connected and together, when administrative power structures, tax regimes and identity cards are put to use to fragment their (and our) world into distinct political, social and cultural spaces?

What is then the connection between the strategies of an individual traveller linked to a globalising religious form on the one hand and those of nomadic bovine identity on the other? They meet each other where the constructions of travel and movement are concerned. Meanings, emotions, decisions and motivations for movement and travel cannot be assumed and cannot be cast in a discourse of rupture alone. The extent to which persons themselves perceive travel and movement as a form of continuity is surprising. It is rather the interruption of travel due to visa problems, lack of money and contacts that is a problem in the case of Ghanaian Pentecostalism. For the Fulbe, a lack of space in which to manoeuvre, the weight of state regulations and the occupation of their pastoral territories are important incentives to move. They have to continue moving if they do not want to become permanently immobilised. In both cases it is clear that people resist being contained by and attached to specific localities.

Questions concerning the relation between the individual, the group and larger wholes in much broader geographical perspectives need to be posed. We are challenged to delve into the traveller's mind, as well as those of the people who stay behind. People do not think in the bipolar models we scientists have developed. The decisions they take every day determine whether they move or not. As such, understanding and analysing cultures of travel can only be done, we argue, from a processual perspective, one which underscores the need to apply concepts and methods that are as dynamic as societal life is in many parts of Africa.

References

Abu-Manga, A.A. 1999, 'Socio-cultural, Socio-economic and Socio-linguistic Diversity among the Fulbe of the Sudan Republic', in V. Azarya, A. Breedveld, M. de Bruijn & H. van Dijk (eds), *Pastoralists under Pressure? Fulbe Societies Confronting Change in West Africa*, Leiden: Brill, pp. 51-68.

Agrawal, A. 1998, *Greener Pastures, Politics, Markets and Community among a Migrant Pastoral People*, Durham and London: Duke University Press.

Appadurai, A. 1991, 'Global Ethnoscapes: Notes and Queries for a Transnational Anthropology' in R.G. Fox (ed.), *Recapturing Anthropology. Working in the Present*, Santa Fé: School of American Research Press.

Appadurai, A. 1995, 'The Production of Locality', in R. Fardon (ed.) *Counterworks. Managing the Diversity of Knowledge*, London: Routledge.

Ba, A.H. & J. Daget 1984, *L'Empire Peul du Macina (1818-1853)*, Abidjan: Les Nouvelles Editions Africaines.

Bah, M.A. 1998, *Fulbe Presence in Sierra Leone: A Case History of Twentieth Century Migration and Settlement among the Kissi of Koindu*, New York: Peter Lang.

Basch, L., N. Glick Schiller & C. Szanton Blanc 1994, *Nations Unbound: Transnational Projects, Postcolonial Predicaments and Deterritorialized Nation-States*, Reading: Gordon & Breach.

Beckwith, C. & M. van Offelen 1983, *Nomads of Niger*, New York: Harry N. Abrams Inc. Publishers.

Bempong, O. 1992, 'Language as a Factor in Ethnographic Research', *Ghana Research Review* 8 (1 & 2): 55-63.

Bernardet, Ph. 1984, *Association Agriculture Elevage en Afrique: Les Peuls Semi-transhumants de Côte d'Ivoire*, Paris: Harmattan.

Blench, R. 1994, 'The Expansion and Adaptation of Fulbe Pastoralism to Subhumid and Humid Conditions in Nigeria', *Cahiers d'Etudes Africaines* XXXIV 1-3 (133-135): 197-212.

Botte, R. & J. Schmitz 1994, 'Paradoxes Identitaires', *Cahiers d'Etudes Africaines* XXXIV 1-3 (133-135): 7-22.

Breedveld, A. 1999, 'Prototypes and Ethnic Categorization on the Terems Pullo and Fulbe in Maasina (Mali)', in V. Azarya, A. Breedveld, M. de Bruijn & H. van Dijk (eds), *Pastoralists under Pressure? Fulbe Societies Confronting Change in West Africa*, Leiden: Brill, pp. 69-89.

Burnham, Ph. & M. Last 1994, 'From Pastoralist to Politician: The Problem of a Fulbe "Aristocracy"', *Cahiers d'Etudes Africaines*, XXXIV 1-3 (133-135): 313-58.

Chazan, N. 1988, 'The Early State in Africa: The Asante Case', in S.N. Eisenstadt, M. Abitbol & N. Chazan (eds), *The Early State in African Perspective: Culture, Power and Division of Labor*, Leiden: Brill, pp. 60-97.

Clifford, J. 1992, 'Travelling Cultures', in L. Grossberg, C. Nelson & P.A. Treichler (eds), *Cultural Studies*, New York: Routledge, pp. 96-116.

Corten, A. & R. Marshall-Fratani (eds) 2001, *Between Babel and Pentecost. Transnational Pentecostalism in Africa and Latin America*, London: Hurst Bloomington, Indiana University Press.

Davis, J. 1992, 'The Anthropology of Suffering', *Journal of Refugee Studies* 5: 149-61.

De Bruijn, M. 2001, 'Those Who Cannot Travel: Staying Behind in Fulbe Society in Central Mali', in M. Bovin & G. Diallo (eds), *Crisis and Culture in Africa*, Uppsala: Nordic Africa Institute.

De Bruijn, M. & H. van Dijk 1994, 'Drought and Coping Strategies in Fulbe Society in the Hayre, Central Mali: A Historical Perspective', *Cahiers d'Etudes Africaines* XXXIV 1-3, (133-135): 85-108.

De Bruijn, M. & H. van Dijk 2001, 'Ecology and Power in the Periphery of Maasina: The Case of the Hayre in the Nineteenth Century', *Journal of African History*.

De Bruijn, M., W.E.A. van Beek & H. van Dijk 1997, 'Antagonisme et Solidarité; les Relations entre Peuls et Dogons du Mali Central', in M. de Bruijn & H. van Dijk (eds), *Peuls et Mandingues: Dialectique des Constructions Identitaires*, Paris: Karthala, pp. 243-66.

De Thouars, B. 1999, '"Go Come". Het remigratieproces van Ghanezen uit het Westen', University of Utrecht, Unpublished MA Thesis.

Delmet, Ch. 2000, 'Les Peuls Nomades au Soudan', in Y. Diallo & G. Schlee (eds), *L'Ethnicité Peule dans des Contexts Nouveaux*, Paris: Karthala, pp. 191-206.

Diallo, Th. 1999, 'Les Stratifications des Structures Politico-sociales de la Société Traditionnelle au Fuuta Jaloo, Evolution et Transformation' in V. Azarya, A. Breedveld, M. de Bruijn & H. van Dijk (eds), *Pastoralists under Pressure? Fulbe Societies Confronting Change in West Africa*, Leiden: Brill, pp. 113-135.

Dupire, M. 1962, *Peuls Nomades: Etude Descriptive des Wodaabe du Sahel Nigérien*, Paris: Institut d'Ethnologie.

Fortes, M. 1975, 'Strangers', in M. Fortes & S. Patterson (eds), *Studies in African Social Anthropology*, London: Academic Press.

Gallais, J. 1975, *Pasteurs et Paysannes du Gourma: La Condition Sahellienne*, Paris: Centre National de la Recherche Scientifique.

Gifford, P. 1998, *African Christianity. Its Public Role*, London, Hurst & Company.

Goody, J. 1975, 'Religion, Social Change and the Sociology of Conversion', in J. Goody (ed.), *Changing Social Structure in Ghana. Essays in the Comparative Sociology of a New State and an Old Tradition*, London: International African Institute.

Hastrup, K. 1993, 'Hunger and the Hardness of Facts', *Man (N.S.)* 28: 727-39.

Hastrup, K. & K.F. Olwig, 1997, 'Introduction', in K. Hastrup & K.F. Olwig (eds), *Siting Culture: The Shifting Anthropological Object*, London and New York: Routledge, pp. 1-14.

Hefner, R.W. (ed.) 1993, *Conversion to Christianity. Historical and Anthropological Perspectives on a Great Transformation*, Berkeley: University of California Press.

Marshall, R. 1998, 'Mediating the Global and the Local in Nigerian Pentecostalism', *Journal of Religion in Africa* 28 (3): 278-315.

Martinelli, B. 1995, 'Trames d'Appartenances et Chaines d'Identité: Entre Dogons et Moose dans le Yatenga et la Plaine du Seno (Burkina Faso et Mali)', *Cahiers des Sciences Humaines* 31 (2): 365-405.

McCaskie, T.C. 1995, *State and Society in Pre-colonial Asante*, Cambridge: Cambridge University Press.

McLeod, M. 1975, 'On the Spread of Anti-Witchcraft Cults in Modern Ashanti', in J. Goody (ed.), *Changing Social Structure in Ghana. Essays in the Comparative Sociology of a New State and an Old Tradition*, London: International African Institute.

Meyer, B. 1995, *Translating the Devil. An African Appropriation of Pietist Protestantism; the Case of the Peki Ewe in Southeastern Ghana, 1847-1992*, University of Amsterdam, PhD Thesis.

Meyer, B. 1998, '"Make a Complete Break with the Past". Time and Modernity in Ghanaian Pentecostalist Discourse', in R.P. Werbner (ed.), *Memory and the Postcolony*, London: Zed Books, Postcolonial Identities Series.

Meyer, B. 1999, 'Christian Mind and Worldly Matters: Religion and Materiality in the Nineteenth-Century Gold Coast', in W. van Binsbergen, R. Fardon & R. van Dijk (eds), *Modernity on a Shoestring. Dimensions of Globalization, Consumption and Development in Africa and Beyond*, London: SOAS/Leiden: ASC.

Mols, D. (ed.) 2000, *Finatawa*, Antwerpen: Zuiderpershuis.

Peil, M. 1979, 'Host Reactions: Aliens in Ghana', in W.A. Shack & E.P. Skinner (eds), *Strangers in African Societies*, Berkeley: University of California Press.

Peil, M. 1995, 'Ghanaians Abroad', *African Affairs* 94: 345-67.

Perbi, A. 1991, 'Mobility in Pre-colonial Asante from a Historical Perspective', *Ghana Research Review* 7 (1 &2) 72-86.

Poewe, K. 1994, *Charismatic Christianity as a Global Culture*, Columbia, S.C.: University of South Carolina Press.

Robinson, D. 1985, *The Holy War of Umar Tal: The Western Sudan in the Mid-Nineteenth Century*, Oxford: Clarendon Press.

Rosenthal, J. 1997, 'Foreign Tongues and Domestic Bodies: Gendered Cultural Regions and Regionalized Sacred Flows', in M. Grosz-Ngate & O.H. Kokole (eds), *Gendered Encounters. Challenging Cultural Boundaries and Social Hierarchies in Africa*, New York: Routledge.

Rouse, R. 1991, 'Mexican Migration and the Social Space of Postmodernism', *Diaspora* 1 (1): 8-23.

Rouse, R. 1995, 'Thinking Through Transnationalism: Notes on the Cultural Politics of Class Relations in the Contemporary United States', *Public Culture* 7 (2) 353-402.

Santoir, C. 1994, 'D'une Rive à l'Autre. Les Peuls Mauritaniens Réfugiés au Sénégal (Départements de Dagona et de Podor)', *Cahiers des Sciences Humaines* XXIX (1): 195-229.

Schildkrout, E. 1979, 'The Ideology of Regionalism in Ghana', in W.A. Shack & E.P. Skinner (eds), *Strangers in African Societies*, Berkeley: University of California Press.

Schmitz, J. 1994, 'Cités Noirs: Les Républiques vVllageoises du Fuuta Tooro (Vallée du Fleuve Sénégal)', *Cahiers d'Études Africaines* XXXIV 1-3, (133-135): 419-60.

Sudarkasa, N. 1979, 'From Stranger to Alien: The Socio-Political History of the Nigerian Yoruba in Ghana, 1900-1970', in W.A. Shack & E.P. Skinner (eds), *Strangers in African Societies*, Berkeley: University of California Press.

Tanoh, 1971, 'Huit Cent Mille Guinéens Ont Fui Leur Pays', *Remarques Africains* 13 (388) 418-19.

Ter Haar, G. 1998, *Halfway to Paradise. African Christians in Europe*, Cardiff: Cardiff Academic Press.

Van Dijk, H. 1999, 'Ecological Insecurity and Fulbe Pastoral Society in the Niger Bend', in V. Azarya, A. Breedveld, M. de Bruijn & H. van Dijk (eds), *Pastoralists under Pressure? Fulbe Societies Confronting Change in West Africa*, Leiden, Brill, pp. 237-265.

Van Dijk, H. 2001, 'Survival on the Margin: Access to Natural Resources of Fulbe Migrants in Central Mali', in M. Bovin & G. Diallo (eds), *Crisis and Culture in Africa*, Uppsala: Nordic Africa Institute.

Van Dijk, R. 1997, 'From Camp to Encompassment: Discourses of Transsubjectivity in the Ghanaian Pentecostal Diaspora', *Journal of Religion in Africa* 27 (2): 135-60.

Van Dijk, R. 1999, 'The Pentecostal Gift: Ghanaian Charismatic Churches and the Moral Innocence of the Global Economy', in W. van Binsbergen, R. Fardon & R. van Dijk (eds), *Modernity on a Shoestring. Dimensions of Globalization, Consumption and Development in Africa and Beyond*, London: SOAS/Leiden: ASC.

Van Dijk, R. 2001a, 'Time and Transcultural Technologies of the Self in the Ghanaian Pentecostal Diaspora', in A. Corten & R. Marshall-Fratani (eds), *Between Babel and Pentecost. Transnational Pentecostalism in Africa and Latin-America*, London: Hurst/Bloomington: Indiana University Press.

Van Dijk, R. 2001b, 'Contesting Silence. The Ban on Drumming and the Musical Politics of Pentecostalism in Ghana', in P. Nugent & B. Meyer (eds), *Religion in the Fourth Republic of Ghana. Ghana Studies Review Special Issue*.

Van Dijk, R. forthcoming, 'Religion, Reciprocity and Restructuring Family Responsibility in the Ghanaian Pentecostal Diaspora', in D.F. Bryceson & V. Vuorela (eds), *Forging New European Frontiers. Transnational Families and their Global Networks*, Oxford, Berg.

Van Steenbrugge, J. 2001, *Movements in a New World: Fulbe Mobility and Survival in Southern Mali*, Leiden: African Studies Centre.

Werbner, R.P. 1989, *Ritual Passage, Sacred Journey. The Process and Organization of Religious Movement*, Washington: Smithsonian.

Wilks, I. 1992, 'On Mentally Mapping Greater Asante: A Study of Time and Motion', *Journal of African History* 33, 175-90.

Wyllie, R.W. 1980, *Spiritism in Ghana: A Study of New Religious Movements*, AAR Studies in Religion No. 21, Missoula: Scholars Press.

6

Mobile workers, urban employment and 'rural' identities: Rural-urban networks of Buhera migrants, Zimbabwe

Jens A. Andersson

Processes of urbanisation and rural-urban mobility in Southern Africa have often been interpreted in terms of macro-economic and policy-induced demographic changes and the behavioural shifts following migrants' movements from 'traditional' rural society to the 'modern' and individualised world of the city. Rather than adopting the a priori assumption of these conventional perspectives that rural-urban mobility involves significant behavioural shifts, this chapter analyses the socio-cultural organisation of this mobility by migrant workers themselves. It is argued that theoretical distinctions between rural and urban social networks are largely irrelevant in the way Buhera workers in Zimbabwe organise their daily lives.

Introduction

Unlike many other forms of mobility, rural-urban population movements have received considerable attention in the social study of Africa, not least because rural-urban migration has been part of wider debates on economic development and modernisation (World Bank 2000: 125-32; Ferguson 1990 and 1999; Mitchell 1956 and 1987; Wilson 1941). Urbanisation, in these debates, has a double meaning. Closely associated with economic growth, it does not simply denote a movement in space but simultaneously represents a wider process of social change. Rural-urban mobility, in this perspective, comes to represent a historical progression from traditional rural society to modern urban society. Rural and urban geographical localities thus become associated with specific behavioural patterns in which the rural is associated with tradition, communality and continuity, as opposed to the urban which is the locus of modernisation, individualisation and change (Ferguson 1999: 35). As a consequence, the understanding of urbanisation processes has been in terms of demographic changes and the accompanying behavioural shifts of those who have moved to urban areas, rather than one of mobility itself.

The economic decline experienced in many African countries in the 1990s poses a challenge to this conventional thinking about urbanisation. Since urbanisation has always been closely associated with economic growth, it was to be expected that the absence of such growth would make some scholars suggest a slow-down and possibly even a reversal of rural-urban population movements (see Potts 1995, 1997 and 2000; Tacoli, this volume). Taking a longer-term perspective, the World Bank (2000: 130) on the other hand has labelled the African situation as unique, finding a 'negative correlation between urbanisation and per capita income'. In the academic literature on urbanisation in Africa these demographic changes in African urban areas are often related to the effects of economic structural adjustment. Seeking to redress structural imbalances in African economies, i.e. distorted terms of trade between rural and urban economic sectors, these programmes have been promoted by the World Bank and the IMF since the early 1980s in an attempt to rectify African governments' policies that contributed to rural-urban migration (World Bank 1981; Bates 1988). By removing these 'urban biases' in African governments' policies, adjustment policies are seen to have contributed to a (short-term) decline in urban employment and living conditions.

From an analysis of demographic changes, urbanisation studies thus link macro and micro levels, as well as rural and urban sectors and their social settings into a powerful explanatory framework. Within this framework certain economic forces and occasionally also state policies are seen as the driving force behind population movements between town and country. These movements, in turn, represent a modern transition between rural and urban patterns of behaviour.[1] The recent debate on relations between economic decline and rural-urban population movements in Africa has, however, turned the relationship between demographic and behavioural change into a problematic one. Where rural-urban migration seemed to represent a progressive social transition towards a modern, urbanised existence, the current debate on 'return-migration' or 'counter-urbanisation' appears as some sort of 'history running in reverse' (Ferguson 1999: 13). It again, however, leaves unexplored the issue of how this mobility is organised.

This chapter on mobile workers originating from Buhera District in Zimbabwe aims to develop a different view of the urbanisation process.[2] It does not study the effects of macro-economic forces and government policies on the demography of rural and urban areas. Nor does it focus on the differential ways in which mobile workers moving from rural to urban areas (or *vice versa*) adapt their behaviour to the urban or rural social setting.[3] Unlike Ferguson (1999) who analysed 'cosmopolitan' and 'localist' cultural styles in urban centres of the Zambian Copperbelt or Mitchell's classic study of the *Kalela Dance* (1956), this study is not confined to an analysis of urban social situations. As will be shown for the migrant society studied here, the theoretical distinction between rural and urban is largely irrelevant to an understanding of how mobile workers organise their

---

[1] Frequently used indicators in urbanisation studies such as sex ratios, level of urbanisation, duration of urban residence, percentage of urban-born urbanites, etc. are indicative in this respect. They presuppose a relation between urban residence and the adoption of some sort of urban behaviour.

[2] Funding for the research described in this chapter was generously provided by the Netherlands Foundation for the Advancement of Tropical Research (Wotro).

[3] This was a major preoccupation of the urbanisation studies in Southern Africa as undertaken by researchers of the Rhodes-Livingstone Institute (see for instance Mitchell 1987; Hannerz 1980: 119-62).

daily lives. For Buhera workers in Harare, social relations that do not encompass both the rural and the urban appear unthinkable. Instead of looking at rural-urban mobility as some sort of socio-economic transition, this chapter aims to analyse rural-urban mobility and the connections between town and countryside as a stable social form. At the level of social actors organising these rural-urban connections, economic preferences do, of course, play a role in shaping behaviour. Yet, the issue is how such economic preferences arise, i.e. how economic decision-making is socio-culturally embedded (Granovetter 1985). Hence, instead of analysing rural-urban mobility as an outcome of economic considerations made by goal-oriented individual actors, the ethnography presented here aims to understand people's socio-cultural dispositions and how these structure the social organisation of rural-urban mobility (Bourdieu 1998: 79-85 and 1990: 52-65).[4]

After a brief outline of the common interpretation of Zimbabwe's history of rural-urban mobility, this chapter analyses the social organisation of this specific type of mobility. It aims to show how specific rural-urban migration practices, such as chain migration, can be understood in relation to certain socio-cultural dispositions like a strong ideology of kinship and identification with the land. There is no need to make *a priori* assumptions as to where such dispositions are situated spatially, i.e. viewing these as urban or rural. The inseparability of rural and urban that emerges from the ethnographic material presented in this chapter follows logically from the research methodology that was applied. Whereas in urbanisation studies migrant behaviour tends to be studied either in urban or in rural settings, this study followed migrants in their mobility from rural Buhera to the urban setting of Harare.

Rural-urban mobility in colonial Zimbabwe: State-regulated urbanisation

It is undeniable that "economic conditions seem to [have] set the basic conditions for the growth of towns" (Mitchell 1987: 46). After the Second World War when industrial growth greatly increased urban employment opportunities, urban centres in Southern Africa expanded rapidly. Southern Rhodesia's capital, Salisbury (now Harare), further benefited from the establishment of the Federation of the Rhodesias and Nyasaland, of which it became the capital in 1953. Since the Second World War the African urban population of (Southern) Rhodesia has more than doubled every decade but by the mid-1970s still less than 20% of Rhodesia's population lived in urban centres (Smout 1976; Mutizwa-Mangiza 1986). The conventional explanation of this relatively low level of urbanisation is not in market terms but in terms of colonial state intervention. Colonial state intervention is perceived as functional to the development of settler capitalism that

---

[4] To argue for the significance of understanding rural-urban migrants' socio-cultural dispositions is not to say that rural-urban relations are important for all categories of urban dwellers. Urban existence may also become disconnected from the rural home. Examples are Harare's street children as discussed in Bourdillon (1994) or specific categories of Copperbelt mine workers studied by Ferguson (1999). In these situations kinship and 'home' are far less important for an understanding of urban social life than they are for the mobile workers discussed here. For a discussion of how the rural and the urban became disconnected in colonial policy discourse, see Andersson (forthcoming).

sought to reduce the cost of wages by localising social reproduction in the rural areas (Wolpe 1972; for an opposing view see Chauncey 1981). The (Southern) Rhodesian government developed a sophisticated legal framework in an attempt to slow down African urbanisation and the formation of a permanently urbanised working class (see Gargett 1977; Mutambirwa & Potts 1987; Zinyama *et al.* 1993). Pass laws restricted urban residence to the duration of employment. A system of compulsory registration of employed urban Africans was developed which enabled the repatriation of unregistered or unemployed Africans to rural areas. Furthermore, urban housing policies for a long time favoured the accommodation of single men. These measures aimed to turn the urban life of male Africans into a temporary affair. As a consequence of the economic and legal insecurity of town life, urban Africans were forced to maintain links with their rural home areas where the women and children were supposed to remain, working the land. This resulted in circulatory migration movements between town and country.

In this brief outline of the origins of rural-urban mobility in colonial Zimbabwe, migratory behaviour is understood as a product of social engineering by the colonial state that operates within a framework of economic incentives triggering labour migration. In other words, state and market are seen as the driving forces of rural-urban mobility. Given this perspective on rural-urban migration and urbanisation, Zimbabwe's independence marks a historical divide. As "restrictions on permanent and family migration to towns were lifted ... it was to be expected that the nature of rural-urban migration would change" (Potts & Mutambirwa 1990: 678). The issue to address thus became "how far family migration was replacing the 'traditional' pattern of single, male migrancy" (Potts & Mutambirwa 1990: 683).

Commonly used demographic indicators such as sex ratios in urban centres, urban growth rates and the level of urbanisation certainly suggest an increase in longer-term and family migration to town in the 1980s (CSO 1994; Potts & Mutambirwa 1990).[5] Yet, at the same time it was found that, as elsewhere in post-colonial Africa (Geschiere & Gugler 1998), rural-urban relations and circulatory migration remained important in post-colonial Zimbabwe (Potts & Mutambirwa 1990: 683). Hence, the 1980s witnessed a diversity of rural-urban links and migration patterns – family migration alongside an established pattern of circulatory rural-urban migration of single men – making aggregated demographic figures increasingly less valuable parameters for the understanding of rural-urban mobility.

In the 1990s, the picture seemed even more complex. Sharp increases in the cost of living, rising transport costs and declining urban job opportunities – possibly aggravated by economic adjustment policies – all contributed to an increase in urban poverty in Zimbabwe. This situation has led some scholars to argue that urban existence has become so expensive that many urban migrants are being forced to return to their rural home areas, resulting in a declining or negative urban population growth (Potts 2000). Yet, as the case material on migrant workers from Buhera presented below shows, rural-urban mobility is not solely determined by economic forces but also influenced by a

---

[5] Urban population growth amounted to 5.6% for the 1982-92 period. Zimbabwe's urban population increased from 24% of the total population in 1982 to 31% in 1992. In Harare the sex distribution changed from 116.9 males per 100 females in 1982 to 110 in 1992 (CSO 1987, 1989 and 1994).

specific value rationality of Buhera workers that informs the way in which they organise their rural-urban migration practices. It is doubtful whether rural return-migration in the 1990s, if it even started to take place, indicates a structural transition in the Zimbabwean economy or a waning of rural-urban mobility. It is more likely that, as this chapter suggests in the conclusion, it is indicative of a re-direction of mobile workers' destinations and economic activities.

Mobile workers, urban houses, rural homes

Farai Machingura and his wife Jane are quite successful small farmers in their early sixties. They live in a small rural village in the Murambinda area of Buhera District (see Map 6.1). The village, which consists of some thirty homesteads along a sandy track, bears the name of Farai's late father, Masanga. In the year 2000, Farai and Jane harvested a surplus of several tonnes of maize, making them one of the biggest maize-producing households in the village. Selling the maize is, however, a major problem as Zimbabwe's cash-strapped Grain Marketing Board offers very low producer prices and delays payments. Farai and Jane are forced to sell their maize locally where the demand for maize is minimal just after the harvest. Despite the marketing problems, Farai and Jane do not appear to be in serious trouble. Their homestead appears prosperous, featuring one of the most impressive houses in the area, a cement plastered four-roomed house with a shiny iron roof. A small vegetable garden, some fruit trees and a private well complete the picture of well-to-do people.

The appearance of a wealthy *farming* family is, however, deceiving. Although there are numerous well-developed homesteads in the district, in an area characterised by poor soils and erratic rainfall both within and between agricultural seasons, it is barely possible to generate the income needed to develop such homesteads. In Buhera District, affluent homesteads are generally a sign of non-agricultural sources of income, i.e. of urban-generated wealth.

Although now a small farmer, Farai was a factory worker in Harare for more than thirty years, while his wife remained in rural Buhera to cultivate the land. The income Farai earned in town is the basis of their wealth and farm enterprise. Farai also has a house (*imba*) in one of Harare's so-called 'high-density' suburbs. He obtained the house in 1980 when the post-independence Harare City Council enabled tenants in the suburbs to buy the house they were renting at the time. Nowadays, Farai's second-born son, Passmore, who raises money for his father by renting out some of the rooms, occupies the house. His urban house thus provides Farai, who has been working the land in his home village since his retirement in 1992, with a small cash income.

Leaving town after spending a working life there – Farai left Harare when he was in his early fifties – is common practice among Buhera migrant workers. Economic considerations naturally play a role in shaping this migration pattern. The relatively high cost of living in town turns a non-working existence there into an expensive affair. However, such economic considerations are merely one factor in the decision to return to the rural area after a working life in the urban context. Returning to the rural area implies an ideology of returning home, to one's (extended) family and ancestral lands. Buhera workers' narratives

Map 6.1: Buhera District, Zimbabwe

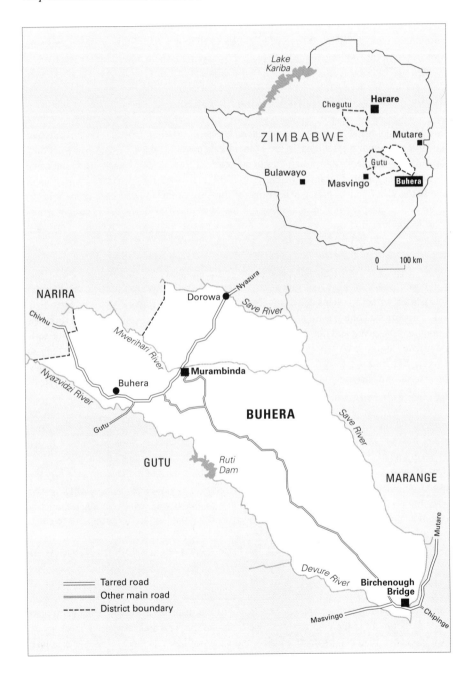

on migration and housing are most illuminating in this respect. Buherans in town clearly distinguish between urban and rural houses. Although one may, like Farai, have lived in town for nearly all one's life – or even been born there – one's house (or parents' house) in the rural area is invariably talked of as 'home' (*kumusha*), whereas houses in town are simply referred to as 'houses' (*imba*). In the same vein, questions such as "where are you from?" and "where do you live?" yield different answers: Buhera and Harare respectively.

The social organisation of rural-urban networks

To understand better the importance of non-economic factors in the structuration of mobile workers' behaviour, Farai's life-history offers an illustrative case. Born in the undeveloped Sabi Native Reserve (now called Save Communal Land) comprising the present-day Buhera District, Farai left in search of work in the mid-1950s. Still a teenager, he went to Hartley (now Chegutu) District where he stayed with his elder (half) brother (*mukoma* B),[6] Jaka, who was a farm worker there. Although with the assistance of his brother he easily found a job on the farm, Farai only stayed briefly. After four months he returned to his parents' home in Buhera District.

Farai could not, however, be typified as a seasonal migrant returning home to farm since it was not the agricultural season that had motivated his return home. Then still a bachelor, "I was not interested in ploughing", he says. Instead, Farai wanted to further his education, and his best chance to do so was in neighbouring Gutu District. In Buhera District itself, education opportunities were very limited as compared to other districts in colonial Zimbabwe. There were only two mission schools in the district, and these only taught up to Standard 6. This lack of schools partly explains why so few Buhera workers were able to reach high positions in the urban labour market during the colonial era. In the field of education, the area was even more disadvantaged than other districts.[7]

Finding your way into the city: Accommodation
When Farai failed to get a place at the school in Gutu, he again tried his luck in the labour market. He returned to his brother Jaka in Hartley, but again, not for long. In 1958 Farai moved on to Umtali (now Mutare). Here, an already established relative offered him accommodation. This time it was his maternal cousin (*mukoma* MZS) who helped him to get a job at the company where he himself was working. When the company was liquidated, Farai once more returned to his parents' home in Buhera District. Yet, he remained a highly mobile worker for he moved on to Bulawayo where he could stay with another cousin (*muzukuru* FZS) who also came originally from Buhera. He did not stay very long in Bulawayo, although not for the lack of urban employment

---

[6] Since it is impossible to translate Shona kinship terminology unequivocally into English, this chapter specifies kinship relations using common categories such as: F (father), M (mother), S (son), D (daughter), B (brother), Z (sister), H (husband), W (wife). Thus, SH denotes sister's husband.
[7] This situation remained largely unaltered up to the mid-1980s when the post-independent government provided more schools in Buhera District, thus enabling Buherans to catch up with people from other districts.

opportunities. Finding a job posed no serious problem in those days he recalls. Farai found a job in a hotel but resigned as he felt he was not fluent enough in Ndebele, the language spoken in Bulawayo.

Being a Shona, he decided to leave for Shona-speaking Salisbury (now Harare) during one of the holidays and expected to find accommodation with his sister's husband (*mukwasha* SH), Chaka Mujiri, from the neighbouring Mujiri village in Buhera District. Chaka occupied a room in a single-men's hostel in Harari (now Mbare), one of the oldest townships in Salisbury. He obtained this accommodation as a 'tied housing' arrangement with his employer. These arrangements, which linked accommodation to employment at a particular company, were common in Rhodesian cities in the 1950s and 1960s. The rapidly expanding urban economy in the post-1945 period not only attracted large numbers of people to work in industry, it simultaneously created a chronic housing shortage.

Accommodating relatives until they found their own accommodation was therefore not only a matter of kindness towards (sometimes distant) relatives, but also often a sheer necessity. Sharing a house, room or even bed with a number of mobile workers originating from one's home district was common in a city like Salisbury. These 'accommodating practices' constituted mobile workers' response to the prevailing 'tied housing' arrangements. The mobilisation of personal networks in finding accommodation made workers flexible because, as Farai explains, "there was always someone you could stay with, if you quit a job".

Finding your way in the city: Employment

Farai's choice of going to Chaka was clever. First, the township of Harari is centrally situated and near a major industrial area, making it possible to go job-hunting on foot – which saved expenditure on bus fares – as recruitment of new workers in Salisbury's industries took place at the factory gate. Second, being with Chaka facilitated finding employment in the tobacco-processing company where Chaka was himself working as a 'baas-boy' (supervisor), a position that enabled him to talk to the company's recruitment officer. Chaka was, thus, able to assist numerous Buhera workers in obtaining jobs.

Unfortunately, Farai had gone to Salisbury without notifying his brother-in-law, and subsequently he discovered that Chaka had left to spend his holidays at home, in Buhera. And so he ended up being accommodated by his 'cousin' (*muzukuru* FZS), Navison, the brother of Farai's cousin in Bulawayo. Through Navison, he found a job at a dry-cleaning company in the nearby industrial area.

Ending up employed in a company in the industrial area in the eastern part of Salisbury was as much accidental as the way in which Farai sought accommodation with Navison. While working at the dry-cleaning company in Salisbury's most centrally situated industrial area, he heard news about a funeral in his home area. Farai took the initiative to inform a 'cousin' (FBS) of the deceased, Tafireyi, who worked in the Masasa industrial area in the eastern part of town. Arriving at the company he told the white South African supervisor he had come to inform his 'brother' about a death in the family. The supervisor, allowing Farai in, asked him whether he was in need of a job. Farai said "yes" and thus he became employed as Tafireyi's 'brother'. He was to stay at the company for more than thirty years.

Farai and Tafireyi were not the only Buherans employed at the company that manufactured industrial clothing (gumboots, gloves, overalls, etc.). Numerous others had found work there, and initially, they were all staying in houses on the company's premises. With the establishment of a new township called Tafara, they moved into newly built houses some four kilometres away. Although the recruitment of new workers at the company took place at the factory gate, the greater distance between workers' houses and the company did not prevent Buhera workers from influencing recruitment practices. As Farai explains:

> The *murungu* [the white supervisor] was taking people at the gate. When I had a relative who needed a job, I gave his name to the *murungu*. At the gate he could call the person's name, and thus he would be employed (…) He [the white supervisor] gave priority to us, workers, to give the names of our relatives who needed jobs.

In this way, Farai found work for his younger half-brother Eland. Eland, in turn, assisted his elder brother's son, Inos, in getting a job. Thus a decentralised network of assistance in finding work and accommodation evolved among mobile workers who knew each other from Buhera (and were often related through kinship or marriage).

Such recruitment practices not only enhanced relations among Buhera workers and between staff and workers, they also facilitated social control at the work place, for if one's employed relative made mistakes or misbehaved, this could jeopardise the future employment chances of one's relatives. Yet, the less well-educated Buhera workers managed in this way to assist numerous relatives in finding employment at the company even when urban employment growth declined in the 1960s. By the end of the 1960s, Farai remembers, there were many Buherans working at the company: "In fact, half of the company [workers] were from Buhera and the other half were from Seke, Murehwa, Hurungwe and Mhondoro [Districts]."

In the post-independence period, the number of Buherans working at the company has steadily declined. With independence in 1980, a fifteen-year economic boycott of Rhodesia came to an end, which not only increased the export possibilities for industries in Zimbabwe but also confronted them with stiff international competition. Furthermore, the introduction of new technologies and the re-organisation of production processes made numerous workers redundant. Employment at Farai's workplace decreased and the number of permanent workers declined as a result of a policy to employ workers more on a temporary basis. Older workers like Farai accepted early retirement packages, while others were retrenched. The number of Buhera workers employed at the company has decreased both in absolute and in proportional terms. This is a result of changes in the staff responsible for recruitment, according to Farai. After independence, the largely white staff in the personnel department were replaced by Zimbabwean managers originating from Masvingo Province. And although contract workers are still recruited at the factory gate and may originate from anywhere in Zimbabwe, when recruiting permanent labourers, the personnel officers "employ more from their area [Masvingo]".

Urban employment through rural connections in contemporary Harare
Farai's migration history is in many ways illustrative of a successful career of the older generation of Buhera workers. During the colonial era, when the urban labour market was racially segmented, upward mobility was limited for African workers. Buhera workers' possibilities for moving beyond unskilled and semi-skilled jobs were further hampered by the limited schooling possibilities within Buhera District. Rather than moving into better paid jobs, urban success meant a good financial package upon retirement after long-term service with one employer and, ultimately, obtaining one's own house in one of Harare's townships that could be rented out upon return to one's rural home in Buhera District.

In the first decade after independence, when the abolishment of discriminatory labour-market policies created new opportunities for Africans, education became an important ingredient for success. Yet, as the case of George Zvarevashe reveals, improved career opportunities in town have not necessarily meant a decrease in the importance of rural-urban connections.

George Zvarevashe, in his forties, owns two houses: one in his home village in Buhera District and another in one of Harare's high-density areas, as the townships were renamed after 1980. Like Farai, George's wife occupies the house in Buhera during the agricultural season, and George comes home once in a while to assist her in cultivating the land as, he claims, a way of relaxation.

George bought his urban house relatively early on in his working career, in the mid-1980s. At that time a government-financed housing scheme provided small, uniform houses in this area. Nowadays these houses are not commonly seen and construction is being undertaken everywhere, hiding the original dwellings behind newly erected walls. House owners try to supplement their incomes by extending their small houses to rent out the extra rooms. George's house is no exception and new asbestos roof sheets are being stored in the living room next to the big television and stereo set. He intends to add three new rooms.

George has a permanent job in the chemical factory at which his father, Tinarwo, started to work in the early 1950s. His father ended his urban career in the late 1960s to become village leader in Buhera District and was an ordinary factory worker who made it to 'baas-boy' (supervisor) and used this position to influence the recruitment of new workers. On his retirement, the company offered his second son, Daniel, a position, in return for Tinarwo's loyal service.[8] While working in town, Tinarwo had invested his income in the education of his older sons who, after entering employment, assisted their father in financing the education of their younger brothers. Thus, George was able to finish Standard 6 in 1974 and obtained a position in the factory's personnel department. With his elder brother Daniel working in a supervisory position in another department, the brothers continued what their father had been doing: employing relatives and

---

[8] This recruitment practice in which jobs are handed down from generation to generation, thus contributing to the emergence of chain migrations, is common in Southern African industry as a whole. See De Vletter (1998: 13) and Cheater (1986: 44). The reason that Tinarwo's second son was offered a job was that his first son was already employed by the company.

friends. Their influence on the recruitment of new personnel is reflected in the large numbers of Buherans who currently work or have worked for the company. In 1997 more than sixty permanent workers originated from the Murambinda area in Buhera District, while Buherans comprised some 40-50% of company's workforce of some 400-500 workers.

The presence of Buherans can easily be observed when one joins George as he leaves his office and meets workers who have just finished their shifts. As he works in the personnel department, it is not surprising that George knows most of them. Yet he frequently calls someone by his clan name, mentions the village in Buhera from which he originates, and then adds: "I recruited him."

Migrant networks and social security: The significance of the land

The histories of Farai and George outlined above make it difficult to talk of rural-urban mobility or the 'maintenance of rural links' in merely economic terms. Buhera workers' involvement[9] in rural affairs is not simply a question of support for rural family members in return for safeguarding a claim to land as some sort of social security arrangement, for, as Van Velsen (1960: 275) already argued:

> ... a person's right to land cannot be isolated from his relationships involving other rights and obligations in the community. ... a member of this society who wants to maintain his status cannot do so only in relation to one aspect of life – he is inevitably drawn into the total life of the community.[10]

Although social security is an important aspect of the migrant networks described above, the productive value of the land is not the source of it. Unlike common perspectives on rural-urban connections that situate mobile workers' social security in (subsistence) farming in the rural area, Buhera migrants invest urban income in the development of their agricultural activities. In Buhera District, characterised by poor soils and erratic rainfall, cultivating the land is not sufficient to generate the cash required each year to buy the necessary farm inputs. Sustainable agriculture in Buhera depends on urban incomes as can be observed towards the beginning of the agricultural season. Visiting urban migrants bring large numbers of bags of hybrid maize seeds and artificial fertilisers.[11]

---

[9] Urban 'involvement' and 'commitment' are frequently used terms in urbanisation studies. They indicate the extent to which an individual has built social relations in town (urban involvement) and the cognitive aspect of this involvement (urban commitment). See Mitchell (1987: 68).

[10] This is even reflected in the way in which migrant workers are involved in land issues at home. Migrants show a keen interest in local struggles over land, although these are hardly motivated by (their own) economic interests. In the Murambinda area of Buhera District, land disputes are predominantly political struggles among village leaders in which migrants may get involved as mobilisers of legal assistance in town (Andersson 1999).

[11] The year 2000 witnessed sharp increases in urban costs of living and Buhera migrants complained that hybrid maize seed had become too expensive. Consequently, many had reduced the size of their maize plots in Buhera District.

Land is significant not for its productive value but because it forms a focal point in Buhera migrants' rural-urban networks. Migration to town and the subsequent maintenance of rural connections are inseparable. Rural connections are presupposed in starting an urban career. As the cases of both Farai Machingura and George Zvarevashe show, social security has to be situated in migrants' networks; in recruitment and accommodating practices in town; and, as the ultimate goal, in having one's own house in the city. As in other countries in Southern Africa where "urban housing is short in supply and prices are skyrocketing, absentee [house] ownership is an important hedge against inflation" (Hansen 1997: 105). Urban houses of migrant workers, like Farai's, are usually not sold but passed on within the family.

Social security arrangements have to be situated in migrants' networks and these networks themselves cannot be reduced to a set of economically motivated links among migrants. Although relations among Buhera migrants are instrumental to an individual migrant's career, economic and social security considerations do not determine the behaviour of these urban migrants or the organisation of their networks. The difference in the way in which migrants like Farai and George deal with housing in town as opposed to the rural area is illustrative. In contrast with houses in town, Buhera migrants' efforts to establish a homestead (*musha*) in the rural area and to construct a house on it cannot be understood from an economic perspective. Similar to observations made by Eades (1993) on Yoruba migrants in the Gold Coast whose success in trading enables them to build houses in their poor rural home area, Buhera migrants' investment in housing in the rural home area has to be understood in relation to their cultural dispositions. It reflects a strong sense of belonging (see De Vletter 1998: 20; Bourdillon 1977: 7). In rural Buhera, as the cases of Farai and George already illustrated, a brick-built house plastered with cement and roofed with asbestos or iron sheets reflects urban success. Besides the round cooking hut with a grass-thatched roof that characterises any Shona homestead, successful urban migrants usually develop their homestead by constructing a brick house. A survey in the Murambinda area in 1997 found that 84% of the homesteads that have such a brick house were owned by (returned) migrant workers or their widows.[12] To construct such a house in the middle of Murambinda Ward, kilometres from any major road, requires substantial capital and considerable effort since building materials often have to be bought and transported from Harare. While such investments may seem irrational from an economic point of view, they are not if one acknowledges the value Buhera migrants attach to belonging to a rural home area.

Migrant networks and socio-cultural dispositions: Kinship and marriage

The case of George Zvarevashe's brother, Daniel, allows a better understanding of the socio-cultural embeddedness of Buhera migrants' economic behaviour. Like his younger brother George, Daniel at first sight seems to represent the modern individual-

---

[12] A survey of four villages (*mabhuku,* singular: *bhuku*) in the Murambinda area found that of the 105 homesteads in these villages, 44 had at least one brick house roofed with iron or asbestos sheets and that 37 (84%) of these brick houses were owned by (ex-)migrant workers or their widows.

ised urban migrant whose rural ties appear to be driven by economic interests. Yet, despite living in town for most of his life and having a successful urban career, he is highly involved in Buhera social life.

Daniel, who has a supervisory position and a reasonable wage, stays in the company house his father used to occupy but also has his own house in a township on the northern side of Harare. He rents out this house to fellow Buherans. In Buhera his wealth is manifested in his *musha* (homestead) that is among the most developed in the area – a brick-built house and nicely thatched huts, all painted in the same colours. However, neither Daniel nor his wife and children spend much time at the rural home (*kumusha*). Daniel's (second) wife is a nurse at Murambinda Hospital (some ten kilometres away) and his children work in town or attend urban schools. Like his father and younger brother, George, Daniel is investing a lot in the education of his children by sending them to urban or boarding schools that generally provide a better education than that available in rural Buhera. To take care of his homestead in Buhera, he employs two young workers from southern Buhera. Daniel pays them to work his fields and graze the cattle when it is his turn in the village herding arrangement. These workers assist in ploughing his father's fields, as well as the fields Daniel has rented from fellow villagers in an attempt to grow sorghum commercially.

Daniel's involvement in both urban and rural life, i.e. his investments in urban housing, his children's careers, his rural homestead, cattle and agriculture, is not simply a matter of economic calculation and, despite having spent most of his life in town both while at school and in employment, he does not represent a modern, individualised urban worker. Daniel's career has to be understood as part of an emerging migrant network that is not confined to the urban space. His adherence to a specific marital custom exemplifies this. He married a daughter of Chiminya, a family ruling a village next to his father's in the Murambinda area. When this wife died, the Zvarevashe family accepted a daughter offered by his in-laws to substitute for his deceased wife. His adherence to this custom, known as *chimutsamapfihwa* ('to [re-]install the cooking stones'), signifies that for Daniel, as in this migrant society as a whole, marriage is more than a transaction between individuals. Marriage relationships involve families (see Holleman 1952: 190) who are often related to one another in a number of ways as rural neighbours, fellow migrants, etc.

That the valuation of marriage relations, rural social relations and the rural home area constitute important dispositions structuring migration practices of Buhera workers also follows from marriage practices among Buhera migrants. Although it is long established that young men leave Buhera in search of work before they marry, marriages in which both the man and wife originate from Buhera remain common. While migrants' sexual relations in town may result in unwanted pregnancies and financial commitments towards the raising of extramarital children, marriage patterns of migrants reveal a preference for women from the rural home area in Buhera. By comparing the marriage patterns of three extended families in the Murambinda area of Buhera District, it was found that the majority brought together partners that both originate from within Buhera District.[13] As Shona

---

[13] These results were derived from family-tree information of three extended families in the Murambinda area of Buhera District. The analysis considered three generations and only family members born before

marriages are exogamous, this means that families maintain marital relations with numerous other families in Buhera District. Customary definitions of blood ties do, of course, somewhat restrict new marriage alliances between these families, yet the preference to marry someone "from a family you already know" is commonly shared, even among the younger generation.[14]

Migrant networks and the idiom of kinship
Migrants predominantly use kinship terminology when talking about their multistranded mutual social relations. Yet, these relations may be very distant and in some cases merely based on shared or related clan membership. A survey[15] of 87 migrants who returned to Buhera for the Christmas holidays illuminates this. When asked who had provided them with accommodation when they first went to town, respondents almost invariably described these relations in kinship terms rather than referring to a common Buhera origin (see Table 6.1). Table 6.1 reflects the strong patrilineal orientation in Shona society with most first-time migrants having relied on patrikin for initial accommodation in town. However, the social organisation of migrant networks in town cannot be understood by reducing it to kinship structures. Kinship and clan membership should primarily be understood as an idiom that Buhera migrants adopt to express their mutual relationships. After all, Buhera migrants do not only mobilise existing kinship relations (and relations through marriage). Non-kin relationships among Buhera migrants in town may also result in the establishment of marriage relations between them. Furthermore, kin and clan membership relations among migrants often overlap with other types of relations such as a common village of origin (*bhuku*) or headmanship (*dunhu*). Asking Buhera migrants who their friends are reveals this as well: friends are often relatives or people known from Buhera. Hence, urban-based social relations do not replace migrants' rural-based social relations but, rather, the former are added to migrants' social relations that span both urban and rural spaces.

Migrant networks and socio-cultural dispositions: Burial practices

A further strong socio-cultural force among urban migrants from Buhera is the wish to be buried *kumusha* (at home, on the homestead) among one's own people and ancestors. Even after a lifetime of urban employment and urban family life, people want to be

---

1970 (i.e. those over 18 years of age). For an overview of kinship relations and marriage practices among the Shona, see Bourdillon (1977) and Holleman (1949 and 1952).

[14] For instance, 'brothers' and 'sisters' (B, FBS, FFBSS, Z, FBD, FFBDD) of George and Daniel (N=29) predominantly married partners from within Buhera District (65% in the Murambinda area, 21% in Buhera District, 14% from outside the district).

[15] The survey was held in the Murambinda area of Buhera District in December 1995 and January 1996. The vast majority of respondents were men (96.6%). On average the respondents were in their early thirties and 69% were married. The partners of 88.4% of the married migrants stay (at least for part of the year) in Buhera District. Migrants were asked the name of the person with whom they stayed when they first went to seek work. They were also asked to mention the relation (in Shona) and to describe this relation. This was done because Shona kinship terms often denote different kinship relations (see Bourdillon 1977; Holleman 1952).

*Table 6.1: Buhera migrants in Harare (N=87): Social relations mobilised in
finding initial accomodation*

	No.	%
Members of the patrilineage	*60*	*69*
a) 'father' (F, FB, FFBS, FFBSS)	22	25.3
b) 'brother' (B, FBS, FFBSS)	33	37.9
c) another member of the patrilineage (Z, FZ, S)	5	5.7
Matrilateril kin	*10*	*12*
d) 'uncle' (MB, MFBS, MBS, MFBSS, MF)		
Relations through marriage:	8	9
e) 'nephew' (ZS, FBDS)	3	2.3
f) 'cousin' (FZS, FFBDS)	4	4.6
g) other (WFBS)	1	1.1
Non-related persons	*6*	*7*
Unknown/not answered	*3*	*3*
Total	87	100

The kinship categories between quotation marks under a) to f), respectively refer to the
following Shona classifications of kin: a) baba, babamukuru, babamunimini; b) mukoma,
muninína; c) handzvadi, vatete, mwanakomana; d) sekuru; e) muzukuru; g) tezvara.

buried at their rural homestead. Thus, a migrant worker's efforts to establish a rural
homestead (*musha*) at some stage in his urban career can be understood. Although he
may stay with his wife and children in town and has no economic need to supplement
his urban income with agricultural production, a 'traditional' round cooking hut has to
be constructed.[16] It is possible, therefore, to see homesteads that are occupied by family
members of absent migrant workers who leave their fields uncultivated or hire people to
work the land for them. Building a homestead on a plot of a few acres is an expression
of a migrant worker's membership of the rural community and of his natural desire to
be buried there.[17]

Urban-based burial societies constitute a more formal organisational expression of
the wish to be buried in the rural home area. Burial societies assist in the transport and
funeral arrangements of a deceased member or family member. Through regular contributions to the society's fund, its members raise the substantial capital that is needed to
transport the body of the deceased from town to the rural home area to be buried. Not
surprisingly, burial societies in town are often organised on the basis of a common rural
background.

---

[16] The round cooking hut or kitchen is also important during the funeral process itself. Before the burial,
it is customary to lay out the deceased for one evening and night in this rondavel, accompanied by female
family members and in-laws.

[17] The funeral process itself is another example of migrant workers' continued involvement in rural
affairs. Migrants not only contribute substantially to the funeral costs, they also finance visits to traditional healers (*n'anga*) or prophets: a common practice that aims to establish the cause of death. Furthermore, they return home to attend funerals and rituals relating to the inheritance of property, the care of a
deceased's wife/wives (*kugara nhaka*) and children, and the succession in the family structure.

Conclusion

Rural-urban mobility and town-country relations have been pertinent issues in the study of Southern Africa for a long time. Conventionally, they have been framed in terms of a classic set of (ideal typical) dichotomies – modernisation-tradition, individualisation-communality, change-continuity, and so on – of which 'the urban' and 'the rural' constitute geographical antipodes. Urbanisation, in this perspective, easily becomes tied into a narrative of modernisation, while state intervention and market forces have generally been depicted as the forces regulating rural-urban mobility. Whereas in the colonial era discriminatory legislation such as housing policies and pass laws regulated urban influx, structural adjustment policies and urban economic decline are seen as the forces behind rural return-migration in the 1990s. Thus, rural-urban mobility is reduced to a function of state regulation and market forces.

This chapter has not denied the importance of the wider political economy on rural-urban mobility and its social organisation. Literature on the Southern African migrant labour system convincingly shows the importance of such forces (O'Laughlin 1998; De Vletter 1998). Instead, this study aimed to show how social forces from below influence and transform such external forces. For instance, Buhera migrants' networks, which encompass rural and urban localities, to some degree mediate the adverse economic circumstances in a city characterised by high urban unemployment and rising costs of living. These networks constitute devices to secure urban employment for people who generally have no access to better-paid jobs. Simultaneously however, because of a lack of formal employment opportunities, these networks gain significance in the re-organisation of mobility patterns and economic activities. For instance, in the absence of urban job opportunities (informal) rural-urban and cross-border trade may gain significance (Muzvidziwa 1997). An indication of such re-organisation of mobility, as opposed to a decrease in mobility, is the number of public bus services that connect Buhera District's major centre, Murambinda, with the country's major urban centres. Despite progressive economic decline in Zimbabwe in the late 1990s, their number has increased substantially from two and five daily buses to Harare and Bulawayo respectively in 1996, to seven and fifteen in the year 2000.

Despite their importance in mediating external forces, the networks of Buhera migrants linking Harare and home cannot be adequately understood if seen only as a strategic reaction to a specific (adverse) economic situation. Although strategic action plays a role, Buhera migrants' participation in these networks that span both urban and rural localities is not a matter of choice or calculation. Buhera migrants cannot escape them. As the cases presented in this chapter have shown, the emergent networks of Buhera migrants are first and foremost an expression of a socio-cultural pattern. The specific ways in which Buhera migrants have organised these networks should primarily be understood in relation to the cultural influences of people in this migrant labour society. Viewing migration practices as observable outcomes of actors' socio-cultural dispositions leads to a better understanding of the preferences that motivate the economic behaviour of mobile workers.

References

Andersson, J.A. 1999, 'The Politics of Land Scarcity: Land Disputes in Save Communal Area, Zimbabwe', *Journal of Southern African Studies* 25 (4): 553-78.

Andersson, J.A. (forthcoming), 'Administrators' Knowledge and State Control in Colonial Zimbabwe; The Invention of the Rural-Urban Divide in Buhera District, 1912-80', *Journal of African History*.

Bates, R. (ed.) 1988, 'Governments and Agricultural Markets in Africa', *Toward a Political Economy of Development*, Berkeley: University of California Press.

Bourdieu, P. 1990, *The Logic of Practice*, Cambridge: Polity Press.

Bourdieu, P. 1998, *Practical Reason: On the Theory of Action*, Cambridge: Polity Press.

Bourdillon, M.F.C. 1977, *The Shona Peoples: An Ethnography of the Contemporary Shona, with Special Reference to their Religion*, Gweru: Mambo Press.

Bourdillon, M.F.C. 1994, 'Street Children in Harare', *Africa* 64 (4): 516-32.

Central Statistical Office 1987, *District Population Sheets: Mashonaland East*, Harare: Central Statistical Office.

Central Statistical Office 1989, *Zimbabwe in Maps: A Census Atlas*, Harare: Central Statistical Office.

Central Statistical Office 1994, *Census 1992: National Report*, Harare: Central Statistical Office.

Chauncey, G. 1981, 'The Locus of Reproduction: Women's Labour in the Zambian Copperbelt, 1927-1953', *Journal of Southern African Studies* 7 (2): 135-64.

Cheater, A.P. 1986, *The Politics of Factory Organization*, Gweru: Mambo Press.

De Vletter, F. 1998, *Sons of Mozambique: Mozambican Miners and Post-apartheid South Africa*, Cape Town: Southern African Migration Project.

Eades, J.S. 1993, *Strangers and Traders; Yoruba Migrants, Markets and the State in Northern Ghana*, London: International African Institute.

Ferguson, J. 1990, 'Mobile Workers, Modernist Narratives: A Critique of the Historiography of Transition on the Zambian Copperbelt', Part I: *Journal of Southern African Studies* 16 (3), 385-412; Part II: *Journal of Southern African Studies* 16 (4): 603-21.

Ferguson, J. 1999, *Expectations of Modernity; Myths and Meaning of Urban Life on the Zambian Copperbelt*, Berkeley: University of California Press.

Gargett, E. 1977, *The Administration of Transition*, Gwelo: Mambo Press.

Geschiere, P. & J. Gugler 1998, 'The Urban-Rural Connection; Changing Issues of Belonging and Identification', *Africa* 68 (3): 309-19.

Granovetter, M. 1985, 'Economic Action and Social Structure: The Problem of Embeddedness', *American Journal of Sociology* 91: 481-510.

Hansen, K.T. 1997, *Keeping House in Lusaka*, New York: Columbia University Press.

Hannerz, U. 1980, *Exploring the City: Inquiries Toward an Urban Anthropology*, New York, Guilford: Columbia University Press.

Holleman, J.F. 1949, *The Pattern of Hera Kinship*, London: Oxford University Press for the Rhodes-Livingstone Institute.

Holleman, J.F. 1952, *Shona Customary Law: With Reference to Kinship, Marriage, the Family and the Estate*, Manchester: Manchester University Press.

Mitchell, J.C. 1956, *The Kalela Dance: Aspects of Social Relationships among Urban Africans in Northern Rhodesia*, Manchester: Manchester University Press.

Mitchell, J.C. 1987, *Cities, Society and Social Perception; A Central African Perspective*, Oxford: Clarendon Press.

Mutambirwa, C.C. & D.H. Potts 1987, 'Changing Patterns of African Rural-Urban Migration and Urbanisation in Zimbabwe', *Eastern and Southern Africa Geographical Journal* 1 (1): 26-39.

Mutizwa-Mangiza, N.D. 1986, 'Urban Centres in Zimbabwe: Intercensal Changes, 1962-1982', *Geography* 71 (2): 148-50.

Muzvidziwa, V. 1997, 'Rural-Urban Linkages: Masvingo's Double-Rooted Female Heads of Households', *Zambezia* 24 (2): 97-123.

O'Laughlin, B. 1998, 'Missing Men? The Debate over Rural Poverty and Women-Headed Households in Southern Africa', *Journal of Peasant Studies* 25 (2): 1-48.

Potts, D. 1995, 'Shall We Go Home? Increasing Urban Poverty in African Cities and Migration Processes', *Geographical Journal* 161(3): 245-64.

Potts, D. 1997, 'Urban Lives: Adopting New Strategies and Adapting Rural Links', in: C. Rakodi (ed.), *The Urban Challenge in Africa: Growth and Management of its Large Cities,* Tokyo: United Nations Press.

Potts, D. 2000, 'Urban Unemployment and Migrants in Africa: Evidence from Harare 1985-1994', *Development and Change* 31 (4): 879-910.

Potts, D.H. & C.C. Mutambirwa 1990, 'Rural-Urban Linkages in Contemporary Harare: Why Migrants Need Their Land', *Journal of Southern African Studies* 16 (4): 677-98.

Smout, M.A.H. 1976, 'Urbanisation of the Rhodesian Population', *Zambezia* 4 (2): 79-91.

Van Velsen, J. 1960, 'Labour Migration as a Positive Factor in the Continuity of Tonga Tribal Society', *Economic Development and Cultural Change* 8 (3): 265-78.

Wilson, G. 1941, *An Essay on the Economics of Detribalization in Northern Rhodesia Parts I & II,* Manchester: Rhodes-Livingstone Institute.

Wolpe, H. 1972, 'Capitalism and Cheap Labour-Power in South Africa: From Segregation to Apartheid', *Economy & Society* 1 (4): 425-54.

World Bank 1981, *Accelerated Development in Sub-Saharan Africa: An Agenda for Action,* Washington DC, World Bank.

World Bank 2000, *World Development Report 2000/2001: Attacking Poverty,* Oxford: Oxford University Press.

Zinyama, L., D. Tevera & S. Cumming (eds) 1993, *Harare, The Growth and Problems of the City,* Harare: University of Zimbabwe Publishers.

7

Migration as a positive response to opportunity and context: The case of Welo, Ethiopia

Jonathan Baker

Recent research has addressed the issue of human migration from a more nuanced perspective in that the central role of the agency of the individual migrant is considered, as well as the importance of structure. The present study, while recognising that the migration experience throws up losers as well as winners, perceives migration as a generally positive response to opportunities elsewhere which can lead to strategies involving survival and accumulation. The data for the present study is from South Welo, an environmentally fragile and degraded region in northeastern Ethiopia. A sample of 75 households, drawn from three separate locations, forms the basis for analysis. While some of the data are presented in aggregated fashion, a number of representative case studies have been selected to reveal the rich detail and insights that inform the complexity of the migration experience.

Introduction

One of the major problems that has characterised or even bedevilled the study of human migration is that all too often simplistic categorisations and classifications have been used to explain what is, after all, a very complex phenomenon. For example, much of the literature concerning migration and migration behaviour has been imbued with simple dichotomies, such as 'push' or 'pull' that seem to imply the absence of free will. Despite the fact that twenty-five years ago Abu-Lughod referred to the demise of such simple notions in the study of migration whereby "human beings, like iron filings, were impelled by forces beyond their conscious control" (1975: 201), such notions still enjoy some degree of currency.

However, more nuanced insights have been introduced into migration studies which open up exciting avenues for further exploration. The migration phenomenon, as with all human experiences, throws up winners and losers. These outcomes are determined by a combination of complex factors that are expressed in and through the interplay of human agency and social structure (Aina & Baker 1995). The agency of the individual migrant is the key explanatory factor from the neo-classical viewpoint, while the structuralist model emphasises the importance of broad structures and particularly the organisation and reorganisation of capitalist development (Wright 1995).

This chapter is concerned with processes of migration in Ethiopia. The main geographical focus is on the area known as South Welo, in the northeastern part of the country. In addition, since migration has also been a central imperative in the creation of the Ethiopian state and its social formation at the end of the nineteenth century, it is appropriate to include a brief review of wider migration processes. Hopefully, this will help demonstrate the congruence of structure and agency.

Imperialism, north-south migrations and state formation
Contemporary Ethiopia is of recent creation. Unlike the situation elsewhere in Africa where European colonialism created dependency and reshaped the map of Africa, Ethiopia developed as the result of a series of brutal conquests by Amhara invaders from the northern highland state of Abyssinia. Through a series of military campaigns, Emperor Menelik II (who ruled as emperor from 1889 until 1913) greatly extended the boundaries of Abyssinia and in the process created a state three times its former size, doubled the population and forcibly incorporated a myriad of religious, ethnic and linguistic groups into the Empire.

Menelik's desire to create a modern, centralised state required the expansion of state revenues, and the extraction of southern resources such as spices, civet, ivory, gold and coffee provided him with the means to achieve this ambition. In the newly conquered southern territories, Menelik established a series of military garrisons (*ketema*) which later developed non-military functions and created a nascent urban system. In addition, soldiers of Menelik's army were rewarded by grants of alienated land as well as obligatory labour and other services that were provided by the newly conquered peoples. The upshot of these processes meant that within the space of two decades, a feudal system had been firmly implanted in the southern regions.

However, a very central consideration in the context of empire building was the importance of the agency of migration. The southern conquests required a steady flow of northern Amhara peasant farmers willing to cultivate alienated land, and thus maintain and consolidate the feudal structure and promote the processes of Amharaisation in non-Amhara regions. Having said this, it should be made clear that the increasing impoverishment of peasant households in the Amhara regions (of which Welo is a part) as a result of increasing land degradation and scarcity meant that there were many peasants who were willing to migrate to the new southern regions. This process continued basically uninterrupted until the rural land nationalisations of 1975, implemented under the Mengistu regime, brought about the collapse of the feudal system. McCann summed up the importance of migration processes to state formation, while concomitantly solving problems of northern land scarcity:

> The north-south migration that took place in Ethiopia between 1890 and the postwar years was perhaps *the most significant single process* in the foundation of the modern Ethiopian social formation. Menelik's conquests meant little without a ready population

of soldier/settler willing to leave the cycle of subsistence production in the north and settle into the huge tracts of alienated land offered in the wake of the imperial conquests (McCann 1986: 39, emphasis added).

As the brief discussion below illustrates little appears to have changed in terms of environmental constraints in Welo since Menelik's conquests a century ago.

Migration processes and experiences in South Welo

The geographical and administrative context of South Welo
The focus of this study is the South Welo Administrative Zone, one of the eleven zones of Region Three that comprises and represents the Amhara ethnic group within the federal ethnic system of contemporary Ethiopia (Map 7.1). This zone is considered to be one of the poorest areas of the country and has long suffered from a combination of factors which have led to processes of underdevelopment, including isolation, poor communications, lack of innovation, irregular and inadequate rainfall which often leads to famine conditions and associated problems of human and livestock mortality and morbidity.

In addition, population growth is exacerbating the problem of shortages of agricultural land. Eighty-three% of land holdings (per household) are one hectare or less in South Welo. This figure should be considered within a context whereby one hectare of cropped land is the minimum amount required to sustain peasant households. Indeed, 40% of all households in South Welo have 0.5 hectares or less of farmland (Kebrom 1999). Given these data it is not surprising that the propensity to migrate elsewhere for work to supplement household income is great. In short, Welo "is a land of humble potentials densely inhabited by millions of small and hardy peasants who have for centuries practiced what they know best, namely subsistence agriculture" (Dessalegn 1991: 58).

Administratively, South Welo is divided into 17 *woreda* (districts within a zone), which in turn are divided into *kebele* (urban dwellers' associations) which have responsibility for urban governance, and *gabarewotch mahber* (peasant associations) which are responsible for development activities in rural localities. While these institutions were established during the early years of the former regime (i.e. in 1975 and 1976), their responsibilities have changed. Broadly speaking, the main responsibility of the peasant associations today is to redistribute agricultural land (all rural land is nationalised but peasants have usufructuary rights) when the number of farm families increases through population growth. In the urban sphere, the *kebele* has responsibility for urban government, the maintenance of infrastructure (where meagre resources permit), the upkeep of the *kebele* shop, and collecting rents from tenants in accommodation nationalised by the former regime. It should be stressed that this description has been simplified and the operations of these institutions may vary considerably, even within the same *woreda* (for more details, see Baker 1994).

The urbanisation level is low in South Welo and the zone only has two urban centres of any regional or national importance: Dessie (with a population of about 100,000) is

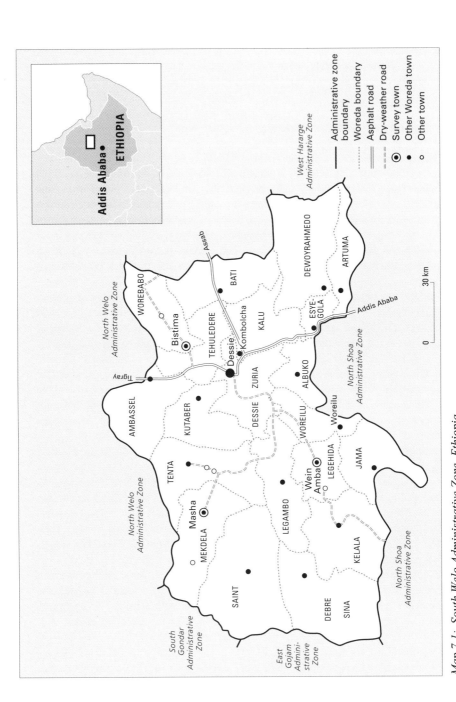

Map 7.1: South Welo Administrative Zone, Ethiopia

the zonal capital, while Kombolcha (with a population of about 40,000) is an important transport and industrial centre. Together, the two centres probably account for about half of South Welo's urban population. The South Welo Zone has a number of small towns with populations of between 2,000 and 4,000 people. Despite their small size, such centres offer a range of essential services including that of *woreda* headquarters for their respective *woreda* populations. Moreover, these towns provide migrant populations with a surprising range of employment options.

The critical influence of agro-climatic conditions
In Ethiopia, it is conventional to categorise agro-climatic zones on the basis of a four-fold classification based on altitude. *Kolla* refers to those regions between 500-1500 metres that have an annual average temperature of between 20-25°C. *Woina dega* regions are between 1500-2500 metres, with an average temperature of 15-20°C. *Dega* regions are between 2500-3500 metres, with temperatures between 10-15°C. *Wirch* regions are above 3500 metres and annual temperatures are 10°C or below.

In the South Welo Zone, 20.4% of land is classified as *kolla*, 45.6% as *woina dega*, 30.6% as *dega*, and only 3.4% as *wirch*. Reference to these categories within the context of this chapter is useful because they influence what plants grow where, disease patterns (for example, the prevalence of malaria), rainfall, and areas which are vulnerable to drought and famine (especially *kolla* areas) and consequently susceptible to poverty.

Major crops grown in the *kolla* zone are *teff* (*Eragrostis Teff*), sorghum, maize, beans and peas. In *woina dega*, barley, wheat, *teff,* sorghum, maize, beans and peas are grown, while wheat and barley are important crops in *dega* zones.

There are two periods of rainfall in the region that are crucial to the prosperity and, indeed, survival of the rural and urban economies. In a normal year the 'short rains' (*belg*) are from about January to March, while the 'long rains' (*maher*) are from late June to the end of September. Obviously the rains are critical for crop production and pasture growth for animal forage, and the failure of these rains can have a disastrous impact. The traditional region of Welo (which also comprises the North Welo Administrative Zone and areas which were formerly part of Welo to the east) has suffered severely at fairly regular intervals from major droughts and famine. For example, in 1973 Welo experienced widespread famine that was probably the precipitating factor leading to the downfall of the imperial regime of Haile Selassie. During 1984-85, Welo was revisited by drought and famine and this resulted in the implementation of a massive resettlement programme devised by the former regime of Mengistu Haile-Mariam. However, in 1994 (when the fieldwork for this study was conducted) and again in the early months of 2000, the failure of the *belg* or small rains created havoc. While it is estimated that these rains are responsible for about 10% of crop production (although considerably more in the marginal areas of Welo and Tigray), their contribution to pasture growth is absolutely critical for livestock survival. Consequently, the very survival of the pastoralist way of life is often under severe threat when the *belg* rains fail. This point was clearly demonstrated by reports of anticipated widespread famine in April/May 2000 (*Africa Confidential*, 14 April 2000). During the fieldwork in 1994, the *belg* rains failed resulting in fairly widespread crop failure and livestock mortality particularly in the *kolla* zones. The result was the introduction of food relief programmes in *woreda* and selected towns for the affected rural populations who often travelled long distances to these urban food-distribution centres. An obvious point to be drawn from the above discussion is that the failure of the *belg* rains severely weakened the rural economy with the result that rural demand for urban goods and services declined quite dramatically. The resultant negative impact of slack rural demand on urban businesses is clear.

The dynamics of migration in South Welo

The literature on migration in Welo presents a picture in which few people migrated into the region (with only 0.9% of the total population enumerated as life-time in-migrants according to the 1984 census) but appreciable numbers out-migrated to find employment on large sugar and cotton farms run as private concerns during the reign of Haile Sellassie or as nationalised entities during the Mengistu regime. It is also clear that many people from Welo have traditionally migrated to Eritrea and other parts of Ethiopia over a period of many years (Office of the Population and Housing Census Commission 1984; Dessalegn 1991; Kloos 1982). However, it appears that many out-migrants eventually return to their places of origin in Welo after a sojourn elsewhere. Data collected during the present research tends to confirm that much migration inside and outside of Welo takes the form of circulation.

Although the data are sketchy, it appears that a good many of the 350,000 people who were resettled from Welo in 1984-85 have returned there (Betemariam & White 2000). Table 7.3 below gives an indication of some of the destinations of the resettlement returnees. Unfortunately, data from the latest census in 1994 do not throw much light on this issue. What the census data do show, however, is that 213,088 individuals (10% of South Welo's population of 2,122,580) were classified as migrants. Unfortunately, no information is available to indicate whether these migrants were internal or external to Welo. However, the distribution of this migrant population by origin and destination is as follows: urban-urban 43,033 (20.3%); rural-urban 46,485 (21.8%); urban-rural 21,920 (10.3%); and rural-rural 101,163 (47.6%) (Office of Population and Housing Census Commission 1994: 11).

Data collected from 75 households in three towns in July 1994 would seem to demonstrate quite clearly that people are very mobile but that, on the face of it at least, many do not move far from their place of origin. Questions regarding mobility were asked of the head of household and spouse (if any). Consequently, a total of 150 responses were possible. The results were as follows: 12% no spouse; 22% were born in the town; 1.3% were born outside Welo. The remainder were born either in a rural area (58%) or in an urban centre (6.7%) of Welo. These data would tend to show that the majority of small-town dwellers in Welo have a close attachment to their home region. Having said this, aggregating migration data tends to miss an astonishing amount of rich detail.

Table 7.1 provides population data for the three surveyed towns. Apart from the obvious fact that these are small central places, the one striking feature is the numerical dominance of females in the urban populations as measured by the use of sex ratios. The sex ratio is an index that measures the number of males per 100 females in a given population. In a hypothetically perfectly balanced population the sex ratio would be 100 and in a fairly well-balanced population the sex ratio would probably fall within the 98.0-102.0 range. Any great deviation from this range suggests that the population is mobile and indicates the in- or out-migration of males or females.

Table 7.1: Population profiles of the three towns, 1993

Town	No. of Households	Population male/female		Total	Household size	Sex ratio
Bistima	835	2,172	2,339	4,511	5.4	92.8
Masha	541	1,349	1,465	2,814	5.2	92.1
Wein Amba	468	990	1,320	2,310	4.9	75.7

The low sex ratios for these towns are evidence of the in-migration of females. This is not to suggest that men do not migrate to these towns (they clearly do), but that the number of female migrants is greater than that of male migrants.

There is nothing unique in the Ethiopian context of women out-numbering men in towns and the phenomenon has been documented for other towns (see Baker 1986 for illustrations from towns in North Gondar Zone, Region Three). There are a number of reasons for this. In rural areas of Welo and indeed in much of rural Ethiopia, paid employment options for women outside agriculture are limited and their participation in agriculture is restricted to weeding, harvesting and threshing. Although women and men have equal land rights, cultural and capital constraints have prevented women from making full use of this resource. Ploughing is entirely the responsibility of men, since cultural constraints associated with the polluting attributes of women, combined with the heavy nature of the activity, excludes women from the task. Consequently, women without men cannot be independent farmers, although they can hire labour to cultivate their land (if they have plough oxen and inputs) or they can let their land be cultivated by others in a share-cropping agreement whereby the oxen and inputs are provided by the farming partner and the output is divided equally. The Ethiopian case can be contrasted to much of the rest of Africa where women are heavily involved in agriculture using simple hoe technology.

Furthermore, early marriage in South Welo means that many girls are married at the age of twelve, occasionally as young as seven, and divorce rates are very high. Thus, if women lose the labour of men in agriculture, their survival options in rural areas are limited. As a result, many go to town in search of work. Common economic activities that require little skill and training and are easy to enter include *tela* and *araki* preparation and selling, domestic service, spinning, petty trade and prostitution.

Table 7.2, which is derived from household interviews, summarises the reasons why migrant householders and their spouses moved to town. Not surprisingly, the most significant single reason was to find a job. In some cases, government employees (all male) were transferred to these towns. Many women followed their husbands, although this does not necessarily mean that they were still married. Some women came because of divorce and a lack of economic opportunities in rural areas.

Table 7.2: Reasons for moving to town: Responses from heads of households and spouses of migrants

	Bistima		Masha		Wein Amba			
	M	F	M	F	M	F	Total	%
Economic reasons								
Job transfer	3		2		3		8	
To seek employment/set up a business	5	1	7	5	6	2	26	
To obtain farmland	1				1		2	
Sub-total							36	40.5
Social reasons								
For marriage/followed husband		8		6		9	23	
Followed relatives/visited relatives	1			1	2	1	5	
After divorce				3		2	5	
For medical treatment				1			1	
Sub-total							34	38.2
Involuntary migration								
Displaced from state farm	2	2	1	1			6	
Expelled from Etritrea/Assab	1	1	2	1			5	
Returnee from Resettlement Area			1		2	1	4	
Ex-soldier	1		2				3	
To escape 1984-85 famine		1					1	
Sub-total							19	21.3
Total							89	100

Just over 20% of all migrants have been classified as involuntary migrants. Almost all involuntary migrants returned to their towns or *woredas* of origin following the collapse of the Mengistu regime in 1991 (Table 7.3). Some left and others escaped from the harsh conditions in the resettlement areas established by the Mengistu regime following the 1984-85 famine that devastated Welo. Some were civilians expelled from Eritrea following the separation of the two countries in 1991. Others were made redundant from state farms as a result of the restructuring policies of the post-Mengistu government (the present government comprises a coalition of ethnic groups under the umbrella of the Ethiopian People's Revolutionary Democratic Front). Yet others were ex-soldiers of the defeated Mengistu army seeking work in town. From our 1994 survey data, only one involuntary migrant left the countryside as a result of the 1984-85 famine and went to town to survive. This figure is misleading in that a certain number of people did take refuge in the many small towns throughout the region. And, of course, more than 350,000 famine-impacted people were resettled in the western areas of Ethiopia. Some *woreda* in Welo were much less seriously affected by famine than others and

Table 7.3: *Numbers of expellees from Eritrea, returnees from resettlement areas, and ex-soldiers in the three towns and their respective* woredas

	Expellees	Returnees	Ex-soldiers
Worebabo Woreda			
Male	286	9,000	452
Female	79	6,000	552 *
Bistima Town			
Male	35	0	100
Female	35	0	0
Mekdela Woreda			
Male	0	1,356	144
Female	0	600	0
Masha Town			
Male	5	30	30
Female	5	20	0
Legehida Woreda			
Male	0	280	550
Female	0	320	0
Wein Amba Town			
Male	0	2	35
Female	0	5	0

* Dependants
Sources: From the *woreda* offices in the respective towns.

consequently far fewer people were obliged to migrate or resettle (Kloos & Aynalem 1989).

As was suggested earlier, aggregating migration data (for the production of tables which provide overviews) is useful but much interesting and rich detail is disregarded in the process. For example, some case histories from the study show that people do not go directly from A to B, but often get from A to B via X, Y and Z. Moreover, a number of these case studies reveal the migration journey to be a long both in space and time.

Long-distance and long-term circulation

Case 1: From poor farmer to successful accumulator
Ato Lema Assefa is a 42-year-old Coptic Christian who was born in the countryside near the town of Masha. He never went to school and describes himself as illiterate. Until he was twenty he worked a small plot of land that barely provided sufficient for subsistence. In 1972, a couple of years before the collapse of the imperial regime of Haile Selassie, he decided to try his luck as a daily labourer in Addis Ababa. While he was there he saved sufficient money to purchase a donkey which he used to transport goods for other people. He bought more donkeys and acquired skills and capital as a trader. He returned to Welo in 1979 and settled in the town of Masha. At the time of the

survey in 1994, Ato Lema was considered to be one of the richest entrepreneurs in town. Apart from his involvement in large-scale trading in coffee, cotton and salt, he had also acquired a six-room lodging house and a *tej-bet*.[1] His wife, aged 40 and educated up to Grade 6, had responsibility for running both the lodging house and the *tej-bet*.

Case 2: Utilisation of local networks as a means of capital accumulation:
From poorly paid labourer to grain mill owner

Ato Yasin Abdu is a Muslim and is 30 years of age. He was born in the countryside about one hour's walk from the town of Masha. At the age of 18, he left Welo to seek employment in the western area of Ethiopia near the town of Metemma, along the Sudanese border.[2] He worked in the area for about 10 years, first becoming a cross-border trader dealing in salt, coffee and grain for a rich wholesale merchant. He was paid 100 Birr a year (worth at the time about US$48) with accommodation and food provided. He later got a job working in a grain mill in Metemma Town. It was during this period of employment that he met three migrant farmers from his home *woreda* in Welo. They decided to pool their economic resources and skills (Ato Yasin's were particularly important) and invest in the construction of a grain mill in Masha. At the time of the investment in 1993, Masha only had one other mill and the market in the town and surrounding countryside was considered sufficient to support an additional mill. The mill represented an enormous investment and the diesel engine alone cost 90,000 Birr (about US$16,423 at the 1993 rate of exchange). To cover such a large investment, a considerable sum of money also had to be borrowed from relatives. Unfortunately, in 1994, future business prospects did not look promising for Ato Yasin and his partners. Two other grain mills had been established in Masha after theirs was set up and this had created fierce competition. The situation was also compounded by weak rural demand because of the failure of the *belg* rains.

Case 3: The acquisition of technical skills while serving in the army:
A radio and watch repairer

Ato Eshetu Shiferaw, born in the town of Masha, is a 32-year-old Coptic Christian. He learnt some technical skills including the maintenance and repair of radios while serving as a captain in the army of the Mengistu regime. He was stationed in Eritrea and was demobilised in 1989. He considers his business of radio and watch repairing to be very successful and has a large rural clientele in addition to customers in the small urban market. There is another watch and radio repairer in the town but since there is plenty of business this does not create problems for either of them. Ato Eshetu repairs at least 3-4 radios a week, although the busy Monday market generates most of his income. He

---

[1] *Tej* is locally produced honey wine, *bet* means house, and in the context used here it means shop or bar.
[2] This region had experienced rapid growth as a result of the development of large-scale capitalist agriculture during the imperial regime and had consequently attracted "tens of thousands of migratory workers" (Imperial Ethiopian 1968: 374.). During the Mengistu regime (1974-1991) this capitalist agricultural system was nationalised and transformed into large state farms.

advertises his business by word of mouth and is assisted in this by his mother who runs a well-known *tela-bet*.[3]

Case 4: The acquisition of technical skills while working on a state farm:
        From daily labourer to skilled carpenter

Ato Nuru Hussein is a 36-year-old Muslim who was born in the town of Bistima where he worked as a poorly-paid daily labourer. In 1976, at the age of 18, he heard of possibilities of better-paid casual work at the Dubti State Cotton Farm in the Tendaho District of the Lower Awash River Valley (now in Region Two to the east of Welo). After nine months working as a labourer, the farm administration offered him the chance to become an apprentice to a carpenter. By 1981 he had successfully completed his apprenticeship and subsequently began working as a carpenter making furniture and constructing houses on the state farm. However, in 1992, Ato Nuru was obliged to return to his birthplace following the closure of the state farm as a result of the present government's economic restructuring programme. At the time of the interview two years after his return to Bistima, Ato Nuru had sufficient work and occasionally even employed additional labour to assist in construction work. His business portfolio included building private houses, offices for the newly decentralised government ministries, and work for a local church NGO.

Case 5: Capital accumulation and skill acquisition through migration
        and the creation and exploitation of a specialised market niche

Ato Ali Endris is a Muslim, aged 28. He was born in Kutaber *Woreda*, west of Bistima, but now works as a pharmacist in the town of Bistima where he has lived for one year. Although he has secondary-school education, he has no formal training as a pharmacist and is entirely self-taught. Before moving to Bistima in 1993 he worked as a pharmacist for a number of years in the town of Dubti (see Case 4) which was the centre for a large state cotton farm (until its closure in 1992) of 5,800 hectares and which in 1975-76 employed 13,000 workers (Kloos 1982). As most of these workers were housed in makeshift labour camps characterised by the scarcity or absence of medical facilities, and given the prevalence of malaria and schistosomiasis, Ato Ali found a large and lucrative market for drugs that he purchased in Addis Ababa. In this way, he was able to accumulate the financial resources necessary to establish and equip the pharmacy in Bistima. His decision to locate the pharmacy in Bistima itself in 1993 was determined by the fact that the *woreda*, with a population of over 140,000 people, did not have a pharmacy although there were three government-run clinics that offered limited stocks of medicines.

Short-distance rural-to-urban migration

As a survival strategy for many independent women with little education and without special skills, short-distance rural-to-urban migration is common. The majority of cases

---

[3] *Tela* is a locally produced beer (from grains such as sorghum, barley and *teff*).

reveal similarities: early marriage for girls and the short duration of marriage, a return to parents in the countryside where there is a lack of rural economic opportunities for females leading to migration to nearby towns (some move further afield) to find low-paid jobs before re-marrying.

Case 6: Short-distance rural-urban migration as a survival strategy: Tela selling
Wizero Birtukan Demissie is 22 years of age, a Coptic Christian, and was born into a farming family in the countryside near the town of Masha. She was married at the age of eight but left her husband after only 17 days and returned to her parents' home. Her parents allowed her to attend junior secondary school in a neighbouring *woreda* but after attaining Grade 8 she had to discontinue her studies because of lack of money. She moved to Masha Town and started business as a *tela* seller. She had a child by one of her customers but the child lives with her parents in the countryside. (Leaving children in the care of parents is common practice and enables the mother the freedom to pursue her business, while the parents often receive some money from the mother and ulti-mately a source of free labour.)

Wizero Birtukan rents a one-room *tela-bet* which she shares with another *tela* seller. The *tela-bet* also provides their accommodation. She estimates that there are about 300 *tela* sellers in the town and that with so much competition her income is meagre. Most of her customers are rural people. It is not uncommon for unmarried *tela* sellers to engage in prostitution to supplement their incomes. However, Wizero said that she did not engage in the practice because she was afraid of getting pregnant again. Although she enjoys town life, she finds selling *tela* tedious work for little reward. But she is in this business because of few other alternatives. She has no great vision for the future but if she had some extra money she would like to sell tea and bread in addition to *tela* in order to increase her income.

Case 7: Short-distance rural-urban migration as a survival strategy:
      Working in a buna-bet[4]
This example has many similarities with the previous case. Wizero Genet Alebachew is 22 years of age and is a Coptic Christian. She was born on a farm in a peasant associa-tion adjacent to the town of Masha. She was married at the age of nine but left her hus-band after only one month and returned to her parents' farm. She was subsequently sent to a junior secondary school in a neighbouring *woreda* where she completed Grade 7. Following this, she was sent by her parents to Addis Ababa to work as a domestic servant and stayed in the city for some years. However, she eventually returned to Welo and settled in the town of Masha so she could be near her parents.

She works as a waitress in a *buna-bet* where she serves tea, coffee, bottled beer and *araki.*[5] While she enjoys living in the town, she dislikes her job because she has to endure sexual harassment from the mainly rural clientele. Her monthly income is fixed at 50 Birr (about US$9 at the 1994 exchange rate). With such a small income she is dependent upon tips to increase her earnings. She clearly stated that she did not engage

---

[4] *Buna-bet* literally means a coffee house.
[5] *Araki* is a locally distilled spirit.

in commercial sex to supplement her income, although many men had approached her. She stated that the general unavailability of condoms and lack of medicine were the most important considerations behind this decision. However, Wizero Genet said that many *tela* sellers engaged in prostitution in the town. As for the future, she would like to improve her economic situation by opening her own bar.

Case 8: Short-distance rural-urban migration as a survival strategy: Prostitution
This example concerns a young divorced Muslim woman, Wizero Fatuma Hussen, who is 23 years of age. She has never been to school and is illiterate. She was married to a farmer in the neighbouring *woreda* of Tenta but after her divorce moved to Masha to find work. At the time of the interview she had been in town for about six months and was renting s small room in a house occupied by a married Muslim couple and their two young children. Wizero Fatuma had originally planned to trade in spices but competition meant that business was very slow. Consequently, she decided to begin producing and selling *keribo,* a non-alcoholic drink commonly consumed by Muslims. (It is interesting to note that the wife of the head of household was producing and selling *tela* which would tend to belie the importance of religious proscription about those who make and sell alcoholic beverages.) But since the selling of *keribo* provided an insufficient income for survival, Wizero Fatuma finally turned to prostitution. She charges customers 10 Birr (a little less than US$2) a night. Because of the fear of AIDS she does not accept many customers, yet paradoxically she does not insist on the use of condoms.

Long-distance urban-to-urban migration

Case 9: Long-distance urban-urban migration as an accumulation strategy:
        From prostitution to araki *seller*
Wizero Tsigie Akalu is 27 years of age and a Coptic Christian who was born in the countryside near the town of Wein Amba in Legehida *Woreda*. She has Grade 4 education and was married at a young age. When she was 16 years old she left the countryside and moved to the large industrial town of Kombolcha (in central South Welo) where she became a bar girl and engaged in prostitution to supplement her earnings. Over the next eleven years she moved to a number of large towns including Goba (the capital of the former province of Bale, now in Region Four) and Debre Zeit (the location of a major military base), as well as to state-farm settlements along the Awash River Valley where she worked as a bar girl and prostitute. While she was working in Awash she had a child who now lives and works as a shepherd with Wizero Tsigie's father in Legehida *Woreda*.

Finally, in 1993, she returned to Legehida *Woreda* and settled in Wein Amba Town. She no longer engages in prostitution and had nearly saved sufficient capital (apart from a 400 Birr loan) to establish her own *tela-bet* where she also makes and sells *araki*. Her decision to stop prostitution was strongly influenced by the fear of AIDS. She does not believe that condom use prevents AIDS. Notwithstanding these considerations however, Wizero Tsigie was in a position to give up prostitution because she had pursued a successful accumulation strategy that enabled her to establish a far less risky and more successful business.

Household splitting as a survival and/or accumulation strategy

Case 10: Short-distance urban-urban household splitting for purposes of household
          survival

Ato Taddesse Abebe is a married Coptic Christian, aged 45. He has lived in the town of Wein Amba for one year where he is employed as a skilled worker in one of the two mills in the town. He lives in one-room accommodation with his 20-year-old daughter who does the housework. However, most of Ato Taddesse's family (his wife, his mother, four sons and three daughters) live in the town of Woreilu in the neighbouring *woreda* of Woreilu. His wife has a successful *araki* and *tela* business and all his children attend school in Woreilu.

The reason why the household is split into two geographical locations is due to the fact that Ato Taddesse lost his job as a mill worker in Woreilu Town where he had worked for 18 years when the mill owner died. Since the mill closed following disagreements over inheritance issues and no other mill work is available in the town, Ato Taddesse was obliged to move to Wein Amba to find appropriate work. The decision to split the household appears to be based on sound economic arguments. His income in Wein Amba is 150 Birr a month (US$27) and, in addition, he receives a number of fringe benefits such as free accommodation, free paraffin and free milling services. No information is available concerning the expenses and income of his wife's part of the household, although *araki* selling can be a good business. Presumably without the two income sources the possibilities of maintaining a reasonable standard of living (such as being able to afford to send all their children to school) or to merely ensure household survival, would be severely compromised.

However, in situations involving household splitting other costs are invariably incurred. Ato Taddesse stated that the greatest disadvantage of living in Wein Amba was the emotional stress of being separated from his wife and family. Having said this, perhaps the person who had suffered the most was the 20-year-old daughter in Wein Amba: she kept house for her father and did not attend school "because she has TB".

Case 11: Long-distance household splitting for purposes of household survival and
          accumulation

Ato Zewdu Berhanu, a 42-year-old Coptic Christian is married. He lives with his wife and six children in the town of Bistima. He was born in the Yejju area which is located east of South Welo in Region Two[6] but has lived in Bistima for the past twelve years. He has Grade 10 education and works as a health assistant in the health centre in Bistima which is operated by the Ministry of Health. He has an income of 370 Birr a month which places him in a fairly well-to-do category of professional people. Two of his children do not attend school: his youngest child, a daughter aged three, and his

---

[6] Prior to the introduction of ethnically-based regions in 1991, Yejju formed part of Welo Region.

eldest child, a son of 22, who is at home with an undiagnosed 'illness'. All the other children, boys aged from seven to sixteen, attend school. Ato Zewdu's large four-roomed house is new and he used all his savings, 10,000 Birr (more than US$1,800), on its construction.

The paradox of this example is that Ato Zewdu's 18-year-old daughter was encouraged to migrate to Saudi Arabia (she had been away for a year at the time of the interview) to work so that she could 'help the family' by remitting some of her earnings. The daughter has Grade 9 education which would imply that she also has English-language skills enabling her to find suitable employment (in the context of Saudi Arabia) as a housemaid or nanny. Given the context and the constraints within which this household operates (for example, no other sources of income such as farmland), investment in the future labour skills of family members through education is considered crucial. I have anecdotal evidence of similar cases from Welo where young women with at least a secondary-school education migrate to the wealthier Arab states to find work.

Measuring migration outcomes

Many migration studies tend to focus on the reasons why migration takes place. This has also been partly the case in this chapter (see Table 7.2). However, while this approach is useful and identifies a main reason for movement, it does not present a holistic picture of the migration situation. It does not describe the migration experience in its totality. Consequently, the case studies in this chapter are an attempt to present a more substantial and fuller explanation behind migration decisions as well as the migration experience itself. One central question that emerges from the analysis is what conclusions can be drawn from migration outcomes. Successful migration may be considered as having two broad implications for migrants: has migration involved a process of accumulation or has migration ensured survival? In both cases, the decision to move led to positive outcomes.

During the course of their journeys, migrants are exposed to a range of experiences that for many individuals can be considered as enhancing their quality of life. As the case studies have demonstrated, migration often leads to processes of accumulation and some individuals, after a sojourn elsewhere, are equipped with capital, skills or goods (or a mixture of all three) which provide them with the wherewithal to enjoy a standard of living superior to that which they would have probably achieved if they had not made the decision to move elsewhere.

Of course, not all migrants become successful accumulators. Among the case studies there is a category of independent women who can be considered as short-distance rural-urban migrants for purposes of ensuring survival. This is a common category both in Welo and throughout Ethiopia. Many independent women (those who are divorced, widowed or single) leave the countryside because of a lack of opportunities and migrate to the nearest town to find low-paid and low-skilled work. However, what emerges from these case studies is that, for the majority of women, coming to town can be liberating. Such a shared experience can best be summed up as follows by quoting a 40-year-old *tela* seller: "Life is hard in rural areas. A woman in the countryside needs a man to plough the land."

Thus, small towns in Welo can be considered as 'nodes of economic and social opportunity' that provide independent women with a range of options. Common and low-paid activities include work in the bar and restaurant sectors as waitresses, petty trade (for example, selling spices, legumes, grains, and firewood), domestic service (often very hard work and badly paid), selling water (considered to be a very low status activity, characteristic of the very poor), and prostitution. The majority of these activities are characterised by ease of entry, the opportunity to switch from one activity to another, and low pay. Having said this, for some occupations (such as bar girls and prostitutes) physical beauty and youth are important attributes in attracting customers. Prostitution has traditionally been an important economic activity for many independent migrant urban women in Ethiopia. It has not necessarily brought with it problems of stigmatisation or marginalisation although much would depend upon the ethnic affiliation of the woman, in addition to where she was engaged in her business. It is not uncommon for some women to engage in prostitution for some time and then to get married. Of all the activities mentioned above, prostitution is the one that probably produces the greatest economic returns. As Case 9 illustrates, prostitution can be used as an accumulation strategy. However, the rapid spread of HIV/AIDS has meant that prostitution has become a high-risk activity and could be characterised as a death strategy. With the increasing awareness of the dangers of HIV/AIDS among independent women, it is possible that prostitution may become increasingly an 'activity of last resort'.

While many women leave the countryside to find new economic opportunities in town as a result of divorce, the paradox of the situation is that many of these women also migrate to town in the hope of finding a new marriage partner. The fact that divorcees have a wider choice of potential husbands in town, for instance, in the many bars on markets days, provides a subsidiary explanation for the attraction of towns (for a insightful analysis of the high incidence of marriage and divorce among the Amhara, see Weissleder 1974).

For the group of migrants classified as involuntary, the apparent problems of disruption from being forced to leave a destination outside Welo (for example, in Eritrea) and return to their areas of origin should not be overstated. As was illustrated through the case studies, the acquisition of specialised skills is a positive experience for some migrants (good examples are Cases 3, 4 and 5) that enabled them to return home and use these skills and capital to improve their standard of living.

The migration phenomenon throws up winners and losers. It would be untrue to state that there have been no losers. Even among the case studies, particular individuals may have been left out of the benefits accruing from migration as a result of chance or accident. In Case 10, the daughter suffering from TB who was given the responsibility of keeping house for her father was excluded from the benefits of education which her siblings could enjoy. In Case 11, the 18-year-old daughter in the household was obliged to migrate to Saudi Arabia so that she could help the family enjoy what appeared to be a good standard of living, in addition to supporting the costs of educating two of her brothers.

However, whether the outcome of migration is perceived as involving a process of accumulation or survival, the central feature which emerges from this study is that migration can be considered as a reaction to constraints at the point of departure and as a positive response to opportunities elsewhere. In other words, the decision to migrate and the migration experience should be viewed as positive behaviour and not considered as dysfunctional or abnormal.

References

Abu-Lughod, J. 1975, 'Comments. The End of the Age of Innocence in Migration Theory', in B.M. DuToit & H.I. Safa (eds), *Migration and Urbanization*, The Hague: Mounton.

Aina, T.A. & J. Baker 1995, 'Introduction', in J. Baker & T.A. Aina (eds), *The Migration Experience in Africa*, Uppsala: Nordiska Afrikainstitutet.

Baker, J. 1986, *The Rural-Urban Dichotomy in the Developing World: A Case Study from Northern Ethiopia*, Oslo: Norwegian University Press.

Baker, J. 1994, 'Small Urban Centres and Their Role in Rural Restructuring', in Abebe Zegeye & S. Pausewang (eds), *Ethiopia in Change: Peasantry, Nationalism and Democracy*, London and New York: British Academic Press.

Betemariam Berhanu & M. White 2000, 'War, Famine, and Female Migration in Ethiopia, 1960-1989', *Economic Development and Cultural Change* 49, 1.

Dessalegn Rahmato 1991, *Famine and Survival Strategies: A Case Study from Northeast Ethiopia*, Uppsala: The Scandinavian Institute of Afican Studies.

Imperial Ethiopian Government 1968, *Third Five-Year Development Plan, 1968-1973*, Addis Ababa.

Kebrom Tekle 1999, 'Land Degradation Problems and Their Implications for Food Shortage in South Wello, Ethiopia', *Environmental Management* 23, 4.

Kloos, H 1982, 'Farm Labor Migrations in the Awash Valley of Ethiopia', *International Migration Review* 16, 1.

Kloos, H. & Aynalem Adugna 1989, 'Settler Migration During the 1984/85 Resettlement Programme in Ethiopia', *Geojournal* 9, 2.

McCann, J. 1986, 'Household Economy, Demography, and the "Push" Factor in Northern Ethiopian History, 1916-35', *Review* IX, 3, Winter.

Office of the Population and Housing Census Commission 1984, *Analytical Report on Wello Region*, January 1991, Addis Ababa.

Office of Population and Housing Census Commission 1994, *The 1994 Population and Housing Census for Ethiopia: Results for Amhara Region: Volume I: Part III Statistical Report on Migration, Fertility and Mortality*, December 1995, Addis Ababa.

Weissleder, W. 1974, 'Amhara Marriage: The Stability of Divorce', *Canadian Review of Sociology and Anthropology* 11, 1.

Wright, C. 1995, 'Gender Awareness in Migration Theory: Synthesizing Actor and Structure in Southern Africa', *Development and Change* 26: 771-91.

8

Multi-spatial livelihoods in Sub-Saharan Africa: Rural farming by urban households - The case of Nakuru Town, Kenya

Dick Foeken & Samuel O. Owuor

Multi-spatial livelihoods refer to households with a livelihood foothold in both urban and rural areas. Although it is well known that multi-spatial households are common in Sub-Saharan Africa, the phenomenon has seldom been looked at from the urban household perspective. Studies so far indicate that rural food and/or income sources are important for urban dwellers. Data from a 1999 survey undertaken in the Kenyan town of Nakuru confirm that over 60% of Nakuru households can be considered as having a multi-spatial livelihood. Although one-adult households and low-income households are relatively under-represented in the survey, multi-spatial livelihoods may be particularly important for the latter group's food security situation. However, the results indicate that rural farming by urban dwellers should be seen mainly in terms of 'opportunity' and not, like urban farming, in terms of 'necessity'.

Introduction

The extent to which urban households in Sub-Saharan Africa depend on rural sources for their livelihood is considered in this chapter. Households in both rural and urban areas seek to diversify their livelihood sources to minimise risks and many have an economic foothold in both areas, which frequently leads to a (temporary but recurrent) splitting up of the household. So far, studies have largely focused on the *rural* perspective, i.e. the contribution of urban sources of income to the livelihood of rural households. The reverse perspective, i.e. of *urban* households, has hardly ever been investigated. This chapter attempts to remedy this situation by looking at the issue in two ways. First, the limited number of studies that have been done in Sub-Saharan Africa are reviewed and second, data are presented from a survey done in Nakuru, Kenya. Despite the incomplete and preliminary character of the data, they show that (rural) agriculture is playing an important role in the livelihoods of the Nakuru townspeople.

Recent changes in urban-rural relations

For urban and rural populations in Sub-Saharan Africa, recent and current global changes have resulted in deepening social differentiation and poverty. Small farmers have become increasingly marginalised due to structural adjustment programmes, trade liberalisation, a focus on export-oriented agriculture, higher costs of agricultural inputs and consumer goods and, at the same time, a relative decline in the price of agricultural produce (Tacoli 1998).

Life in urban areas has become more expensive while employment opportunities in the formal sector have decreased and real wages have not kept up with price increases or have even declined in absolute terms (UNCHS/Habitat 1996). In many Sub-Saharan countries, employment in the public sector has been seriously cut, particularly in the lower echelons. Women, who tend to be concentrated at the lower end of the occupational hierarchy, have been affected to a greater degree than men (ILO/JASPA 1992). The manufacturing sector was also badly hit due to the effects of structural adjustment such as shortages of imported materials, reduced investment, declining demand, etc. (Gilbert 1994). This has led to the 'informalisation' of the urban economy in Africa (Stren 1992). Nowadays, "the majority of the urban workforce are (...) engaged in a highly differentiated range of small-scale, micro-enterprise or informal activities" (Rogerson 1997: 346). For some time now, the informal sector has been the most rapidly expanding employment sector of African urban economies.

In the context of urban-rural linkages, these processes have caused two fundamental changes. First, the "dynamics of income distribution between urban and rural areas has changed" (Jamal & Weeks 1988: 274). The rural-urban income gap has, according to Jamal and Weeks, substantially narrowed or, in some cases, even closed. Second, there has been a relative shift over time in the locus of poverty, from rural towards urban areas (Kanji 1996). And although there is still far more rural poverty than urban poverty in tropical Africa, urban poverty is increasing at a faster rate (Baker 1997). In many ways, the harsh economic conditions of the 1980s and 1990s have been felt even more acutely in the cities than in the rural areas, as life is generally more expensive in urban areas (O'Connor 1991; Mougeot 1993). According to Potts (1995: 248), "the fall in real urban incomes has been devastating", particularly for what is sometimes referred to as the 'new urban poor', a group who, during the 1980s and 1990s, "have become much poorer in many countries" and whose lives "have become an almost incredible struggle" (p. 250).

One of the consequences of these processes concerns the sectoral changes in both rural and urban areas (Tacoli 1997, 1998). Typical urban activities, like manufacturing, are increasingly taking place in rural areas as well. In general, non-agricultural rural activities have become a widespread feature of Sub-Saharan Africa (Tellegen 1993, 1997; Bryceson 1996). On the other hand, agriculture, an activity typically associated with the rural areas, has become common in urban areas (Obudho & Foeken 1999). Urban farming is now a permanent feature of the landscape in most African towns and cities. This is sometimes referred to as the 'ruralisation' of African cities (Rogerson 1997: 358; Bigsten & Kayizzi-Mugerwa 1992: 1430). Vennetier (1989) described the process of 'rurbanisation', whereby urban dwellers are 'colonising' villages and agricultural land around the cities of Brazzaville (Congo) and Cotonou (Benin). The growth of urban agriculture since the late 1970s is largely understood as a response to escalating poverty and to rising food prices or shortages exacerbated by the implementation of structural adjustment policies in the 1980s (Drakakis-Smith 1992; Foeken 1998; Tacoli 1998).

What these changes in the two areas have in common is the element of risk spreading or risk management (Painter 1996): households perform a wide range of different activities in order to maintain a certain standard of living or even just to avoid starvation. This is what Jamal and Weeks (1988: 288) call the "trader-cum-wage earner-cum-*shamba* growing class". In Kampala, for example, households have a multiplicity of income sources from all kinds of activities in the informal sector to farming (both crop cultivation and livestock keeping) to remittances, mostly from relatives in the rural areas (Bigsten & Kayizzi-Mugerwa 1992).

These global changes have had an impact on rural-urban linkages in Sub-Saharan Africa. First, new forms of migration have emerged or old ones have slowed down or intensified (Tacoli 1997). There are indications that the rate of rural-urban migration has decreased, while return migration, i.e. from the city to the rural 'home', is emerging (see, for example, Tripp 1996; Baker 1997; Potts 1997) and circular migration between urban and rural areas is increasing (for example, Smit 1998).

Second, rural links have become "vital safety-valves and welfare options for urban people who are very vulnerable to economic fluctuations" (Potts 1997: 461). There is evidence of significant shifts in the nature of transfers of goods and cash between urban and rural households, with remittances from urban to rural areas on the decline while transfers of food from rural to urban areas are increasing.

Finally, risk spreading or income diversification often implies a permanent or temporary split within the household, with one or more household members living in town and the other(s) in the rural home. This is sometimes referred to as 'multi-spatial households' (e.g. Tacoli 1998: 149) or 'multiple-home households' (Smit 1998: 82). However, the term 'multi-spatial livelihood' seems more appropriate because to perform different income-generating activities in different geographical areas does not necessarily imply a residential split of the household. With 'multi-spatial livelihood', a household has both urban and rural sources of food and/or income. As such, this is not new, as many rural households have for a long time enjoyed an urban foothold from which an income supplement has been derived (see, for example, Foeken 1997). Less well known, and probably more recent, is the reverse situation, namely urban households partly dependent on rural sources for their livelihood, either with or without a physical foothold in the rural area.

Multi-spatial livelihoods in Sub-Saharan Africa: An overview of the literature

Multi-spatial livelihoods in Sub-Saharan Africa are not new. For instance, in the early 1940s, Read (1942) noticed that the majority of (temporarily) urbanised Africans maintained links with their village of origin. Yet, studies specifically focusing on *rural* livelihood sources of *urban* households in Sub-Saharan Africa have up to now not been effected. This is surprising because there are increasing indications that rural farming is an important livelihood element of urban dwellers. What is known about the topic is derived from mostly urban studies that were broader in scope and usually mention the aspect of rural livelihood sources but only in passing. These literature sources are few in number but continent-wide in coverage: Nigeria (Gugler 1971, 1991; Andræ 1992), Congo-Kinshasa (Makwala 1972; Nicolaï 1989), Tanzania (Baker 1996; Tripp 1996), Zimbabwe (Potts & Mutambirwa 1990; Drakakis-Smith 1992; Kamete 1998), Senegal (Fall 1998), South Africa (Smit 1998), Botswana (Krüger 1998) and Kenya (Lee-Smith *et al.* 1987; Lee-Smith & Memon 1994; Mwangi 1995; Mwangi & Foeken 1996; Foeken & Mwangi 1998).

The most common finding in all these studies is the high percentage of urban households claiming to have access to rural land, i.e. a plot of land in their rural 'home village'. In general samples of urban households, these percentages range from 35% in Harare, Zimbabwe (Drakakis-Smith 1992) to 80% or more in Biharamulo, Tanzania (Baker 1996) and Enugu, Nigeria (Gugler 1971, 1991). Among the low-income households, percentages ranged from 24% in Harare (Drakakis-Smith 1992) to 64% in Nairobi, Kenya (Mwangi 1995). In the only general survey of urban agriculture on a national scale, that undertaken in Kenya in the mid-1980s, 52% of households claimed to have access to rural land (Lee-Smith *et al.* 1987). Moreover, at least one third of the households stated that they had livestock back in their rural area (Lee-Smith & Memon 1994). In Gaborone and Francistown (Botswana), 37% of the low-income households were cattle owners, with average herd sizes of more than 20 animals (Krüger 1998).

From a number of studies it is clear that claiming access to a plot of rural land does not imply its actual use by the urban household. In fact, very few of the urban workers in Kano and Kaduna took full advantage of such land (Andræ 1992). In Harare, various surveys revealed figures ranging from 50% to 75% (Potts & Mutambirwa 1990). Among poor households in Harare, Drakakis-Smith (1992) found that only 21% of the households with access to rural land cultivated it themselves. However, among the households in the slum of Korogocho in Nairobi, the figure reached about 50% (Mwangi 1995).

The importance of rural produce for urban households with access to rural land should not be underestimated. Many low-income households in Enugu, Nigeria "partly relied on food produced in the rural home", both in the 1960s and later in the 1980s (Gugler 1971, 1991). For textile workers in Kano and Kaduna, Nigeria, the claim to rural land was "important as a security mechanism" during adverse times (Andræ 1992). In Harare, rural produce represented "a fairly significant addition" to household incomes (Potts & Mutambirwa 1992). According to Krüger (1998: 128), the "long-lasting rural-urban linkages" in Botswana were more important for the food security situation of the urban households than urban farming. In the slum of Korogocho, Nairobi, over a third of those with access to rural land stated that the plot was "a regular food and/or income source". Finally, in a study by Baker (1996) in the small town of Biharamulo in northern Tanzania, an attempt was made to calculate the contribution of the sale of rural agricultural produce to urban households' incomes, which resulted in the surprisingly high figure of 70%.

In addition to food from urban households' rural plots, donations of food and gifts from rural to urban households were invaluable. In Harare, 20% of respondents appeared to receive gifts of food, mainly traditional basic crops, from the rural areas, which led Drakakis-Smith (1992: 276) to conclude that "there is still a substantial subsidy from rural to urban households". Also in Dakar, Senegal, there was a considerable flow of cash and food supplies from rural homes to urban areas (Fall 1998).

A comparison was made in a few studies between households with an economic base in both urban and rural areas (multi-spatial livelihoods) and households with only one spatial-economic base. Baker (1996: 46) found that "the most economically successful and most secure group of households are those which combine crop production and marketing with a variety of non-farm and off-farm income-generating activities". These households had a foot in both economies and were not only found in Biharamulo but also in the surrounding villages. Among slum dwellers in Nairobi, those with access to both urban and rural land were somewhat better off in terms of welfare level, food intake and the nutritional condition of their children than those without such access (Foeken & Mwangi 1998). Likewise, Krüger (1998: 134) found that a number of poor urban households in Botswana lacking a rural foothold were "living under severe risk".

From the aforementioned examples, it emerges that access to *rural* food and/or income sources is a crucial element in the livelihood of many urban dwellers particularly in the present circumstances of urban unemployment and poverty. Without a foothold in the rural economy, poor urban households are likely to face severe hardships. A number of the studies indicated that households with access to both urban and rural economies (multi-spatial livelihoods) are relatively better off than those with one spatial-economic base only (mono-spatial livelihood). Most of the studies discussed did *not* focus on multi-spatial livelihoods, let alone specifically on the topic of rural sources in the livelihood of urban households. Although this applies to the Nakuru study as well, the data presented below are richer than those offered in most studies to date.[1]

The Nakuru survey of 1999-2000

Introduction
Nakuru Town is located in Kenya's Rift Valley, 160 km north-west of Nairobi. It is the fourth largest town in Kenya (after Nairobi, Mombasa and Kisumu), with a population in 1999 of 239,000 (Kenya 2000). The town functions as an administrative centre and a major agricultural centre with many of its industries being agro-based (MCN 1999). Its location on the main highway between Mombasa/Nairobi and the highlands, Uganda

---

[1] A detailed study on the topic for which these data form the basis is planned for 2001-03.

and other East African regions makes it a key communications centre as well. Tourism is also significant thanks to Lake Nakuru National Park that lies within its boundaries.

In June-July 1999, a general survey was carried out among a representative sample of 594 households.[2] Of these, 366 (62%) could be classified as 'rural farmers', i.e. those who had indicated either cultivating crops or keeping livestock (or both) in the rural areas. A large majority (361 or 61% of the total sample) of these rural farmers cultivated crops, while 222 (37%) kept livestock. These figures indicate that five of the rural farmers did not grow crops but only kept livestock, while 144 cultivated crops only and the remaining 217 practiced mixed farming. Another 5% of the Nakuru households obtained some income from renting out rural land. Table 8.1 shows that rural farming is equally distributed between the various income categories. Nevertheless, it seems that the lowest income category is somewhat less rurally oriented than the three higher income classes.

Table 8.1: Rural farming by income class (%)

Income class (Ksh/month)*	N	Rural crop cultivation	Rural live- stock keeping	Rural land renting
Up to 5,000	310	55.5	31.3	5.2
5,001 - 10,000	167	65.9	42.5	4.8
10,001 - 20,000	74	67.6	44.6	4.1
More than 20,000	32	65.6	43.8	-.-

* 1,000 Kenyan shillings = US$ 13.7 (on 31-12-1999)
Source: Kenya 2000

In September-October 2000, an in-depth survey was carried out among 29 randomly selected households. Although this survey focused again on *urban* farming, some more information on *rural* farming was obtained as well. Almost all (27) of the 29 appeared to have access to rural land. Two of these households had access to two rural plots and one household to three.

Rural plots: Size and location
Table 8.2 offers data on numbers and sizes of rural plots. On average, a rural farmer has access to 1.17 plots outside town, with an average plot size of 4.4 acres. This means that the average rural farmer in Nakuru Town has more than five acres of rural land at his/her disposal. This figure is much higher for the highest income group (15.4 acres). They have more plots on average per household (1.33) while the average size of the plots is bigger (11.6 acres) than those of other income groups.

When considering the figures in Table 8.2, the substantial variation between numbers and sizes should be recognised. For instance, 15% of the plots of the Nakuru rural farmers were less than one acre in size. The four income groups did not differ greatly in this respect except for the fact that the smaller plots were more common among the poorest

---

[2] The survey was restricted to the built-up area of Nakuru Town. The peri-urban zone between the built-up area and the town boundary, where farming is a predominant activity, was not included.

Table 8.2: Rural plots (%; N=467)

(1) Mean number of plots/household	1.17
(2) Mean plot size (acres)	4.4
(3) Mean acreage per household (1 x 2)	5.1

group (21% versus 9% - 13% in the other three groups). It is not surprising that the highest income group was over-represented in the 10+ acres category (30% versus 6% - 13%).

Map 8.1 shows the geographical distribution of the rural plots. (To avoid confusion, the old districts, i.e. before the large-scale subdivision of districts started, have been used.) By province, three areas of concentration can be distinguished: Rift Valley, Western and Nyanza Provinces, together accounting for 90% of all plots. A closer look reveals that three districts in particular stand out as accounting for over half of the plots: Nakuru (31%), Kakamega (13%) and Siaya (11%). Nandi District is conspicuous by its absence as far as the location of rural plots is concerned.

In Kenya it is highly desirable for urban dwellers to have access to land in a rural area and even more advantageous if it is located in their home area. A strong relationship is to be expected between the location of the rural plots, on the one hand, and the district of origin of the Nakuru townspeople, on the other. Although data on both place of origin and location of rural plots *below* the district level are not available, it may be safely assumed that if the district is the same for the two variables, the plot is very likely to be located in the home area. The majority (71%) of rural farmers did indeed have at least one plot in their home district (Table 9.3), although some had plots in another district as well. However, almost 30% of rural farmers had his/her plot(s) in a district other than his/her district of origin. Of all the plots outside the home district, the majority (66%) appeared to be located in Nakuru District, i.e. at a relatively short distance from the person's place of residence.

Table 8.3: Location of rural plots and district of origin of rural
farmers (%; N=327*)

At least one plot in district of origin	66.7
At least one plot in district of origin *and* in another district	4.6
At least one plot in other district (outside district of origin)	28.7
Total	100

* Immigrants only.

Rural plots: Ownership and use

Table 8.4 presents some basic data regarding ownership and use of rural plots. Over half (56%) of the rural plots were owned by the Nakuru households themselves. The rest was mainly land belonging to the family 'back home'. Some plots (5%) were rented from a landlord. Ownership of rural plots differs substantially in relation to income class: as

Map 8.1: Geographical distribution of rural plots, Kenya (by district)

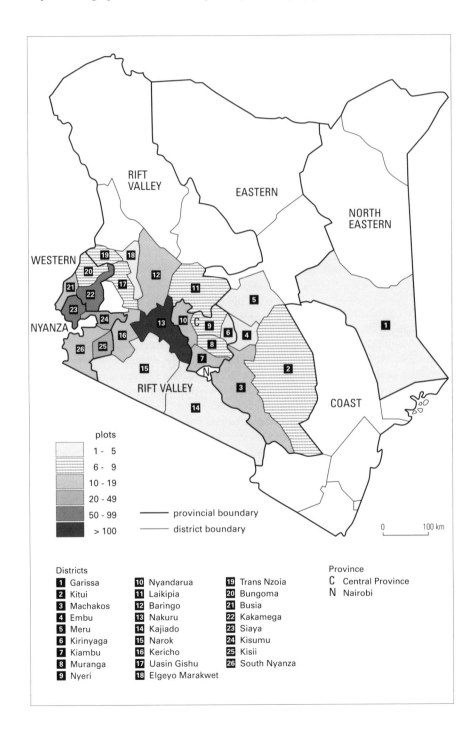

plots
1 - 5
6 - 9
10 - 19
20 - 49
50 - 99
> 100

—— provincial boundary
—— district boundary

0   100 km

Districts

1	Garissa	10	Nyandarua	19	Trans Nzoia
2	Kitui	11	Laikipia	20	Bungoma
3	Machakos	12	Baringo	21	Busia
4	Embu	13	Nakuru	22	Kakamega
5	Meru	14	Kajiado	23	Siaya
6	Kirinyaga	15	Narok	24	Kisumu
7	Kiambu	16	Kericho	25	Kisii
8	Muranga	17	Uasin Gishu	26	South Nyanza
9	Nyeri	18	Elgeyo Marakwet		

Province
C Central Province
N Nairobi

household income is higher, the percentage of plots owned by the respondent him/herself is higher and the percentage of plots owned by the (rural) family is lower. For instance, the majority (87%) of the highest income group owned the plot, while for the poorest this applied to less than half (48%) of the plots, the other half (47%) being denoted as family land.

Table 8.4: Ownership and use of rural plots (%; N=467)

Ownership of plot	own land	56.2
	family land[a]	38.5
User of plot	myself[b]	57.2
	other family[c]	32.3
Usage of plot	crops only	42.1
	crops + livestock	49.2

Notes: a) includes 'relative's land' (4 out of 179 cases)
           b) in 14 (out of the 267) cases the plot was partly used by 'other family'
               and in 3 cases was partly rented out
           c) in 1 case the land was partly rented out

Rural plots have been acquired either through inheritance or through purchase. Out of 27 plots in the in-depth survey, 16 had been inherited and the other 11 had been bought. Of the latter, seven had been purchased in Nakuru District within a reasonable distance of Nakuru Town, and the others were in the district of origin of the household head.

The same pattern can be seen with the person(s) actually cultivating the plot (Table 8.4). Not surprisingly, ownership on the one hand and the person using the plot are related. Two-thirds of those who stated that they were the owners of the plot used it themselves (and over half of the remaining plots were used by other family members). Of the plots indicated as being family land, 61% were used by other family members (and almost all the other plots were being used either by the Nakuru household or together with the family). However, there were also plots that were used by people other than the Nakuru townspeople or their families back home: 19 plots (4%) were rented out, 9 plots were used by somebody else, while another 21 were not used by anyone. This occurred in all income categories.

Of the 31 plots belonging to the 27 in-depth cases with access to rural land, 14 were in use by the Nakuru households themselves. In four cases, the spouse of the head of the urban household was responsible for crop cultivation. One of these ladies lived permanently in the rural area, the others were there for part of the time, for example 9-10 months per year. These are examples of not only multi-spatial livelihoods but at the same time (temporary) multi-spatial households. There were also examples of households where another family member was the one responsible for the rural plot, such as a sister of the household head (as in two cases), the mother of the household head (two cases), the daughter of the household head (one case) and the spouse's mother (one case). These are examples of multi-spatial livelihoods with no physical division of the household.

The large majority of the plots (over 90%) were used to grow crops and on just over half of these, livestock were kept as well (Table 8.4). Very few plots were solely used to keep livestock. Twenty-nine plots (6%) had been left idle. Although the percentage of plots left idle was higher in the highest income group (13%) than in the other three income groups (5% - 6%), half of the idle plots were owned by households from the lowest income category.

Importance of rural plots
The importance in qualitative terms of the rural plots for the Nakuru townspeople is shown in Table 8.5. Almost three-quarters of the plots were a source of food, while almost half were a source of additional income. The income component was more important for the highest income group (63%) than for the others. Almost one fifth of the plots were considered as neither food nor income sources.

Table 8.5: Importance of rural plots (%; N=467)

Food source only	32.3
Both food and income source	39.7
Income source only	8.6
Neither food source nor income source	19.4
Total	100

Further information is available on the importance of rural land from 24 households visited during-the in-depth survey. For 13 of them, the plot was a food source, mainly from the crops cultivated there. For eight households, it formed a regular income source, through sales of crop surpluses, animals and animal products, or through renting out the plot. An example was a plot in Murang'a District planted with tea and which was in the charge of a sister of the Nakuru household head. Three households intended to make money out of their rural plots in another way. For one, the plot was considered too far away (Migori District) to be able to use it productively for farming, so the owner wanted to build some residential houses there for letting purposes. Another household with no access to rural land hoped to obtain a rural plot for exactly the same purpose. The other two households intended to sell their rural plot(s) in order to buy land in Nakuru Town, also for commercial purposes.

For several households, the rural plot was not only a source of food and/or income but also a safety net in times of need (seven cases) and/or a place to go on retirement (nine cases). However, there was one respondent who specifically stated that he would not return to the rural area after retirement because "when one is used to town life, rural life is difficult due to lack of amenities". Finally, for six respondents, the rural land had a specific meaning because "it runs in the family". For one, the plot served as the burial place for the household head. (This is common among, for example, the Luo and the Kisii.) Two other observations can be made. Firstly, the three values attached to the rural land, namely as a safety net, for retirement and 'from the family lineage', were usually mentioned in combination with each other. Secondly, family land has not only a material value but also a sentimental value for many people.

'Rural farmers' and 'non-farmers'

There are some marked differences between urban households having access to rural land ('rural farmers') and those who do not ('non-farmers'). Table 8.6 presents some household characteristics and characteristics of the household heads of the two groups. The three household characteristics refer to three possible reasons for urban households practicing rural farming: the number of mouths to fill (household size), the purchasing power of the household (income class) and the amount of space in the (urban) residential area (population density of estate). The figures indicate that none of these variables seems to be a determinant for engaging in rural farming. Poorer households do not practice rural farming more frequently than richer households and the lack of space for *urban* farming in the urban residential area seems not to be compensated for by a higher frequency of *rural* farming.

Table 8.6: Rural farmers and non-farmers: Household characteristics (%)

		Rural farmers (N=366)	Non-farmers (N=228)
Household size (members)	5 or more	35.2	34.6
Household income class (Ksh./month)	up to 5,000	47.8	61.8
	more than 10,000	20.1	15.1
Population density of estate	high	45.6	40.4
Sex of household head	female	14.8	27.6
Marital status of hh head	single/divorced/separated/widowed	18.6	36.0
Ethnic background of hh head	Kikuyu	36.2	56.6
	Luo	24.4	12.7
	Luhya	20.8	12.3

The question as to whether rural farming and urban farming are substitutes of each other can also be posed as follows: Do urban dwellers who practice rural farming refrain from urban farming and *vice versa*? This appeared not to be the case. The percentages of urban farmers among both 'rural farmers' and 'non-farmers' are exactly the same, namely 35%. This applies to crop cultivators (25% and 30% respectively) as well as to livestock keepers (20% and 21% respectively). In other words, those urban dwellers in Nakuru who do not have access to a rural plot are not more inclined to engage in urban farming than those who do have access to a rural plot.

As for the characteristics of the household heads of 'rural farmers' and 'non-farmers' respectively, only those variables are presented in Table 9.6 that show a difference between the two groups. Regarding such characteristics as age, type of residence, educational level and occupational status, the two groups appear to be very similar. However, as far as sex, marital status and ethnic group go, the situation is different. The percentage of male-headed households with access to rural land is almost twice as high as among female-headed households. This is to some extent related to the fact that many of the one-adult households (single, divorced, separated or widowed) are female-headed households. For these households it is much more problematic logistically to farm outside town than for households with a head and a spouse. Another 'sex difference' concerns the distance to the plot. The rural plots of the female-headed households are generally nearer to Nakuru Town than those of male-headed households.

Finally, as far as ethnic background is concerned, it is conspicuous that, in relative terms, the Kikuyu (accounting for 44% of all household heads and by far the largest group in Nakuru Town) engage in much less rural farming than the other major ethnic groups. Of all the Kikuyu households in Nakuru, about half farmed in rural areas, compared with about two-thirds to over three-quarters of the Luo, Luhya, Kalenjin, Kisii and Kamba (this is also visible on Map 8.1).

Conclusions

The recent and current global changes (e.g. structural adjustment programmes) and their resultant consequences have had an impact on rural-urban linkages in Sub-Saharan Africa. One of these consequences concerns risk spreading or income diversification through multi-spatial sourcing of food and/or income.

From the 1999-2000 survey in Nakuru Town, it is evident that rural plots are an important livelihood source for the townspeople. Over 60% of households can be said to have multi-spatial livelihoods. In addition to their income-generating activities in the urban economy of Nakuru Town they also have a rural livelihood base, either in the form of cultivating one or more rural plots themselves or by sharing in the produce from plots cultivated by relatives. Multi-spatial livelihoods apply to households in all income classes, and contrary to general opinion and to what has been reported in the literature to date, a reasonable number (almost 30%) of those rural plots are not located in the home areas of the Nakuru townspeople. This may be due to the specific situation in this part of Kenya where many of the large farms that used to be owned by white settlers have been subdivided since independence, making many plots available in the town and its environs.

For most of the 'rural farmers' in Nakuru Town, their rural plots are a source of food and for many also a source of income. However, for quite a number (20%) it appeared to be neither a food nor an income source. This has also been found in several other studies elsewhere in Sub-Saharan Africa. The Nakuru study reveals that for many households their rural land has a non-material value. In addition to being a resource on which to fall back in times of economic stress, it is a place to retire to and has an emotional attachment simply because it belongs to the family and always has. Only in the study by Andræ (1992), is the rural plot mentioned as a security mechanism.

Not all Nakuru households have equal access to rural land. For instance, low-income households are under-represented among the households with multi-spatial livelihoods. Moreover, their rural plots are usually smaller and they are less likely to be the owners of the plots. Female-headed households and one-adult households in general have less access to rural land and their plots are generally closer to the town. As these households frequently belong to the lower income groups in town, the distance factor is crucial both in terms of cost (hiring labour is too expensive) and in terms of time (the single adult cannot leave the Nakuru house for too long). Finally, there is a difference between the ethnic groups in Nakuru Town. The largest group, the Kikuyu, is much less rurally oriented than the Luo and the Luhya (the second and third largest groups). This may partly be related to differences in urban occupations since the Kikuyu are more heavily involved in business, and partly due to the availability of space in the areas of origin.

Except for these differences, households with multi-spatial and with mono-spatial livelihoods appear to be very similar, implying that there are no clear determinants for engaging in rural farming. In this respect, rural farming by urban dwellers differs from urban farming because one of the main determinants of urban farming is household size, i.e. the number of mouths to be filled (or 'family life-cycle'). Hence, rural and urban farming are no substitutes for each other. In terms of 'necessity' and 'opportunity', urban farming can be considered as a necessity (i.e. to maintain a certain standard of living), while rural farming is more opportunistic and related to whether one happens to have access to a plot of land (through marriage, inheritance or purchase) in the rural areas or not. This does not mean that rural farming cannot be an important livelihood source for urban dwellers, a fact that applies especially to the lower income households, as the findings of the Nakuru study indicate. The study confirms what has been mentioned in other studies as well, notably that households with a foot in both the urban and rural economies, i.e. with multi-spatial livelihoods, are on average relatively better off than those with only one spatial-economic base.

References

Andræ, G. 1992, 'Urban Workers as Farmers: Agro-Links of Nigerian Textile Workers in the Crisis of the 1980s', in J. Baker & P. Ove Pedersen (eds), *The Rural-Urban Interface in Africa: Expansion and Adaptation*, Uppsala: Scandinavian Institute of African Studies, Seminar Proceedings no. 27, pp. 200-22.

Baker, J. 1996, 'Rural-Urban Links and Economic Differentiation in Northwest Tanzania', *African Rural and Urban Studies* 3 (1), 25-48.

Baker, J. 1997, 'Introduction', in J. Baker (ed.), *Rural-Urban Dynamics in Francophone Africa*, Uppsala: Scandinavian Institute of African Studies, pp. 11-25.

Bigsten, A. & S. Kayizzi-Mugerwa 1992, 'Adaptation and Distress in the Urban Economy: A Study of Kampala Households', *World Development* 20 (10): 1423-41.

Bryceson, D.F. 1996, 'De-agrarianisation and Rural Employment in Sub-Saharan Africa: A Sectoral Perspective', *World Development* 24 (1), 97-111.

Drakakis-Smith, D. 1992, 'Strategies for Meeting Basic Food Needs in Harare', in J. Baker & P. Ove Pedersen (eds), *The Rural-Urban Interface in Africa: Expansion and Adaptation*, Uppsala: The Scandinavian Institute of African Studies, pp. 258-83.

Fall, A.S. 1998, 'Migrants' Long-Distance Relationships and Social Networks in Dakar', *Environment and Urbanization* 10 (1): 135-45.

Foeken, D. 1997, 'Urban Trajectories in Rural Livelihood Strategies: Household Employment Patterns in Kenya's Coast Province', in D.F. Bryceson & V. Jamal (eds), *Farewell to Farms: De-agrarianisation and Employment in Africa*, Aldershot: Ashgate, pp. 119-36.

Foeken, D. 1998, 'Coping with Urban Poverty in Sub-Saharan Africa, with Special Emphasis on Urban Farming', Paper presented at the international symposium on *The Development Perspective of Africa toward the 21st Century*, Beijing, 21-23 October 1998.

138   *Foeken & Owuor*

Foeken, D. & A.M. Mwangi 1998, 'Does Access to Land Have a Positive Impact on the Food Situation of the Urban Poor? A Case Study in Nairobi', *East African Social Science Research Review* 14 (1): 19-32.

Gilbert, A. 1994, 'Third World Cities: Poverty, Employment, Gender Roles and the Environment during a Time of Restructuring', *Urban Studies* 31: 605-33.

Gugler, J. 1971, 'Life in a Dual System: Eastern Nigerians in Town, 1961', *Cahiers d'Etudes Africaines* 11 (43): 400-21.

Gugler, J. 1991, 'Life in a Dual System Revisited: Urban-Rural Ties in Enugu, Nigeria, 1961-87', *World Development* 19 (5): 399-409.

ILO/JASPA 1992, *African Employment Report*, Addis Ababa: International Labour Office.

Jamal, V. & J. Weeks 1988, 'The Vanishing Rural-Urban Gap in Sub-Saharan Africa', *International Labour Review* 127 (3): 271-92.

Kamete, A.Y. 1998, 'Interlocking Livelihoods: Farm and Small Town in Zimbabwe', *Environment and Urbanization* 10 (1): 23-34.

Kanji, N. 1996, *Review of Urbanization Issues Affecting Children and Women in the Eastern and Southern African Region*, Unicef.

Kenya, Republic of 1997, *Nakuru District Development Plan 1997-2001*, Nairobi: Government Printer.

Kenya, Republic of 2000, *Economic Survey 2000*, Nairobi: Government Printer.

Krüger, F. 1998, 'Taking Advantage of Rural Assets as a Coping Strategy for the Urban Poor: The Case of Rural-Urban Interrelations in Botswana', *Environment and Urbanization* 10 (1): 119-34.

Lee-Smith, D., M. Manundu, D. Lamba and P.K. Gathuru 1987, *Urban Food Production and the Cooking Fuel Situation in Urban Kenya: National Report*, Nairobi: Mazingira Institute.

Lee-Smith, D. & P.A. Memon 1994, 'Urban Agriculture in Kenya', in A.G. Egziabher *et al.*, *Cities Feeding People. An Examination of Urban Agriculture in East Africa*, Ottawa: International Development Research Centre, pp. 67-84.

Makwala M.M.Y.B. 1972, *Le Réseau Urbain du Bas-Zaïre. Contribution à l'Etude des Relations Ville-Campagne*, Brussels: Free University. Unpublished PhD thesis (3 vols).

MCN 1999, *Strategic Nakuru Structure Plan. Action Plan for Sustainable Urban Development of Nakuru Town and the Environs*, Nakuru: Nakuru Municipal Council.

Mougeot, L. 1993, 'Urban Food Self-reliance: Significance and Challenges', Ottawa: International Development Research Centre, unpublished mimeographed report.

Mwangi, A.M. 1995, *The Role of Urban Agriculture for Food Security in Low Income Areas in Nairobi*, Nairobi/Leiden: Ministry of Planning and National Development/African Studies Centre, Food and Nutrition Studies Programme, Report no. 54.

Mwangi, A.M. & D. Foeken 1996, 'Urban Agriculture, Food Security and Nutrition in Low Income Areas in Nairobi', *African Urban Quarterly* 11 (2/3): 170-79.

Nicolaï, H. 1989, 'Le Citadien et Son Village. Un Aspect de la Relation Ville-Campagne au Zaïre', in Singaravelou (ed.), *Pauvreté et Développement dans les Pays Tropicaux*, Bordeaux: University of Bordeaux III, pp. 499-507.

Obudho, R.A. & D. Foeken 1999, *Urban Agriculture in Africa. A Bibliographical Survey*. Leiden / Nairobi: African Studies Centre / Centre for Urban Research, ASC Research Report 58.

O'Connor, A. 1991, *Poverty in Africa. A Geographical Approach*, London: Belhaven Press.

Painter, T.M. 1996, 'Space, Time and Rural-Urban Linkages in Africa', *African Rural and Urban Studies* 3 (1): 79-98.

Potts, D. 1995, 'Shall We Go Home? Increasing Urban Poverty in African Cities and Migration Processes', *The Geographical Journal* 161 (3): 245-64.

Potts, D. 1997, 'Urban Lives: Adopting New Strategies and Adapting Rural Links', in C. Rakodi (ed.), *The Urban Challenge in Africa: Growth and Management of the Large Cities*, Tokyo/New York: United Nations University Press, pp. 447-94.

Potts, D. & C. Mutambirwa 1990, 'Rural-Urban Linkages in Contemporary Harare: Why Migrants Need their Land', *Journal of Southern African Studies* 16 (4): 677-98.

Read, M. 1942, 'Migrant Labour in Africa and its Effects on Tribal Life', *International Labour Review* 45 (6): 605-31.

Rogerson, C.M. 1997, 'Globalization or Informalization? African Urban Economies in the 1990s', in C. Rakodi (ed.), *The Urban Challenge in Africa: Growth and Management of its Large Cities*, Tokyo / New York: United Nations University Press, pp. 337-70.

Smit, W. 1998, 'The Rural Linkages of Urban Households in Durban, South Africa', *Environment and Urbanization* 10 (1): 77-87.

Stren, R. 1992, 'African Urban Research since the Late 1980s: Responses to Poverty and Urban Growth', *Urban Studies* 29: 533-55.

Tacoli, C. 1997, 'The Changing Scale and Nature of Rural-Urban Interactions: Recent Developments and New Agendas', in UNCHS/Habitat, *Regional Development Planning and Management of Urbanization. Experiences from Developing Countries*, Nairobi: UNCHS/Habitat, pp. 150-61.

Tacoli, C. 1998, 'Rural-Urban Interactions: A Guide to the Literature', *Environment and Urbanization* 10 (1): 147-66.

Tellegen, N. 1993, *Rural Employment in Sub-Saharan Africa. A Bibliography*, Leiden: African Studies Centre, Working Paper 18.

Tellegen, N. 1997, *Rural Enterprises in Malawi: Necessity or Opportunity?*, Aldershot: Ashgate.

Tripp, A.M. 1996, 'Urban Farming and Changing Rural-Urban Interactions in Tanzania', in M.L. Swantz & A.M. Tripp (eds), *What Went Right in Tanzania: People's Response to Directed Development*, Dar es Salaam: Dar es Salaam University Press, pp. 98-116.

UNCHS/Habitat 1996, *An Urbanizing World: Global Report on Human Settlements*, London: Oxford University Press (for United Nations Centre for Human Settlements).

Vennetier, P. 1989, 'Evolution des Espaces Péri-urbains à Brazzaville (Congo) et Cotonou (Bénin)', in P. Vennetier (ed.), *La Peri-urbanisation dans les Pays Tropicaux*, Bordeaux: Universitaire de Bordeaux, Centre d'Etudes de Géographie Tropicale.

9

Urbanisation and migration in Sub-Saharan Africa: Changing patterns and trends

Cecilia Tacoli

The increase in urban poverty in the 1980s in most African countries is likely to have affected the directions of population movement and subsequent regional and national urbanisation trends. It is thought to have slowed, sometimes significantly, the growth rates of urban centres. However, population and urban change in Africa in the last two decades has been insufficiently documented, and census data are often non-existent or unreliable. This chapter reviews some of the recent literature on urbanisation and migration in nations south of the Sahara, with a particular focus on the argument that return migration is resulting in de-urbanisation. Drawing on recent research in Tanzania, Nigeria and Mali, it suggests that migration is still playing an important role in the livelihoods of many African people but also that movement patterns have indeed changed in the last few decades. While links between rural and urban areas and populations tend to remain strong, transformations in economic and non-economic factors underpin the sometimes important variations in the migration decisions of different groups, Gender, generation and access to assets are critical in determining who goes, who stays and who returns.

Introduction

Migration has been one of the major factors shaping urbanisation in Africa since pre-colonial periods. Colonial interests and, later, urban bias in independent states' policies have influenced the direction of movement from the rural areas towards the urban centres. However, more than two decades of economic crisis and reform packages and, more recently, the internationalisation of trade and production have deeply transformed relations between town and countryside in many countries south of the Sahara. This has affected the direction of migrations as well as the composition of the flows and the types of movement. There is also some evidence of changes in the way populations are spatially distributed. The importance of the constantly evolving and complex inter-relationships between socio-economic and cultural change, migration and urbanisation is becoming increasingly recognised. At the same time, it is essential to understand the diversity of these interrelationships, which depend largely on local circumstances and on the ways they are integrated in wider contexts.

The aim of this chapter is not to provide an exhaustive review of the evidence on migration and urbanisation trends in Sub-Saharan Africa. It is rather to point to key issues emerging from recent work which may prove helpful in disentangling the economic/social/cultural change, migration and urbanisation relationships. Perhaps inevitably, the discussion is highly selective, both in terms of the issues addressed and of the geographical areas covered. This also applies to the main forms of mobility discussed which, because of the chapter's focus on urbanisation, tend to exclude movement between rural areas. This certainly does not imply that rural-rural migration is not important; indeed, in many countries south of the Sahara it is likely to be the prevailing type of mobility. This chapter's underlying argument is that mobility is a critical component of the livelihoods of many African people, and in many cases increasingly so. However, while rural-urban movement is still very important and an essential element of urbanisation in the region, it needs to be considered within the wider context of different forms of movement such as international migration, urban-urban and urban-rural movements.

The chapter is divided into three sections. The first summarises recent trends in urban change in the continent. In doing so, it also highlights some of the problems in data availability and reliability, and therefore the need to treat most general statements on urbanisation in Africa with a considerable degree of caution. The second section examines the links between de-urbanisation, return migration and wider changes in population movement in the past two decades, with examples from Nigeria and Ghana. A brief description of the main socio-economic and cultural transformations in the region since the 1980s provides the backdrop for the final section which turns to the micro-level and an analysis of migration as a livelihood strategy, and its implications for the understanding of its diversity – who moves, who stays and who returns – drawing from recent research in Mali, Nigeria and Tanzania.

Recent trends in urbanisation in Sub-Saharan Africa

The urban population of Sub-Saharan Africa has been characterised by high rates of growth since the 1950s. In most countries in the decade following independence, the expansion of employment in the public sector, in parastatal agencies and in the private sector attracted large numbers of migrants and urban centres grew rapidly. However, not all regions have experienced the same rates of urbanisation, and there are considerable variations, for example between Eastern Africa, with only around 22% of its population estimated to be living in urban areas and Southern Africa with around 48% (Chen *et al.* 1998). In addition, there are often significant variations within sub-regions, for example between the coastal nations and the Sahelian nations of West Africa, as well as diversity within the same nation that is often linked to ecological characteristics.

A second problem relates to the availability and reliability of national level data for the calculation of estimates of the components of urban growth – natural growth, internal migration and reclassification. Population censuses are the main source of data for measuring population movement and its affect on urban growth. However, they can be of limited use since collecting information on migration is not usually their purpose and they do not include specific questions on movement. In part, this reflects the persistence of fertility reduction as the main area of interest for the international donors and agencies that fund census exercises (Bilsborrow 1998). In addition, long intercensal intervals and delays in processing the information can increase the difficulties in data use. While this is a common problem for many countries, it is more pronounced in Africa where deteriorating economic conditions have often resulted in the information not being published or in data collection being suspended altogether. Of the 1980 round of census data, fewer than ten African countries have published figures allowing an estimation of the scale and direction of internal migration (Oucho 1998). The result is that, in many cases, data are estimates derived from censuses held in the years of rapid urban growth, thus raising questions of accuracy.[1]

Intra-regional comparisons are also hindered by the different definitions of 'urban centres' used by different nations. Changes in the definitions of urban and rural areas between census dates within the same country can be an additional difficulty for data comparability: for example, the 1952 Nigerian population census considered as 'urban' all centres with a population in excess of 5,000. This threshold was increased to 20,000 in the following census in 1963, a reclassification that affected the status of over 2,350 settlements.

Despite these problems and bearing in mind that in most cases estimates are based on projections and are, therefore, more indicative than substantive, it is possible to identify some clear trends in African urbanisation. First, the contribution of rural-urban migration to urban growth appears to have declined. In the 1960s and 1970s, rural-urban migration was thought to account for over 40% of urban growth, most of it directed towards large cities. In the 1980s and 1990s, large cities continued to grow although natural population increase has recently accounted for the main growth while rural-urban migration is estimated to account for only around 25%. The other significant trend is that, in many countries, small and medium-sized urban centres have grown more quickly than the largest cities. These changes are likely to be the result of a combination of factors, including the generally more difficult economic conditions facing urban dwellers in the last two decades, the on-going deterioration of infrastructure and public services and, since the 1990s, the spatial decentralisation of investment and planning decisions (Chen *et al.* 1998; UNCHS 1996). Finally, in some regions urbanisation trends are affected by the forced movement of people escaping from drought, famine, ethnic conflicts, civil strife and war. These can either result in de-urbanisation trends (for example in Uganda and Rwanda) or in the concentration of refugees in urban areas.

---

[1] Census data can also be less reliable because of a clash of interests. As a result, figures may be manipulated for political reasons, though obviously this is difficult to prove.

Urban poverty, migration patterns and de-urbanisation

Urbanisation processes in the majority of African countries have not gone hand in hand with the growth of the industrial sector. It is rather the expansion of the public sector, related to the creation of new administrations at independence, which has acted as the main engine of urban growth. The demand for services from this sector has in turn spurred the growth of a large urban informal sector that has acted as the main provider of employment for low-income urban groups. Both sectors were severely affected by the economic crisis and structural adjustment programmes implemented by several nations in the 1980s. As a result, urban incomes in most countries fell dramatically and the relative position of urban dwellers compared to their rural counterparts drastically changed (Jamal & Weeks 1988).

The impact of the economic crisis on urban populations has been well documented. Several elements of structural adjustment packages have exacerbated urban poverty, and reductions in subsidies and increases in food prices have particularly affected urban consumers, who rely largely on purchased food items. Retrenchments among public-sector workers and restrictions on wage levels have affected both formal-sector workers and the informal-sector activities that depend on their demand. Moreover, retrenched formal-sector workers who switched to informal-sector activities have contributed to the imbalance between increasing supply and declining demand. Increases in service charges, and cuts in public spending on health and education and in urban infrastructure expenditure have also contributed to making life more difficult for low-income urban residents (see for example Amis 1995; Kanji 1995; Wratten 1995).

A number of empirical studies have examined the consequences of economic hardship on the linkages that urban residents maintain with relatives and kin in home areas. Financial support from urban dwellers to rural relatives has been shown to have declined (see for example Fall 1998; Potts with Mutambirwa 1998), although in other contexts, urban dwellers' investments in home areas as a form of safety net have continued if not increased due to growing uncertainty in the cities and towns (Krüger 1998; Smit 1998). Some authors have suggested that this may have involved some degree of urban-to-rural migration, for example retrenched workers deciding to go home earlier than planned because of the narrowing of the gap between rural and urban incomes, and because the strength of rural-urban linkages often means that migrants can keep their claim on land in home areas (Potts 1995). However, evidence on return migration is anecdotal and findings are not uniform. Indeed, this reflects the wide variations in migration patterns between and within African countries as well as the lack of reliable demographic data to support and expand on the findings of small-scale studies.

Other studies have pointed to the role of additional factors in determining migration directions. In Nigeria, the retrenchment of workers in both the public and private sectors since the early 1980s is thought to have increased urban-to-rural movement since the most appealing solution for the unemployed was often to return home and take up farming. This was accompanied by the creation of new states and Local Government Areas provided with start-up grants by the federal state aimed at attracting private

investment. Since the mid-1980s, the federal state has also invested in rural development projects including the provision of physical infrastructure and the creation of over
200 new rural branches of commercial banks. The impact of these efforts in encouraging
urban-rural migration and in stemming rural-urban movement cannot be verified because of a lack of census data for that period. However, evidence suggests that these
projects have not been as successful as expected; partly because of macro-level constraints such as the 'hidden' impact of structural adjustment on agriculture through the
rising costs of agricultural production inputs (Meagher & Mustapha 1997); partly due to
inadequate funding and official corruption; and partly because of delays in the payment
of entitlements to redundant and retired workers who, without this income, could not set
up small-scale enterprises (Onyeonoru 1994). These authors suggest that rather than
one-way return migration, the emerging pattern is the intensification of circular migration involving a number of rural and urban destinations as a response to declining
income-earning opportunities in both areas.

A recent analysis of urban change in Ghana based on the admittedly limited available
census data (1960 to 1984) shows that in order to understand the impact of migration on
urbanisation trends, it is necessary to examine it in the wider regional context (Songsore
2000). All regions in Ghana experienced increased urbanisation in the period 1960-
1970. However, between 1970 and 1984, the Western, Central and Greater Accra
Regions experienced slight de-urbanisation, with the percentage of their urban population declining from 27.6 to 22.8 for the Western Region, from 28.5 to 26.5 for the
Central Region and from 85.3 to 83.5 for the Greater Accra Region. It is worth noting
that during the same period, urbanisation rates in all the other regions continued to
grow, and that the population of Ghana overall has become increasingly urban-based.

De-urbanisation trends in the three regions are due to a combination of factors.
Decline in specific sectors of the regions' economies, for example mining and timber
industries in the Western Region and the collapse of the cocoa industry in the Central
Region, resulted in population loss for small towns, which were subsequently reclassi-
fied as rural settlements because they fell below the 5,000 population threshold. The
slight drop for the Greater Accra Region can be explained by the fact that while the city
remained the main pole of attraction for internal migrants, it was also used as a staging
post for emigration, as travel documents could only be processed in the capital. In other
words, outward movement from the city did not necessarily only involve return migration or urban-rural migration, but also international migration. As Songsore (2000: 9)
noted, between 1973 and 1983 "there was hardly any extended family in the metropolis
that remained untouched by this outward flow to the high-wage regional growth pole of
oil-rich Nigeria".

Other emerging destinations for people moving out of the industrial core and large
regional administrative capitals during that period were smaller and medium-sized
towns. An important reason for this is that in these less densely populated centres, urban
and peri-urban agriculture could more easily be combined with other urban occupations
as a livelihood strategy (Songsore 2000). A similar process appears to have taken place
in Tanzania where, in the 1980s, smaller towns of between 20,000 and 50,000 were
preferred destinations because of the easier self-provisioning of food for urban house-

holds. However, municipal estimates in the 1990s suggested that the concentration of wealth caused by market liberalisation and the reinstatement of foreign-aid flows have again changed the direction of population movement towards the rapid growth of Dar es Salaam (Bryceson 1997).

While there is little doubt that the economic crisis of the past two decades has profoundly affected urbanisation trends and migration patterns in most countries south of the Sahara, it is also clear from small scale studies and from analyses of census data that it is difficult if not impossible to make generalisations on the nature and scale of these changes (see De Haan 1999). However, what the evidence shows is that migration and urbanisation are indeed still very important issues in the African context. Return migration needs, therefore, to be understood as one specific form of movement within the wider patterns of migration involving different groups of people and different destinations.

Migration as a livelihood strategy:
Who goes, who stays and who comes back?

Declining economic opportunities in urban centres and narrowing rural-urban income gaps are respectively 'push' and 'pull' factors which provide useful pointers to changes in the direction of movement. However, traditional push-pull approaches to migration fail to account for culturally and socially specific aspects, which play important roles in determining not only the direction but also the composition of the flows as well as the type of movement. Access to resources in home areas is likely to be a critical factor and one that varies according to individuals' wealth, gender and generation. At the same time, labour markets at destination are often segmented along lines of gender, age and ethnicity, the latter reflecting the migrant networks' control over specific sections of the urban labour market. However, not all migrants leave because they have no access to resources at home, and not all migrants end up in low-paid, unskilled jobs in urban areas. Indeed, for some groups migration can be a strategy to increase individual or, more often, household capital with a view to re-investing it in assets in the home village. On the other hand, the non-economic perception of migration as an important rite of passage means that in many instances those who 'do not make it' in the city may find it particularly difficult to return home.

The discussion in this section draws heavily on the first results of collaborative research conducted in Tanzania, Nigeria and to a lesser extent in Mali into the role of rural-urban interactions in the livelihood strategies of different groups.[2] Migration is a

---

[2]   As part of the research programme 'Rural-Urban Interactions, Livelihood Strategies and Socio-Economic Change', case studies were conducted in Mali by the Groupe Recherche Actions pour le Développement (GRAD) based in Bamako, in Nigeria by the Nigerian Environmental Study-Action Group (NEST) based in Ibadan, and in Tanzania by researchers from the University College for Land and Architectural Studies (UCLAS) and the Tanzania Gender Networking Group (TGNP), both based in Dar es Salaam. The research programme is coordinated by the International Institute for Environment and Development, London. Funding from the UK Department for International Development, the European Union, the International Development Research Centre, the Swedish International Development Agency

central interaction between town and countryside in all three countries, although in recent years there have been significant changes in the composition and direction of flows. This is the result of constraints in home areas and opportunities elsewhere, which in turn are important factors in determining who moves, who stays and who comes back.

Who moves? Gender composition and migration destinations

Young men have traditionally formed the bulk of migrants in African countries. While overall this would still appear to be the case, there is evidence that the independent movement of women has increased in recent years (Gadio & Rakowski 1995; Ouedraogo 1995). This reflects the growing demand for housemaids and nannies but also for barmaids and for women in what is often euphemistically called the 'entertainment industry'. For example, the international tourist resorts on the Kenyan coast are an important destination for young women from the Kilimanjaro region in northern Tanzania (Diyamett *et al.* 2000). Young women from villages around the town of Mopti in Mali find employment as maids both in the capital Bamako and in the regional urban poles such as Abidjan (GRAD 2000). In south-east Nigeria, destinations include local centres such as Aba and Port Harcourt but also Lagos as well as Cotonou in neighbouring Benin (NEST 1999). In view of the fact that some types of employment can attract considerable social stigma, access to more distant destinations may have increased the opportunities for moving. This is the case not only for young women working in the entertainment industry but also for men doing menial jobs. In southern Tanzania, for instance, it is not uncommon for men to engage in seasonal rural-rural migration seeking work as waged agricultural labour even if similar employment is available in their home villages (Lerise *et al.* 2000).

Increasing out-migration from rural areas to international destinations reflects the growing dependency of labour markets on foreign-resource flows, which in turn tend to be concentrated in fewer centres. For example, in West Africa, migrants from rural areas tend to bypass internal urban centres and concentrate on Côte d'Ivoire, heading both to rural destinations dominated by plantation agriculture (Brock & Coulibaly 1999) and to the regional urban centre of Abidjan. As in the case of Ghana in the early 1980s (Songsore 2000), the result is de-urbanisation without a decrease in rural out-migration. Indeed, international migration is likely to be an important factor in Mali, where the preliminary results of the 1997 population census show that, since 1986, the overall percentage of the urban population has declined from 22 to 18.9%, although Bamako has continued to grow (République du Mali 1998).

Non-economic supply-side factors are also important in migration decisions. In rural settlements in southeastern Nigeria, migration to urban centres is considered essential for economic and social success. Young people who do not migrate or commute to town are often considered to be shying away from hard work and may become the object of ridicule (NEST 1999). At the same time, young people see the demands on their time in the form of village community work as conflicting with their own wish to make money.

and the Swiss Agency for Development and Cooperation is gratefully acknowledged. The views expressed here are, however, only those of the author.

For both young men and women, migration is often a way to escape from obligations and control by their elders. This in turn is likely to affect their decision to return.

Remittances, investments and return migration
Remittances are an essential component of rural incomes and are mainly destined for consumption purposes as well as education and health expenditures. Investing in more tangible assets, for example in housing and land, is usually linked to an intention to return (De la Brière *et al.* 1997). Both remittances and investments in home areas are evidence of strong linkages between migrants and non-migrants. However, in many parts of Africa, links with home areas are considered as an essential part of one's identity, and therefore socio-cultural factors may play a more important role than economic considerations (Mbiba 1999). Investing in home villages may be part of the accumulation strategy of successful migrants who increase their household's assets. On the other hand, it may also be the outcome of the survival strategy of migrants for whom life in urban centres involves economic and social insecurity (Krüger 1998; Smit 1998). However, even this option may be limited or non-existent for migrants who are marginalised in home settlements. Migrants' links with home areas and their contribution to the well-being of relatives and communities depend on the specific socio-economic circumstances of those involved, and on the opportunities available in home areas. Conversely, the migrants may require their support in times of crisis.

The Tanzanian studies show how both intra-household relations and the general socio-economic conditions in home areas contribute to determine whether remittances are sent, investments are made and finally whether migrants return. Of the four rural settlements studied, only Lotima and Marawe Kyura, both in the Kilimanjaro region, showed any evidence of return migration. In Lotima, there is no shortage of land on the plain around the village, much of it irrigated. At the same time, there is little influx of permanent migrants, suggesting that the village is able to control access to land. Probably the most important factor is that access to other villages, towns and even areas across the border in Kenya is relatively easy. The result is that while farming remains the main occupation for village inhabitants, over half combine it with some form of trading activity. Continued access to land and the opportunity for income diversification are likely to be important factors attracting return migrants.

It is important to note that out-migration remains significant in the village, and that its composition and direction have changed in the past few years. Young women are excluded from land inheritance and have limited access to parental land, especially irrigated plots. This, combined with the proximity of employment opportunities in Kenya, especially in the coastal tourist resorts, has resulted in important out-migration flows of young women, who usually return only when forced to do so due to child-bearing or illness (Diyamett *et al.* 2000). Thus, while continued access to land is important in encouraging return migration, it implies the exclusion of other groups and becomes an important factor in their out-migration.

The other village, Marawe Kyura, lies on the slopes of Mount Kilimanjaro and suffers from a severe shortage of land, with family plots usually being inherited by only one child in the family. Traditionally this was a son but increasingly nowadays daughters are inheriting family land. Decisions as to who will inherit are frequently made by fathers in favour of the child who has provided the most support to the family. Remittances have therefore become an important way of ensuring access to land through inheritance. However, the acute land shortage means that returning to the village is usually only on retirement. Alternatively, returnee migrants find employment in non-agricultural activities that involve commuting to surrounding urban centres. Investment in the village, therefore, concentrates on housing improvements rather than on agricultural production (Diyamett *et al.* 2000).

By contrast, the villages around the town of Lindi in southern Tanzania show very little return migration and high rates of out-migration of young men and, to a lesser extent, of young women to both rural and urban destinations. There is no shortage of agricultural land in the region. However, what makes a desirable farm is the number of mature cash-crop trees such as cashew nuts and coconuts (which require five to seven years to become fully productive) and proximity to settlements or to feeder roads. Transport infrastructure in the area is extremely poor and acts as a bottleneck in the marketing of agricultural produce as well as creating difficulties for farming, especially with regard to protecting crops from wild animals (Lerise *et al.* 2000).

Young people's access to mature farms is limited by their elders' control over them and may be a source of inter-generational tension and conflict. In this context, migration is perceived by young people as an attractive alternative. However, the available employment is usually in low-skilled, low-income sections of the urban informal sector. Indeed, the majority of young street-vendors in Dar es Salaam are thought to come from the country's southern regions, including Lindi. The lack of return migration to the Lindi area can be explained by a combination of two factors. First, opportunities for investment in the home area are limited due to poor infrastructure and to the socially determined access to the main resource, tree-crop farms. Although many residents also engage in trading activities, revenue from them is very low due to transport limitations and to the generally low incomes in the region, which act as a brake on demand. Second, unlike their counterparts from the Kilimanjaro region where education was traditionally highly valued, access to the urban labour market for the relatively unskilled and uneducated migrants from the Lindi region is limited to low-income activities, making the sending of remittances and investment in the home area a luxury few can afford (Lerise *et al.* 2000).

Social networks and obligations towards home areas
The absence of return migration in the Lindi region does not imply that relations between migrants and non-migrants are being severed. On the contrary, links are cultivated through cultural practices such as children's initiation ceremonies and clan-based activities that all members are expected to attend whether they live in the settlement or not. Non-attendance at these week-long events is considered as socially incorrect as not attending the burial ceremony of a relative. Social links and networks are reinforced by such ceremonies, which often include gifts of food to urban-based relatives, much to the dismay of the local authorities in areas subject to food shortages. Rural residents are also aware that this increases food insecurity but the gains in terms of social networks and

security seem to outweigh the risks, at least for the time being, although some house-holds are now attempting to reduce expenditure levels (Lerise *et al*. 2000).

The importance of participating in home-based social networks is also evident in southeastern Nigeria, where, as in most African countries, it is inconceivable to be buried elsewhere than in one's ancestral home. At weekends, roads are busy with hearses and funeral guests attending ceremonies in rural areas. In the rural settlements around the town of Aba, age groups formed during the initiation ceremonies remain active and migrants' contributions through them to community welfare activities are often significant. The construction of schools, public fountains and other high-profile initiatives contribute to raising the status of successful migrants while reinforcing traditional social structures (NEST 1999). Unlike their counterparts in southern Tanzania, migrants tend to invest in private housing. However, few migrants return prior to retirement. This is attributed to limited land availability in the rural settlements and to increased insecurity in the urban centres, which makes it difficult for migrants to accumulate capital to later reinvest in a rural-based enterprise. Unless it is linked to retirement, return migration appears to be perceived as somewhat of a failure, and as the inability to cope with the demands of urban life (NEST 1999).

The examples of southern Tanzania and southeastern Nigeria suggest that the existence of strong linkages between urban-based and rural-based kin, and between migrants and non-migrants from the same village does not necessarily encourage return migration. This may be due, on the one hand, to limited opportunities in the home place, as is the case in Tanzania, while, on the other hand, it may be related to the high social expectations of 'success' in the urban centres, which makes return migration difficult for those who face future potential hardship at their rural destination. Returnees are expected to return for retirement or to have done well enough in town to be able to start their own business.

Conclusions

Migration patterns in Africa appear to be increasingly complex. Access to information and to transport, however limited, and new employment opportunities in the service sector attract different types of migrants, such as young women moving on their own. These transformations, which go hand in hand with the economic crisis and reforms that together have radically changed urban labour markets in the larger cities, and agricul-tural production have generally increased social polarisation in both urban and rural areas.

The changes in the direction and composition of migration flows have affected urbanisation trends in most countries, although a lack of reliable and relevant data makes it difficult to quantify these transformations. Bearing in mind that generalisations are likely to be inaccurate, what follows are tentative suggestions that require further investigation. First, return migration is likely to be an element of population redistri-bution although its significance varies according to the characteristics of home areas and those of the migrants. Second, in some countries international migration, both within the continent and more recently to southern Europe and other non-traditional destinations, may be more important than migration to internal urban centres. This is, for example, the case in West Africa where migrants moving from Sahelian countries to the coast often bypass local centres, and in Ghana, where the de-urbanisation process may partly be due to the migration of urban dwellers to Europe. Third, de-urbanisation may appear to be increasing as small centres fall below the threshold of 'urban centres' and are being re-defined as 'rural settlements'. This underlies the fourth point, that de-urbanisation is usually a local phenomenon, with some regions experiencing a decline in the proportion of their urban populations but with the country as a whole still becoming increasingly urban, as is the case in Ghana. However, this is not always true, as shown by the data on Mali that require a better understanding at a sub-regional (West African) level.

Finally, it is essential to consider the complexity of livelihood strategies that provide the context for understanding migration at the individual and household level. Taking into account the wider picture including economic and non-economic factors, it becomes possible to identify the opportunities and constraints influencing the migration decisions of different groups. These often include socially-embedded and culturally-specific dimensions which in turn determine access to assets such as land, but also to labour markets. In addition to wealth and social status, gender and generation are essential factors ultimately determining who goes, where they go, and, to a large extent, who returns.

References

Amis, P. 1995, 'Making Sense of Urban Poverty'', *Environment and Urbanisation* 7 (1): 145-58.

Bilsborrow, R. 1998, 'The State of the Art and Overview of the Chapters', in R. Bilsborrow (ed.), *Migration, Urbanisation and Development: New Directions and Issues*, Norwell, Mass.: UNFP, pp. 1-58.

Brock, K. & N. Coulibaly 1999, *Sustainable Rural Livelihoods in Mali*. Brighton: Institute of Development Studies, Research Report 35.

Bryceson, D. 1997, 'De-agrarianisation in Sub-Saharan Africa: Acknowledging the Inevitable', in D.F. Bryceson & V. Jamal (eds), *Farewell to Farms: De-agrarianisation and Employment in Africa*, Aldershot: Ashgate, pp. 3-20.

Chen, N., P. Valente & H. Zlotnik 1998, 'What Do We Know about Recent Trends in Urbanisation?', in R. Bilsborrow (ed.), *Migration, Urbanisation and Development: New Directions and Issues*, Norwell, Mass.: UNFP, pp. 59-88.

De Haan, A. 1999, 'Migration and Poverty in Africa: Is There a Link?', Background paper for the World Bank SPA Status Report on Poverty.

De la Brière, B., A. de Janvry, S. Lambert & E. Sadoulet 1997, 'Why Do Migrants Remit? An Analysis for the Dominican Sierra', Washington: IFPRI, FCND Discussion Paper no 37.

Diyamett, B., M. Diyamett, J. James & R. Mabala 2000, *Rural-Urban Interactions and Livelihood Strategies in a Changing Economic Environment: The Case of Himo and Its Region in Northern Tanzania*, London: International Institute for Environment and Development.

Fall, A.S. 1998, 'Migrants' Long Distance Relationships and Social Networks in Dakar', *Environment and Urbanisation* 10 (1): 135-46.

Gadio, C.M. & C.A. Rakowski 1995, 'Survival or Empowerment? Crisis and Temporary Migration among the Serer Millet Pounders of Senegal', *Women's Studies International Forum* 18 (4): 431-43.

GRAD 2000, 'Les Interactions entre Milieux Rural et Urbain au Mali: Potentialités et Conflits en Zones Péri-urbaines', Bamako: Groupe Recherche Actions pour le Développement (Preliminary report of the qualitative phase).

Jamal, V. & J. Weeks 1988, 'The Vanishing Rural-Urban Gap in Sub-Saharan Africa', *International Labour Review* 127 (3), 271-92.

Kanji, N. 1995, 'Gender, Poverty and Economic Adjustment in Harare, Zimbabwe', *Environment and Urbanisation* 7 (1): 37-56.

Krüger, F. 1998, 'Taking Advantage of Rural Assets as a Coping Strategy for the Urban Poor', *Environment and Urbanisation* 10 (1): 119-34.

Lerise, F., A. Kibadu, E. Mbutolwe & N. Mushi 2000, *Rural-Urban Interactions and Livelihood Strategies in a Changing Economic Environment: The Case of Lindi and its Region in Southern Tanzania*, London: International Institute for Environment and Development.

Mbiba, B. 1999, 'Urban-Rural Relations: Communal Land Rights as African Culture and Religion in Zimbabwe', Mimeo.

Meagher, K. & A.R. Mustapha 1997, 'Not by Farming Alone', in D.F. Bryceson & V. Jamal (eds), *Farewell to Farms: De-agrarianisation and Employment in Africa*, Aldershot: Ashgate, 63-84.

NEST 1999, 'The Rural-Urban Divide: Changing Dimensions of Rural-Urban Interactions in Southeastern Nigeria', Ibadan: Nigerian Environmental Study-Action Group (Report of the qualitative phase).

Onyeonoru, I.P. 1994, 'Labour Migration and Rural Transformation in Nigeria', *International Sociology* 9 (2): 217-21.

Oucho, J. 1998, 'Recent Internal Migration Processes in Sub-Saharan Africa: Determinants, Consequences and Data Adequacy Issues', in R. Bilsborrow (ed.), *Migration, Urbanisation and Development: New Directions and Issues* Norwell, Mass.: UNFP, 89-120.

Ouedraogo, J.-B. 1995, 'The Girls of Nyovuuru: Dagara Female Labour Migrations to Bobo-Dioulasso', in J. Baker & T.A. Aina (eds), *The Migration Experience in Africa*, Uppsala: Nordiska Afrikainstitutet, 303-20.

Potts, D. 1995, 'Shall We Go Home? Increasing Urban Poverty in African Cities and Migration Processes', *The Geographical Journal* 161 (3): 245-64.

Potts, D. with C. Mutambirwa 1998, 'Basics Are Now a Luxury: Perceptions of the Impact of Structural Adjustment on Urban and Rural Areas in Zimbabwe', *Environment and Urbanisation* 10 (1): 55-76.

République du Mali 1998, 'Recensement Général de la Population et de l'Habitat (Avril 1998), Résultats Provisoires, Juin 1998', Bamako: Ministère du Plan et de l'Intégration, Direction Nationale de la Statistique et de l'Informatique.

Smit, W. 1998, 'The Rural Linkages of Urban Households in Durban, South Africa', *Environment and Urbanisation* 10 (1): 77-88.

Songsore, J. 2000, *Towards a Better Understanding of Urban Change: The Ghana Case Study*, London: International Institute for Environment and Development.

UNCHS 1996, *An Urbanizing World: Global Report on Human Settlements 1996*, Oxford: Oxford University Press.

Wratten, E. 1995, 'Conceptualizing Urban Poverty', *Environment and Urbanisation* 7 (1): 11-36.

10

Processes and types of pastoral migration in northern Côte d'Ivoire

Youssouf Diallo

Migration and mobility are part of the history and daily life of pastoral Fulbe. For the Fulbe in West Africa different movements and migratory flows have been well described in the literature. The more recent moves to the south of West Africa are less well known. In this chapter, one of these moves, from Burkina Faso and Mali to northern Côte d'Ivoire, is described and explained as an expansionist tendency of Fulbe migration. Attention is paid to the different patterns of this movement and to the socio-political conditions in which it took place.

Introduction

The migration process and geographical patterns of Fulbe mobility have generally been well documented. However, the pastoral migrations from Sahelian areas into West African sub-humid zones are a relatively recent phenomenon and not as well known. This chapter describes one of these southward-oriented migration waves, from western Burkina Faso and Mali to northern Côte d'Ivoire.

In the early 1960s Fulbe from present-day Burkina Faso and Mali started to move into the north of Côte d'Ivoire, a process that continues today. The majority of Fulbe who come from western Burkina Faso and have settled in the north of Côte d'Ivoire are originally from the old Fulbe centre of Barani, located in the Nouna region, also called Boobola (Bwaland). The Boobola region was a popular residence for various Fulbe groups and one of the most important cattle-breeding zones in Burkina Faso. Recent changes, however, have diminished its pastoral interest, leading to an increased out-migration of Fulbe pastoralists.

This migration cannot be understood as a simple geographical displacement. Pastoral peoples are especially mobile and this mobility forms a major part of their culture. Their movements have a complex geographical, social and cultural character, and pastoralists and their neighbours have developed socio-cultural institutions to deal with movement and integration. As is shown in this chapter, this process of integration has led in some cases to profound identity transformations and even ethnic changes among the Fulbe. On the other hand, some social institutions stress the complementary relationships Fulbe pastoralists have with their neighbours, enabling them to keep their pastoral identity. Behind the complexity of geographical mobility and the accompanying social and cultural transformations are a variety of reasons, causes and consequences that can be traced back to personal motivations, to group characteristics, etc. The case study of Foulabougou reveals part of this complexity behind mobility.

This chapter describes the different forms of Fulbe movements from an area in western Burkina Faso to the sub-humid savannah of Côte d'Ivoire and the conditions under which these movements took place.[1] After a general overview of the various forms of nomadic movements as described in the literature, the focus turns to Burkina Faso. The pastoral migrations of Fulbe in the area before the second half of the twentieth century are reconstructed, with a reflection on possible identity transformations that have taken place. Then the recent mobility patterns that lead from Burkina Faso to Mali and Côte d'Ivoire are examined. This study contributes to the research on rural migration forms and processes (group formation, residential change, etc.) within pastoralist societies in relation to multi-ethnic coexistence, the impact of national policies, and competition for control over natural resources.

Pastoral mobility

Migration is generally defined as "any kind of movement of groups or individuals to another place, which result in a change of residence" (Braukämper 1993: 26). However, when considering pastoral societies, their mobility can neither be described nor explained in terms of migration. Pastoralists are mobile by nature and changes in residence are difficult to foresee.

Early studies go far beyond the simplistic push-pull model so often used in migrant studies, and have already considered the dynamic patterns of pastoral mobility and the many forms it may take. Stenning (1959) was one of the first to differentiate mobility among the Fulbe in West Africa, distinguishing three types of mobility among the pastoral Fulbe in northern Nigeria: transhumance, migratory drift and migration. Whereas 'transhumance' is a seasonal movement, 'migratory drift' is a long-term process by which cattle-herders gain access to new pastures. Stenning considered 'migration' as the flight of pastoral groups resulting from ecological constraints or political pressure exercised by powerful states. In the past, such migrations occurred as massive movements following critical and historical events such as conflict, warfare or cattle disease. However, there is no clear-cut division between the three different processes and, in practice, these pastoral movements are all inter-related.

Anthropologists working in East African pastoral societies have developed a similar analysis. According to Turton (1991: 145-69), for example, three types of movement can be observed among the agro-pastoral Mursi in the Lower Omo Valley of southwestern

---

[1] Information presented here was collected in Burkina Faso and Côte d'Ivoire between August 1996 and March 1997. I would like to express my gratitude to the German Founding Board (DFG) for its generous support that made this research possible.

Ethiopia: a 'breakaway' or separation from a parent group, a steady infiltration across an ethnic boundary through inter-marriage, and a gradual occupation of new territory claimed by another ethnic group. More generally, Galaty & Bonte (1991: 18) distinguished between mobility, expansion and conflict. Mobility is a form of nomadic, semi-nomadic or migratory movement of humans and herds. Expansion might be used to describe change in a political domain, while conflict is a significant feature in East African pastoralism resulting in clashes of interest between groups (see also Schlee 1994). Competition, sometimes resulting in conflict, is common between different resource users (for example between agriculturalists and herders) but also between various sectors of the same migratory group.

In a comparative study of conditions of pastoral migrations, Dupire (1970) made the distinction between internal migration and external migration, the difference between migration considered as a pastoral mode of life and migration as a possibility of escape. While the former has emerged as a result of socio-economic choices and decision-making at a family or even individual level, the latter is caused by ecological or political disaster or administrative pressure. A central notion on which Dupire focused is that of 'migratory group', which has been re-examined more recently by Burnham (1996) and Botte, Boutrais & Schmitz (1999). From recent Fulbe studies, and in line with Dupire's argument, it appears that the notion of a migratory group includes not only a territorial but also a social-relational dimension. The former points to access to pastures and water, or access to a new territory through perpetual migration (Galaty & Bonte 1991; Burnham 1996; Bonfiglioli 1988). The second refers to a certain form of flexibility within lineages whereby constant reconstructions of kinship relations emerge.

The best definition of expansion is probably that of Irwin (1981) who studied the history of movement and settlement patterns among the Fulbe of Liptako in present-day north-east Burkina Faso. Irwin showed that expansion involves both demographic and territorial aspects and is defined as a specific "type of movement which leads to the enlargement in area of a lineage's territory. It may eventually lead to a change in geographical location of the lineage territory; it does not affect the overall juxtaposition of lineage areas" (Bohannan 1954: 2; Irwin 1981). It is the slow movement of neighbouring lineages gradually expanding and occupying new land, moving in such a way that they remain neighbours. The contrary also exists: separation of neighbouring groups in a certain place due to movement that is known as 'disjunction'.

The concept of expansion is relevant for the description of the specific movements of Fulbe in this chapter. It is a slow and continuous process and is used in the description of long-term movements and displacements of Fulbe cattle-herders in the Ivorian semi-humid zone. To understand the mechanism of Fulbe expansion into the semi-humid savannah it is important to distinguish between two types of mobility: direct or intentional migration, on the one hand, and indirect or non-intentional migration, on the other. In western Burkina Faso, direct and intentional migrations were usually a form of 'escape' (*perol*) related primarily to political events such as warfare, exactions and insecurity. As in the past, direct migrations today, from Burkina Faso to Côte d'Ivoire, are rapid and seasonal movements. Although not always perceived as such by Fulbe migrants, the movements may be understood as a form of long-distance transhumance because they are carried out mainly during the dry season. In addition, there is the traditional practice of north-south transhumance. The Fulbe cattle-herders in northern Côte d'Ivoire make the distinction between dry-season transhumance (*seddorè*) and rainy-season transhumance (*luumordè*), both concerning short-distance mobility of milk herds (*suraadi*). Braukämper (1993) suggested that this kind of nomadic movement combined with cycles of transhumance be called 'circulation'. As a continual form of mobility, it is important in the traditional herding strategies in northern Côte d'Ivoire but since it does not involve a change in residence it cannot be considered a distinct form of migration.

Unlike direct migration, indirect migration is a long-term movement carried out in successive stages. This type of mobility is comparable with the 'migratory drift' known among nomadic groups in northern Nigeria. Even if direct and indirect migrations are opposed in duration, phasing and rhythm of their achievements, there is no sharp dividing-line since the Fulbe refer to both direct migration and indirect migration as *eggugol*. The boundary between the two types of migration varies due to the diversity of motivation and strategies of the pastoral groups. But such fluctuations are also due to circumstances that govern the displacement of the Fulbe. For a mobile group like the Fulbe pastoralists, indirect migration can sometimes be pursued as direct migration, particularly when a household undertakes a journey to join other members of their lineage group who have settled in a new zone with the intention of exploiting fodder potentialities favourable to cattle-herding.

Many case studies in northern Côte d'Ivoire show the combination of the two forms of migration. Direct migration or indirect migration, as strategies and pastoral behaviour, were undertaken in the 1960-1980 period in response to political pressure (persecution, exaction) and ecological constraints (lack of water, overgrazing). Table 10.1 shows the movements of people and herds as well as the main ecological and sociological factors to which each type of mobility is due.

Table 10.1: Fulbe movements of herds and people

Movements	Motives	Herd	People
Transhumance: - Dry season (south) (*seddorè*) - Wet season (north) (*luumordè*)	Better pastures Better pastures	*seddorde* *na'iddin* *luumorde* *na'iddin*	Herder Herder
Nomadic transhumance or circulation (*Garki*)	Better pastures	*Garki suraadi*	Herder (*Garki gori*)
Migration (*eggugol*)	Ecological or sociological constraint	*na'i eggooji*	Household
Migration as 'flight' (*perol*)	Conflict, cattle disease	Cattle	Household

Past and present migrations

Fulbe in western Burkina Faso, early movements in the eighteenth and nineteenth centuries

The history of the Fulbe in western Burkina Faso is one of movement, displacement and inter-ethnic relations but it is difficult to discern all the different movements. This section attempts to reconstruct the history of Fulbe mobility in the area.

During the eighteenth century various pastoral groups coming from the Niger Valley moved to Bwa communities in the Boobola region (Diallo 1997) and further to the east to Yatenga villages that formed part of the Mossi Kingdom (Izard 1985). Most of these Fulbe groups and sub-groups are classified by reference to the areas in which they reside or from which they have come. This geographical system of classification and internal differentiation coincides sometimes with clan lineage divisions. A classic example is the Fulbe ruling clan in northern Nigeria known among the Hausa as *Toronkawa*, which is equivalent to the Fulbe word *Toroobe*, meaning 'those who come from Fuuta Toro'. This identity paradigm is used among Fulbe communities in the study, where the name *Boobolankoobe*, for example, derives its meaning from a place of residence ('people from Boobola').

The exact date when the first Fulbe groups appeared in the Bwa area is not known but from historical data it is assumed that their arrival in present-day western Burkina Faso was before the second half of the eighteenth century when some of them left the chieftaincy of Barani. Barani and Dokwi were important settlements from where small Fulbe groups migrated southwards into Bobo, Bwa and Marka societies. The reasons behind such small-scale migrations were conflicts or the search for new pastures. According to oral tradition, relations between members of the ruling clan in Barani and other Fulbe groups were of a conflictual nature. This was the main cause of the migration of a Fulbe sub-group, the Diallube, to the Mossi region where they obtained the protection of the head of Fulbe communities settled among the Mossi people.

Other Fulbe groups left Barani with their large herds in search of new pastures. They crossed the Black Volta (Mouhoun) River and settled in the eastern area of Dédougou (see Map 10.1 below). Other Fulbe who fled from Barani during a dynastic conflict joined them later. Some of these refugees returned after the conflict, while others chose to stay near Dédougou or elsewhere in Bwa communities. The latter are known as *Feroobe* or *Fereebe* (sing. *Pereejo*).

During the nineteenth century, the Boobola were under the political influence of two Fulbe chieftaincies, Barani and Dokwi, to which Bwa and Bobo peasants were obliged to pay tribute. The most important villages inland from the Black Volta River were also under the political influence of the Barani and Dokwi. Fulbe from these chieftaincies who had established themselves in village communities generally maintained good relations with their hosts and the tradition of sedentary peasants entrusting their livestock to Fulbe was widespread. Some Fulbe who migrated to the Bobo-Dioulasso area in the south settled among the Bobo peasants and developed a complementary relationship with their hosts. Difficult conditions, due to bovine tryponosomiasis, forced some to return and settle permanently in Bondoukwi near the northern bend of the Black Volta.

In the Bondoukwi area, the Fulbe represent one of the oldest foreign ethnic groups, having arrived before both the Marka Muslim families and the Mossi migrants who moved into the area in search of agricultural lands and cash incomes. Emigration by the first groups of Fulbe Diallube near Boromo at the beginning of the nineteenth century coincided with the arrival of Fulbe Sidibé from Barani in the Bondoukwi region. Another group of Fulbe migrants joined the existing pastoral settlements.[2]

In the 1970s, the Bondoukwi area became one of Burkina Faso's principal cotton zones. The Fulbe pastoralists living in this cotton-producing area developed complementary relations with the Bwa and Mossi agriculturalists but cooperation was not the only aspect of peasant-herder relations. Competition for control over local resources is becoming increasingly acute. The Fulbe cattle-herders accuse the peasant migrants of contributing to land scarcity while the Mossi clear land to the detriment of pasture land, which is gradually being relegated to interstitial zones. The Mossi migration is similar to the pastoral expansion in its geographical orientation, since both are directed towards the south and west of Burkina Faso. But Mossi residential practices differ from those of the Fulbe and of the autochthonous groups of the region. The Mossi live in scattered hamlets and their cultivated fields are widely dispersed. Any expansion of pasture and agricultural land makes pastoralism more difficult.

The Fulbe from the cotton-producing zone of Bondoukwi go on dry-season transhumance in the Banfora and Lobi areas. Although they settled a long time ago near Bobo-Dioulasso, the Fulbe have never had direct or historical relations with the population in the neighbouring area of Banfora.

Migration and identity transformations
Fulbe identity is linked to migration. During the migration process new groups may be formed and ethnic identities change, with processes of fission and fusion emerging. In the course of pastoral mobility Fulbe migrants split up into smaller groups or are joined by other semi-nomadic groups.

In the past, Fulbe expansion led to two types of integration. The first was the political incorporation of non-Fulbe populations into Fulbe state and administrative systems, such as in Adamawa in northern Cameroon (Burnham 1996). The opposite process also occurred with the gradual pastoral expansion resulting at times in the assimilation of the Fulbe in village communities and earlier state organisations. For example, some Fulbe who worked as herders for the Senufo have been gradually incorporated into Senufo society and have became known as 'Black Fulbe'.[3] Other Fulbe, originating from the Malinke chieftaincy of Wasulu (in present-day Mali) and whose activity is hunting, have adopted the Senufo culture.

---

[2] This group is formed by Wolarbe (patronymic Boli), Fulbe from Jelgooji (in the north-east of Burkina Faso) and other cattle-herders from the Mossi country of Yatenga.
[3] In Bobo and Senufo societies, the dichotomy between 'red' and 'black' Fulbe is used to distinguish assimilated from non-assimilated Fulbe. This distinction is sometimes confusing. 'Black Fulbe' are considered to be an aristocratic group, while 'red' or 'white' Fulbe are viewed as nomads, pastoralists and pagans.

The second type of integration is found among the Fulbe who lived in the Mossi kingdoms. They adopted the Mossi language and married Mossi women. Skinner (1964: 12) pointed out that these Fulbe "gained the good will of the Mossi rulers and spread throughout the territory. Many of them married Mossi women, giving rise to a new group known as Silmi-Mossi, who continued to raise cattle but also practiced agriculture and adopted many of the cultural traits of their hosts."

Other Fulbe groups were assimilated in the same way into local cultures in Boobola. The Fulbe in western Burkina express the movement of groups across ethnic boundaries by using the metaphor of 'entrance' (see also Burnham 1996; Stenning 1959). Those Fulbe assimilated into the Bwa culture 'have come into' the Bwa groups. Cultural assimilation of the Fulbe into the Bobo and Bwa societies was a gradual, long-term process, sometimes followed by ethnic assimilation when a new group emerged.

Bobo, Bwa and Marka cultural influences affected those Fulbe living in closer contact with Bwa groups and whose language and culture they adopted. These Fulbe are pejoratively called *Fulamuru* or *Murube*. They are only recognisable by their initial patronymic (Sangare). The Fulfulde word *Murube* (sing. *Murunke*) means 'the Fulbe ignorant of their culture'. However, the Fulamuru are not the only ones who assimilated into local cultures. Other Fulbe groups interacted with Marka and married Marka women. According to oral tradition, the first Fulbe clan to 'lose' its original identity (i.e. its 'Fulbeness') was the Yiirlaabe. The Yiirlaabe settled among the Marka ethnic group of Nouna with whom they had close relations and whose language they later adopted. The cultural boundaries between the Yiirlaabe and the Sidibe ruling clan of Barani, whose leading members define their Fulbe identity in terms of prestige connected with political power, appear to be rigid.

The movement of Fulbe groups across ethnic boundaries occurs not only after peaceful migration but also as a result of political events such as wars and revolts. In present-day western Burkina Faso, Fulbe migrations in peripheral areas and village communities were often prompted by warfare. This is the case for most of the Fulbe from Boobola, known as *Jonkaarinkoobe* (Fulbe from Jonkaari), who fled from powerful armies during the nineteenth century and migrated to the peripheral San area in Mali. Other Fulbe took refuge in the Samoland in the east after the first military intervention of the army of Maasina in Boobola in 1830. In Bondoukwi, the current descendants of former refugees are divided into seven families living on the periphery of the village. They all speak the Bwa language but have maintained their identity through their religion and a pastoral way of life.

However, other migrating Fulbe groups have not integrated to such an extent into other communities. They have developed, through their mobile lifestyle, socio-cultural institutions that help them integrate as Fulbe in a new area. These relationships play a role in current relations between immigrants and authochtohonous populations. Such is the case in western Burkina Faso where the Bobo and Bwa, and in northern Côte d'Ivoire where the Senufo are the dominant sedentary groups, and where the Fulbe have had to develop different strategies to deal with their new neighbours. Traditionally, the Bobo, Bwa and Senufo were hospitable to strangers and groups of migrants because they could contribute to the diversification of their economy and were easily incorporated into their village communities. Two socio-cultural institutions associated with mobility and migration are important for settlement in a foreign area. These are the relationship with the 'Master of the Earth' and that between 'host' (*yaatigi*) and stranger. Both represent the means by which ethnic or professional groups of different origin become integrated into the Bobo-Bwa and Senufo village communities.

Pastoral expansion in the Ivorian sub-humid zone

The first migrants: Opening up the route
The large majority of Fulbe stockowners from western Burkina initially passed through Mali before settling in the north of Côte d'Ivoire. These included the Fulbe Sidibe who provided the initial impetus to pastoral expansion, hereby opening up migratory routes to the Ivorian semi-humid zone that became the point of convergence of several groups of Sahelian cattle-owners. Due to the continuous changes in the configuration of pastoral settlements, it is difficult to determine the exact number of Fulbe living in the north of Côte d'Ivoire. Arditi (1990: 139) estimated a total of 50,000 people. This low figure is due to the pattern of settlement generally based on small groups of migrant Fulbe and individuals.

In northern Côte d'Ivoire peasant cattle-owners entrust their livestock to Fulbe herders. The Fulbe are paid in cash for their services and they get the usufruct of the milk. These labour divisions have led to the movement of a large number of Fulbe herdsmen in search of wage labour. The development of cattle-herding activities in northern Côte d'Ivoire has turned this area into a centre of attraction for 'proletarian' young Fulbe who work as hired herdsmen for individual cattle-owners or, occasionally, in public farm companies. The migration of young herders, which started in the 1960s, was temporary. Initially, the hired herders came from Yatenga (Mossiland) and Mopti (Mali) and went to the Kong region. During their absence, Fulbe migrants maintained matrimonial and religious relationships with their home area in Burkina Faso, generally, returning home after a few years' service.

Migration flows: Indirect migrations: Burkina Faso-Mali-Côte d'Ivoire
Information from the Fulbe of Barani now living in the north of Côte d'Ivoire confirms the ideas of Benoît (1979: 167), who stated that the migration of pastoralists can be understood if not only the chronology of events and processes but also the reasons for migration are taken into account. From this, it is possible to distinguish two successive migratory trends. The initial movement involved Fulbe cattle-herders who migrated to the San area in Mali during the 1950s, while the second migration, directed towards the south-west of Burkina Faso dates from the 1970s.

Ecological and political changes in western Burkina Faso (Nouna District) during the 1940s resulted in the pastoral migration to San. This migration of stockowners must be understood in the context of political and social change marked by the suppression of the chieftaincy of Barani and the slow process of emancipation of former slaves (*rimaaybe*). Degradation of natural resources, on the one hand, and heavy cattle taxation (*jangal*)

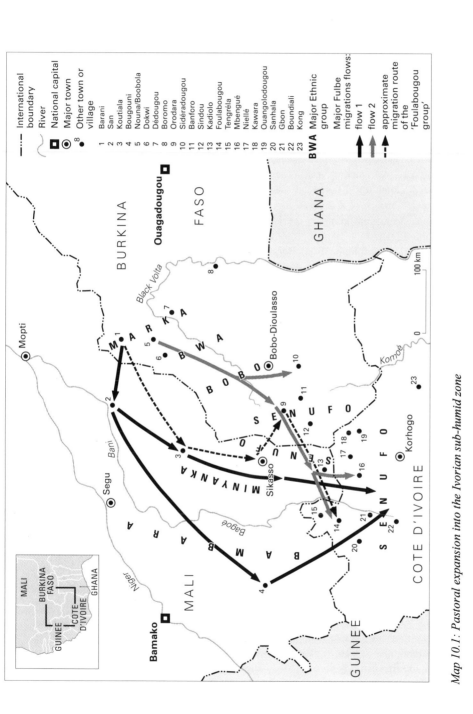

Map 10.1: Pastoral expansion into the Ivorian sub-humid zone

imposed by the Chief of Barani Belko Widi (1937-1959), on the other hand, caused large numbers of Fulbe, particularly members of the Diallube clan, to abandon the area.

Initial migration was characterised by several phases. A short period of stability due to an administrative intervention followed after the first movements. Confronted with the impact of increased out-migration, the Chief of Barani requested the assistance of the French administration (Benoît 1979: 169). Since health aspects were an important matter of concern to the French administration, they tried to control the spread of cattle diseases by limiting nomadic movements. The colonial authorities forced Fulbe migrants who had settled in the San and Koutiala regions to return to Barani to pay their taxes.

In spite of these provisions, the pastoral migratory process continued and even gained in importance. A French census in the main districts of northern Côte d'Ivoire in early 1950 listed a total of 942 Fulbe who had settled in the border area between Côte d'Ivoire and Mali (Holas 1966). Except for seasonal migrants coming from Bambaraland (Bougouni, Segu) and going to the Ivorian central savannah, most of the Fulbe who settled among Senufo peasants in Mali worked as hired herders during that period.

The migration of Fulbe from Barani continued until the beginning of the 1970s. Cattle-owners of the chieftaincy started to move to the south-west of Burkina Faso and some crossed the border into Mali. The majority of Fulbe informants explained their movements as due in the first place to a lack of sufficient pasture land rather than a shortage of rain or unfavourable rainfall distribution. The first arrivals established themselves in the Bougouni area, in particular in Gwanadougou, where there is a long-standing Fulbe population. Oral traditions mention Fulbe cattle-herders finding water and open spaces in southern Mali where cultivated fields did not impede their herds' mobility.

In the literature dealing with pastoral migrations to Côte d'Ivoire, the argument of the accessibility of the international border between Mali and Côte d'Ivoire has been used as an explanation for crossing from Burkina Faso to Mali (Bernardet 1984). This tends to accredit the idea that the first Fulbe migrants intentionally crossed into Mali. The southern Sikasso area was open to the transhumans coming from Segu and even from Barani but the accessibility of southern Mali and its border do not account for the choice of itinerary passing through Mali to reach Côte d'Ivoire.

The areas of San, Koutiala and Sikasso are zones of concentration and dispersion of Fulbe stockowners from Burkina Faso, and also the principal places of origin of their Malian counterparts. The Fulbe from Burkina Faso mentioned the lack of pasture as the main reason for their migration. The Fulbe from Mali left in the wake of a pastoral dispersion, and as the main reason for their departure to Côte d'Ivoire they emphasised the desire to make money in order to increase their livestock numbers. These Fulbe were part of a general movement provoked by the dispersion of the Fulbe from Barani who were leaving San. Information on family migrations of Malian Fulbe show they followed the majority of Fulbe originating from Burkina Faso by taking the same migratory routes leading to Bougouni and Sikasso. The fodder and water possibilities in Sikasso made this region an attractive meeting place for several pastoral groups. From Sikasso, the first cattle-herders entered Côte d'Ivoire between 1960 and 1965 for political reasons (see below), after having lived in Mali for more than two decades. Some other groups came to Côte d'Ivoire due to ecological constraints. The main points of entry are located to the east of the Kolondieba-Tengréla road axis, with Fulbe groups from the north-east generally moving towards Korhogo District.

Only a few Fulbe migrants from Bougouni passed Kolondieba before entering Côte d'Ivoire. The majority crossed the border (formed by the Bagoé River) between Mali and Côte d'Ivoire at Débété, about thirty kilometres to the west of Tengréla. In the border area, located between the Sudanese and the sub-Sudanese ecological zones, the two villages of Sanhala and Gbon were important during pastoral migration into the sub-Sudanese zone. Some Zebu cattle-owners from the Sahelian zone spent between five and ten years in this climatic transitional area to allow their cattle to adapt to the semi-humid conditions. Small groups of cattle-owners in search of pastures and water accounted for most of these migratory movements from Burkina Faso as far as the town of Boundiali in Mali.

Migration flows: The entry into Côte d'Ivoire through southwestern Burkina Faso
The second migratory group was made up of Fulbe cattle-owners who entered the north of Côte d'Ivoire from the extreme south-west of Burkina Faso and the south of Mali (Kadiolo District). The first groups arrived in northern Côte d'Ivoire during the reign of Fulbe Chief Douramane Sidibé (1959-1972).

Having spent a few years in southwestern Burkina Faso, and especially in the area around Orodara or on the north of the Banfora Plain, Fulbe migrants moved on to Mali, crossing Kadiolo District. Here, in the extreme south of Sikasso, the migratory routes split. The first route goes to Tengréla District in the west, while the second heads for Korhogo District in the south. Mbengué and Niellé in the Korhogo region are two important centres of Fulbe dispersion in Côte d'Ivoire. Various pastoral groups were established in Niellé at the beginning of the 1960s and, in 1965, the first families came from Mali and other places. Some of the Fulbe migrants, who initially lived in the south of Bobo-Dioulasso and near Orodara, went directly to Ouangolodougou. They were attracted by its location in the border area because it was sparsely inhabited and therefore a favourable place for their herds. Various factors drew the Fulbe to Kawara. It is one of the oldest Muslim centres and a local Fulbe chief performs the role of host (*yaatigi*) for Fulbe migrants.

Some semi-nomadic Fulbe groups of varying sizes live in the border area between Burkina Faso and Côte d'Ivoire. Some came from Burkina Faso but others were originally from the Niger Delta in Mali.

Migration flows: Direct and intentional migrations (Burkina Faso-Côte d'Ivoire)
Of all the movements into the north of Côte d'Ivoire, the direct and intentional migrations in the 1970s and 1980s were the most important. It was during this period that the national livestock policy operated under optimal political and institutional conditions. The advantages Fulbe migrants could benefit from on their arrival, including for example free veterinary care, suggest that the Ivorian livestock policy contributed to increased pastoral migration into the country.

Two examples of direct and intentional migration of Fulbe families that settled in the north of Côte d'Ivoire allow an understanding of the main characteristics and mechanisms of pastoral movement. In the first example, a family of Fulbe Sidibé left Loulouni, a village south of Sikasso, intending to migrate to Boundiali District. The second concerns Fulbe Diallube who left Bama, thirty kilometres north of Bobo, to go to Kawara in the border district of Ouangolodougou. The two families, who made direct displacements, show similarities concerning the period of migration (1980), the time-span of their movement (about six weeks) and the total distance covered (200 to 300 km). Direct migrations, with the clear aim of reaching a certain destination, are seasonal movements only carried out in the dry season. This is an exhausting form of mobility during which herds are moved by young herders, while the other members of the household travel by car. Soon after departure from the camp, the group moves in such a way that no animal can detach itself from the herd. The daily distance covered varies from between ten to twenty kilometres, with breaks of one to three nights so that the animals can rest. By so doing, Fulbe herders try to prevent dramatic weight losses among the animals. Water and the birth of calves are two factors that influence the rhythm and progress of the herd. For example, if the distance between two watering points is too long or too short, herders may decide to accelerate or to slow down the pace of the herd accordingly.

The impact of national and regional livestock policies on Fulbe migration
With the arrival of Fulbe pastoral groups in Côte d'Ivoire came the widespread practice of herding and related activities. National and international livestock policies towards Fulbe transhumants, at least in the Ivorian case, contributed to an increase in pastoral migration from the Sahelian semi-arid zones to the sub-humid zones. In the latter areas, the Ivorian government developed a market-oriented policy to promote the livestock economy and the sedentarisation of mobile populations. Pastoral production of meat for urban markets was promoted and development planners launched projects to encourage the settlement of cattle-herders, like that in La Palé in the northern part of the country (Arditi 1990; Bernardet 1984; Diallo 1999).

At a regional level, the control of cattle diseases related to pastoral mobility required the cooperation of several countries. Côte d'Ivoire and neighbouring Burkina Faso and Mali signed agreements regarding the cattle trade and transnational movement of herds. The *Communauté Economique du Bétail et de la Viande* (CEBV) agreement determined that cattle could only cross national boundaries by predetermined passages, and defined administrative and health prerequisites. At the border between Mali and Côte d'Ivoire two crossings were created (at Tienko and Tengréla) and three checkpoints (Niellé, Ouangolo and Doropo) were set up between Burkina Faso and Côte d'Ivoire. While cattle-traders use these crossings, cattle-herders very often avoid the authorities' checkpoints. According to the Ministry of Agriculture, the total percentage of controlled cattle fell from 64 per cent in 1983 to 16% in 1993.

Another example illustrating the impact of national policies on Fulbe rural migration is the attitude adopted by the Malian government at the beginning of the 1960s. After independence, the cattle trade between Mali and Côte d'Ivoire was considered an illegal activity for political and economic reasons. The two countries had different national economies at that time: Mali had a socialist regime (1960-1968) and Côte d'Ivoire a market-oriented system. Unlike most West African countries that were using the CFA Franc as their official currency, the Malian government decided to introduce a new local currency. Simultaneously a rigid regulatory system was introduced to curb smuggling and illicit trade activities. Incidents of the unjust confiscation of Fulbe cattle on the assumption that the herd was destined for trade created misunderstandings and increased tensions between the Fulbe and local authorities.

Within the framework of several policies aimed at protecting environmental resources, the Malian government outlawed the practice of bush fires. The perception by Malian local authorities of semi-nomadic Fulbe as anarchic users of space had a considerable impact on pastoral mobility. For the first Fulbe groups on their way to Côte d'Ivoire via Sikasso, the beginning of Modibo Kéita's rule as the first president of independent Mali was a difficult period. Relations between the Fulbe and the administrative authorities in Sikasso deteriorated to the point where a considerable number of cattle-herders were even starting to leave the district. It is said that Modibo Kéita carried out a raid in Sikasso after which Fulbe cattle-herders became the target of National Forestry Commission agents, with members of Fulbe groups often being wrongly accused of starting bush fires and forced to pay fines. Such events forced many Fulbe cattle-herders to go to Côte d'Ivoire around 1962 where they settled in Boundiali District. In 1960, others returned to Burkina Faso, not to their area of origin but to the south-west of the country, among them the founders of Foulabougou in Tengréla District.

Foulabougou, a 'Fulbe village' in Côte d'Ivoire: A case study

Foulabougou is one of the most important pastoral settlements from where many Fulbe spread over the northern savannah in Côte d'Ivoire. The 1988 National Census indicates 706 inhabitants in Foulabougou. The foundation of Foulabougou (meaning 'Fulbe residence') in Tengréla District marked a significant stage in the history of pastoral migration. The Fulbe who left Barani in the 1940s and 1850s founded the village in 1963. They were among the first Fulbe to move into Côte d'Ivoire not via Tengréla (as was the case of many migrants at that time) but via southwestern Burkina Faso. From Barani, they went initially to Koutiala, where they became followers of an influential religious leader, Alfa Yeroru, who acted as spiritual guide and leader at the same time. After having spent more than ten years in Farakoro, he moved with his group to the Sikasso area. One year after their immigration into the area, Alfa Yeroru's group left Mali in the early 1960s due to the political problems mentioned above. The group moved eastwards to Burkina Faso, in particular to the area of Orodara. The tsetse fly is a major constraint to cattle-herding in this area and it, combined with a lack of hygiene, caused many casualties among both the human and livestock populations, and forced the Fulbe three years after their arrival to leave Orodara. They moved on to join their parents who had settled close to the current site of Foulabougou.

Foulabougou changed from being a nomadic camp to a sedentary village and, in the context of nomadism or transhumance, also a centre of dispersion. Some Sidibé families left Foulabougou to settle in the Korhogo region. Unlike other Fulbe camps with round huts and thatched roofs, the houses built in Foulabougou were rectangular and covered with leaves. In 1996, the population of the village was distributed over thirty-one Fulbe families and four Riimaybe families who had followed their former masters. The Fulbe say that the Riimaybe are employed as labourers but members of this group do not appear to be engaged in cattle keeping for their former masters. The Riimaaybe of Foulabougou, who are all Muslims, cultivate rice and cotton and invest their agricultural incomes in cattle. The camp of Foulabougou shifted from a pastoral vocation to an intellectual and religious centre whose role is still increasing among the Fulbe diaspora in Côte d'Ivoire. Traditionally, three people occupy positions of leadership in the Fulbe community: the political leader, the spiritual leader and the imam. In reality, Al Hajj Ali Sidibé, a marabout, son and successor of the first religious leader, remains a central character. He has an excellent reputation across the Ivorian savannah and many Fulbe pay him regular visits to receive his blessing.

Another type of Fulbe mobility due to religious factors is the pilgrimage to religious centres to participate in events celebrated in the Muslim calendar. The Fulbe from Burkina Faso maintain religious ties with the Islamic elites of the religious centre of Luunkan (close to Barani). Luunkan, a former local centre of diffusion of Tijaaniya in western Burkina Faso, is today an active centre of pilgrimage that the Fulbe visit annually either to take part in the prayer of the *haram* or in the anniversary of the birth of the prophet Mohammed. During these special celebrations, Fulbe living in Côte d'Ivoire pay a financial contribution to the imam's delegate. In the diaspora situation, the role of religious centres and leaders will probably become increasingly important as indicated by the growing number of visitors. However the practical problems of organising travel to Luunkan explain why relations with this centre in Burkina Faso are decreasing. Fulbe living in Côte d'Ivoire now prefer to go to Foulabougou.

Conclusion

Pastoralists are mobile by nature. The Fulbe's complex mobility is adopting new forms under changing circumstances and cannot only be explained in terms of migration. In this chapter an attempt was made to study Fulbe movements from western Burkina Faso and Mali to the north of Côte d'Ivoire as a form of 'expansion'. A distinction has been made between direct or intentional and indirect or non-intentional migration. The direct form is characterised by flight from a range of insecurities but also rapid, seasonal movements, such as dry-season and rainy-season transhumance (also known as 'circulation'). Indirect migration is understood as a long-term movement carried out in successive stages (similar to 'migratory drift'). In practice, the forms occur in combination and the Fulbe themselves do not distinguish between them.

The indirect migrations in search of new migratory routes were initiated by ecological and political changes in western Burkina Faso (Barani) resulting in pastoral movements to the San area in Mali. Ecological factors and administrative pressure pushed people further via Koutiala and Sikasso into Côte d'Ivoire. A second migratory group comes from Orodara and Banfora in the extreme south-west of Burkina Faso. By crossing Kadiolo District they moved on to Mali and from there, some followed the route to Tengréla, while others headed for Korhogo in Côte d'Ivoire.

The most important movements into Côte d'Ivoire were the direct migrations in the 1970s and 1980s. A favourable livestock policy in Côte d'Ivoire at that time allowed many Fulbe migrants to profit from free veterinary care and contributed to increased movements into the country. These direct migrations may best be compared to seasonal movements, an exhausting form of mobility with daily distances varying from ten to twenty kilometres and the route going more or less straight to the final destination.

The dispersion of the Fulbe throughout the Sahelian zone and their gradual infiltration into the West African sub-humid zones has resulted in the occupation of ecological niches and cooperation and coexistence with peasants. At present, population pressure, internal migration and increases in the cattle population are imposing limitations on Fulbe movements in northern Côte d'Ivoire where competition for natural resources is resulting in conflicts between them and the peasants. The pastoral way of life that generally implies a high degree of mobility has become a matter of concern not only for the pastoralists themselves and for their neighbours, but also for governments and development planners who are trying to control the Fulbe by promoting sedentarisation. However, the movement of people with its own internal logic and dynamics is an ongoing process, characteristic of this part of the West African savannah where people are on the move for ritual, economic and political reasons.

References

Arditi, C. 1990. 'Les Peuls, les Senufo et les Veterinaires', *Cahiers des Sciences Humaines* 26 (1/2): 137-53.

Benoît, M. 1979, *Le Chemin des Peuls du Boobola*, Paris: Orstom.

Bernardet, P. 1984, *Les Peuls Semi-transhumants de Côte d'Ivoire*, Paris: L'Harmattan.

Bohannan, P. 1954, 'The Migration and Expansion of the Tiv', *Africa* XXIV: 2-16.

Bonfiglioli, A.M. 1988, *Dudal. Histoire de Famille et Histoire de Troupeau Chez un Groupe Wodaabe du Niger*, Paris: Editions de la MSH, Cambridge University Press.

Botte, R., J. Boutrais & J. Schmitz (eds) 1999, *Figures Peules*, Paris: Karthala.

Braukämper, U. 1993, *Migration und ethnischer Wandel*, Stuttgart: Franz Steiner.

Burnham, P. 1996, *The Politics of Cultural Difference in Northern Cameroon*, Washington: Smithsonian Institution Press.

Diallo, Y. 1997, *Les Fulbe du Boobola. Genèse et Evolution de l'État de Barani (Burkina Faso)*, Köln: Rüdiger Köppe Verlag.

Diallo, Y. 1999, 'Dimensions Sociales et Politiques de l'Expansion Pastorale en Zone Semi-humide Ivoirienne', in V. Azarya, A. Breedveld, M. de Bruijn & H. van Dijk, *Pastoralists Under Pressure? Fulbe Societies Confronting Change in West Africa*, Leiden: Brill, pp. 211-36.

Dupire, M. 1970, *Organisation Sociale des Peul*, Paris: Plon.

Galaty, J.G. & P. Bonte 1991, *Herders, Warriors and Traders. Pastoralism in Africa*, Boulder, San Francisco, Oxford: Westview Press.

Holas, B. 1966, *Les Sénoufo (y Compris les Minyanka)*, Paris: PUF.

Irwin, P. 1981, *Liptako Speaks. History from Oral Tradition in Africa*, Princeton N.J.: Princeton University Press.

Izard, M. 1985, *Le Yatenga Précolonial*, Paris: Karthala.

Schlee, G. 1994, *Identities on the Move*, Nairobi: Gideon S. Were Press.

Skinner, E.P. 1964, *The Mossi of the Upper Volta: The Political Development of a Sudanese People*, Stanford: Stanford University Press.

Stenning, D.J. 1959, *Savannah Nomads*, London: IAI.

Turton, D. 1991, 'Movement and Warfare in the Lower Omo Valley', in J.G. Galaty. & P. Bonte (eds), *Herders, Warriors and Traders. Pastoralism in Africa*, Boulder, San Francisco, Oxford: Westview Press, pp. 145-69.

11

Mobility and exclusion: Conflicts between autochthons and allochthons during political liberalisation in Cameroon

Piet Konings

Political liberalisation in Africa has often been accompanied by a somewhat paradoxical obsession with autochthony, leading to more or less violent forms of exclusion of migrants. South West Province, one of the two provinces in the Anglophone region of Cameroon, provides an interesting case study to illustrate this striking phenomenon. In an area where a plantation economy was established during German colonial rule, massive labour migration has been encouraged from elsewhere in the country, particularly from the other Anglophone province, North West Province. Following large-scale settlement of northwestern migrants in the South West, the 'autochthonous' population began to resent their increasing domination in demographic, economic and political terms. When the government and its regional allies felt threatened by widespread opposition and federalist/-secessionist tendencies in the Anglophone region during the political liberalisation process in the 1990s, they started exploiting existing tensions between the 'autochthonous' and 'allochthonous' populations to boost South-West identity, promote various forms of ethnic cleansing, and thus split the Anglophone front.

Introduction

It is striking and somewhat paradoxical that the current processes of globalisation and liberalisation often appear to restrict rather than to promote a free flow of people and labour. Throughout the world, various forms of exclusion of migrants can be observed, even of second and third-generation immigrants. Western countries are witnessing not only widespread attempts to control and regulate the increased flow of migrants, particularly from less-developed countries but also the development of serious tensions between 'autochthons' and 'allochthons', the former fearing loss of identity and preferential access to scarce resources such as employment, the growth of right-wing movements and parties and, in extreme situations, such as Bosnia, attempts at ethnic cleansing (cf. Geschiere & Nyamnjoh 2000). In many parts of Africa, too, mobility appears to have become more and more problematic during economic and political liberalisation, as is manifest in the intensification of conflicts between people who claim to be indigenous to a certain territory and settlers or strangers, even long-standing migrants of the same nationality.

Economic and political liberalisation in Africa has created space for autochthons to articulate their long entrenched feelings about allochthonous domination in demographic, economic and political terms. Their struggles for control over economic and political resources are mostly instigated or fuelled by political entrepreneurs. With the introduction of multipartyism, the ruling party and government often fear being outvoted during local and regional elections by 'strangers' who tend to support the opposition for the representation and defence of their interests. They are inclined to encourage a distinction between 'ethnic citizens' and 'ethnic strangers' rather than to emphasise national integration and national citizenship (Mamdani 1996). Such a strategy naturally serves the purpose of winning votes and consolidating power at national and regional levels.

Some of the struggles between autochthons and allochthons have occurred at the local level, notably over control of land (cf. Simo 1997; Mvondo 1998). Others have occurred at the national level between nationals and immigrants of African, Asian and European origin especially regarding control over employment and business. In Gabon, for instance, there have been violent actions by nationals against immigrants from neighbouring African countries, Lebanon and France (Gray 1998). Economic and political liberalisation in Tanzania has been accompanied by a rise in social tensions between Tanzanians and the prosperous Asian business community and calls for the indigenisation of the latter's property (Heilman 1998). Most clashes, however, appear to have taken place at the regional level, particularly where autochthonous ethnic groups feel dominated by allochthonous ethnic groups. One serious conflict between autochthonous and allochthonous ethnic groups took place in Rift Valley Province in Kenya between the Kalenjin and Maasai on the one hand, and the Kikuyu and Luo on the other (Médard 1996; Heilman 1998; Ogachi 1999). Another outbreak of violence occurred in 1993-1996 between the autochthonous ethnic minority groups and the allochthonous Banyarwarda (migrants from Rwanda) in Northern Kivou in the Democratic Republic of Congo (Mathieu & Tsongo 1998; Pourtier 1996).

Several conflicts between autochthons and allochthons have emerged during political liberalisation in Cameroon, albeit in most cases of a less violent nature than in Kenya and the Democratic Republic of Congo (cf. Socpa 1999; Tabapssi 1999). In this chapter the focus is on the deteriorating relations between autochthons and allochthons in the coastal forest area of Anglophone Cameroon, present-day South West Province (see Map 11.1). This province provides an interesting case study as it is one of the few regions along the West African coast where a plantation economy was established during the German colonial period (1884-1916) (Epale 1985; Konings 1993). The plantation economy stimulated large-scale labour migration to the coastal estates and, more importantly, increased the settlement of plantation labour in the area after retirement. This chapter considers why the current obsession with the autochthony-allochthony issue in South West Province relates foremost to relations between the inhabitants of the two provinces of Anglophone Cameroon: autochthonous South Westerners versus allochthonous North Westerners. This is all the more surprising since political liberalisation has created space for the emergence and rapid growth of several Anglophone associations, stressing their Anglophone identity and solidarity. These movements have attempted to mobilise the Anglophone population as a whole against the Francophone-dominated unitary state, which is accused of 'marginalising, exploiting and assimilating' the Anglophone minority (All Anglophone Conference 1993), and demand a return to the federal state or outright secession (Konings 1996a; Konings & Nyamnjoh 1997). The South-West elite's fear of renewed North-West domination during political liberalisation was one of the main reasons for their incitement of the autochthonous minority against the dominant and exploitative northwestern settlers and their request for government protection.

The South-West plantation economy and labour mobility

The continuous support given by the German colonial state (1884-1916) to plantation production led to the large-scale expropriation of approximately 300,000 acres of very fertile volcanic soil around Mount Cameroon in the South West Province and the expulsion of the original occupants of the expropriated lands, in particular the Bakweri, to prescribed native reserves (Courade 1981/82; Molua 1985). Nearly all the estates in the area were held by German planters.

During the First World War, the British occupied the area and confiscated the German planters' estates. By 1922, however, the British Mandate Authority had already decided to get rid of them, as the administrative costs of maintaining them were prohibitive. It seriously considered returning the plantation lands to their original owners but finally dropped the idea. Instead, it was decided that it would be in the best interests of the territory and its inhabitants to place the plantations back in the hands of foreign private enterprise. They were put up for auction in 1922 and 1924. For a variety of reasons, the vast majority of the estates were bought back by the former German owners (Konings 1993). One notable exception was the estates acquired by the United Africa Company (UAC), a well-known Unilever subsidiary (Fieldhouse 1978 and 1994). After its foundation in 1929, the UAC took over three local estates from the African and Eastern Trading Company (AETC) and, in 1932, bought another estate from the *West-afrikanische Handelsgesellschaft* at Lobe. Its most important estates are located in today's Ndian Division of South West Province, bordering eastern Nigeria. Its estates came to be known as Pamol Ltd, the principal private agro-industrial enterprise in the country (Konings 1998).

At the beginning of the Second World War, the German estates were expropriated again by the Custodian of Enemy Property. After the war, a decision had to be reached once more on how to dispose of the properties. The educated Bakweri elite, organised in the so-called Bakweri Land Committee, immediately started to agitate for the retrieval of its ancestral lands. It sent several petitions, first to the British Crown and subse-

Map 11.1: Republic of Cameroon

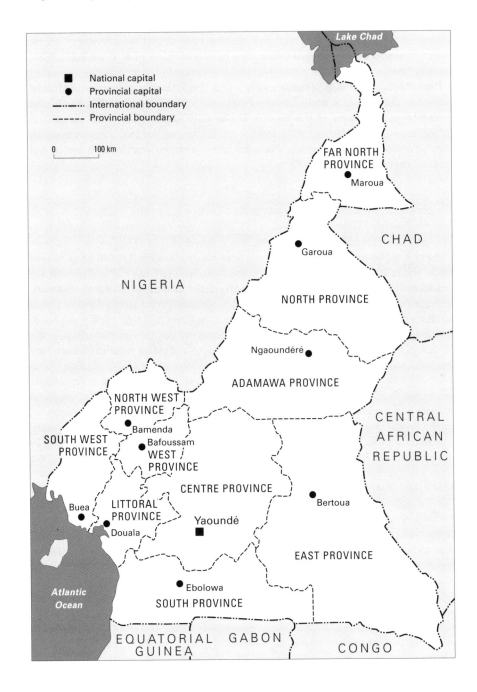

quently to the United Nations, as Britain had assumed responsibility for the administration of the territory under United Nations' Trusteeship after the war (Molua 1985). However, after considerable deliberation, the British Trusteeship Authority declined to surrender the ex-German plantation lands to their original owners and announced in November 1946 that the lands would be leased to a newly established statutory corporation, the Cameroon Development Corporation (CDC) (Ardener *et al.* 1960; Epale 1985; Konings 1993).

Plantation agriculture is labour-intensive and by 1914, German planters needed about 18,000 workers. Pamol's labour force gradually rose from 1,200 to 3,500. The CDC, the second largest employer in the country (being only surpassed by the government) initially employed between 20,000 and 25,000 labourers. Today it employs approximately 14,000 labourers (Konings 1993 and 1998). The procurement of a regular and adequate supply of labour was for a long time a major problem for plantation production. The German planters experienced almost insurmountable problems procuring sufficient labour from the local communities which were not only sparsely populated but also hated working for the expropriators of their land. This compelled them to import a considerable number of labourers from outside Cameroon, in particular from various West African countries (Rudin 1938; Rüger 1960). This imported labour, however, could not solve the acute labour problem. It also turned out to be expensive which was a major reason for its quick abandonment. The gradual opening up and pacification of the more densely populated areas of the interior revealed their enormous potential for solving the labour problem. The large majority of people in the interior, however, were not ready to accept voluntary labour contracts so various forms of coercion were employed during the entire German period to 'free' labour from the interior to the plantations. Initially, large numbers of men from rebellious areas were simply seized and sent to the plantations for up to six years as a kind of penal labour force, sometimes receiving no pay at all. Later on, a labour recruitment system was developed based on the continuous coercive pressures of private recruiters, local officials and suitably bribed African chiefs (Halldén 1968; Chilver 1971; Clarence-Smith 1989). Near the end of German colonial rule, limited head taxes and hut taxes were imposed which encouraged Africans to work on the plantations. Persons unable to pay taxes in cash would be turned over to private employers who paid the tax and the fee of ten Marks per head.

The most important inland recruitment areas were the Yaounde region and the Grassfields area, both in the Francophone part of Cameroon and occupied by the Bamileke, and present-day North West Province, part of the later Anglophone region and occupied by various ethnic groups closely related to the Bamileke. It was during the British Mandate period that a gradual transition occurred from forced to voluntary labour migration. This was facilitated by a variety of factors including the growing need for cash, improved conditions of service (especially the provision of land for food cultivation, the so-called 'chop farms') and active recruitment through ethnic, community and family networks.

There were initially remarkable differences between the CDC and Pamol concerning labour recruitment areas (Konings 1993 and 1998). When the CDC was established in

1946/47, it was faced with a serious decline in the supply of labour from Francophone Cameroon. Labour mobility from this area used to be encouraged by forms of forced labour imposed by the French (Kaptue 1986). By 1926 approximately 52% of the plantation labour force originated from the French Mandate area (Table 11.1). This figure gradually declined to only 1% in the 1980s. The efforts of the French Mandate Authority to stabilise labour within its home regions and to prevent it from leaving the French Mandate area greatly contributed to this decline. The expansion of more remunerative employment opportunities in Francophone Cameroon and the rising cost of living in Anglophone Cameroon in the aftermath of independence and reunification in 1961 brought about a further reduction in labour migration from Francophone to Anglophone Cameroon (Ndongko 1975). Apart from a temporary influx of labour from neighbouring eastern Nigeria (Ardener *et al.* 1960) and a steady labour force from South West Province, this decline was largely compensated for by an increasing number of labour migrants from North West Province. This province had a higher population density, was much later in developing cash-crop production, and lacked job opportunities outside the traditional sector.

Table 11.1: Regional composition of the CDC and Pamol labour forces (%)

	1926	1941	1950	1960s	1970s	1980s	1990s
CDC							
North West Province	14.0	37.0	32.5	43.5	54.5	73.5	71.0
South West Province	33.0	27.5	33.0	25.0	38.0	24.5	27.0
Francophone Cameroon	52.0	25.0	13.0	4.5	5.0	1.0	1.0
Eastern Nigeria	1.0	10.5	21.5	27.0	2.5	1.0	1.0
Total	100	100	100	100	100	100	100
Pamol							
North West Province	n.a.	n.a.	n.a.	5.0	27.0	41.8	54.0
South West Province	n.a.	n.a.	n.a.	13.0	47.0	44.4	33.5
Francophone Cameroon	n.a.	n.a.	n.a.	1.7	1.7	1.3	1.0
Eastern Nigeria	n.a.	n.a.	n.a.	80.3	24.3	12.5	11.5
Total	n.a.	n.a.	n.a.	100	100	100	100

Source: Konings 1993 and 1998

Pamol faced even more problems than the CDC in recruiting sufficient labour. Its main estates are located in one of the most marginalised areas of Cameroon where the cost of living is extremely high due to regular food shortages. Cameroonian workers were, consequently, inclined to seek employment on the CDC estates. In these circumstances, neighbouring eastern Nigeria readily became the main supplier of labour to the Pamol estates. In 1961, eastern Nigerians accounted for 80% of the total Pamol labour force (Table 11.1). Since independence and reunification, the dominant position of Nigerian workers on the Pamol estates has rapidly declined. However, managerial failure to recruit sufficient labour in Anglophone Cameroon formed an insurmountable obstacle to the complete realisation of the government's Cameroonisation policy: in 1970 Nigerian workers still accounted for a quarter of the total Pamol labour force. From the 1970s onwards, a certain stabilisation in labour recruitment from Nigeria can be seen at around 12%. Under constant pressure to 'cameroonise', the management staged a renewed recruiting drive in Anglophone Cameroon, first in the nearby Ndian and Manyu Divisions of South West Province and later in various divisions of North West Province. As at the CDC, northwestern workers at present account for the majority of the labour force on the Pamol estates (54%).

Labour mobility and relations between autochthons and allochthons on the southwestern estates prior to political liberalisation

It is striking that there have been few serious clashes between autochthonous and stranger ethnic groups on the southwestern estates. Tensions between autochthons and allochthons are most likely to arise when stranger ethno-regional groups appear to occupy a dominant position on the estates.

The dominant position of eastern Nigerian workers on the CDC and particularly on the Pamol estates in the nationalist climate after the Second World War gave rise to serious frictions between autochthonous Anglophone Cameroonian workers and eastern Nigerian strangers. During the 1947-1960 period, Anglophone Cameroonian workers on the CDC and Pamol estates undertook a series of collective and informal actions aimed at the removal of Igbo and Ibibio supervisory staff and management (Konings 1993: 69 and 1998: 80), repeatedly calling upon management and government to promote a rapid Cameroonisation of the labour force and management staff. Since independence and reunification, former animosities between Anglophone Cameroonian and Nigerian workers appear to have largely subsided, probably because Nigerians have become a relatively small, stranger minority group on the estates, and are thus no longer perceived by Anglophone Cameroonians as a threat. During fieldwork, some Nigerian workers expressed the view that their best strategy was to assume a low profile so as not to encourage envy and arouse tensions (cf. Kleis 1975). Although conflicts have not disappeared altogether, the social distance between Nigerian and Cameroonian workers appears to have diminished (DeLancey 1973).

After the conflict between Anglophone Cameroonian and Nigerian workers, a new potential source of friction could be in relations between the autochthonous southwestern minority and the northwestern majority on the estates. Extended clashes between these two groups have not yet occurred. On the contrary, all researchers on estate labour agree that southwestern and northwestern workers usually live and work together peacefully (Ardener *et al.* 1960; DeLancey 1973; Kofele-Kale 1981; Konings 1993 and 1998). Both groups tend to organise not only on an ethnic but also on an inter-ethnic basis, as is seen in the membership of churches and trade unions. They have engaged from time to time in common struggles against managerial control and exploitation in the workplace. One reason for this unexpected phenomenon is the consistent policy of the management, as well as church and union leaders, to mobilise and organise workers on a multi-ethnic basis. This policy seems to have created a certain measure of understanding and tolerance among the workers for each other's socio-cultural backgrounds, thus fostering bonds of companionship and friendship across ethno-regional boundaries. Another reason is the general use of Pidgin English, which has helped overcome communication barriers between the various ethnic groups. A third reason is the marked preference of workers themselves for ethnically-mixed living and working arrangements, partly stemming from their belief that witchcraft is most likely to occur among close relatives and tribesmen (Ardener *et al.* 1960; Konings 1993). The most important reason, however, appears to be the shared living and working conditions on the estates, which are classical examples of occupational communities. However, while relations between southwestern and northwestern workers appear to be more or less peaceful, relations between southwestern and northwestern *managers* have been marked by fierce conflicts caused by the persistent attempts of the southwestern managerial minority to establish control over agro-industrial enterprises located in 'their' region (see below).[1]

The effects of labour mobility on the relations between autochthons and allochthons in local communities in the South West appear to have been more dramatic. While initially most migrant workers returned to their region of origin after short spells of work on the estates, an increasing number gradually decided to settle in the South West after retirement. The CDC and Pamol management also proved incapable of accommodating all their workers in the labour camps on the estates and some workers were obliged to find accommodation in the villages and towns surrounding the estates. Settlers were soon joined by fellow members of their ethnic group who wanted to grow food or cash crops on the fertile lands or to become artisans, traders or employees in local enterprises. In some coastal districts, like Victoria District, the local population "almost became overwhelmed by these strangers even before the Second World War" (Gwan 1975). Indeed, strangers rapidly found themselves in the majority in local towns and villages.

Initially, strangers were welcomed by the local population and given land in usufruct, thus becoming more or less incorporated in the land-giving lineage. They were usually expected to provide a small recompense in kind as a token of appreciation for the land-giver. According to Ardener *et al.* (1960), the procedure for a stranger to have access to land in the Bakweri area was to provide a pig for the villagers. He was then accorded a usufruct without further payments of rents. Yet, it soon became evident that the local tenure system could not cope with the increasing flow of strangers and that local institutions were too weak to enforce the existing norms and rules. The system collapsed. A

---

[1] Unlike on the CDC and Pamol estates in Anglophone Cameroon, some severe clashes between autochthonous and stranger workers have reportedly occurred on agro-industrial enterprises situated in the southern part of Francophone Cameroon, especially on the SOSUCAM sugar estates at Mbandjock (Barbier *et al.* 1980; Ngend 1982). Two factors seem to be responsible for the violent confrontation between southern and northern workers on the latter enterprise in 1976. First of all, the existence of occupational and ethno-regional overlapping has always constituted a potentially explosive situation at SOSUCAM: the higher-paid jobs are occupied by the better-educated and skilled workers from the south and the less well-paid jobs by the uneducated and unskilled workers from the north. And secondly, the unskilled northern sugar-cane cutters tend to oppose any integrative efforts and prefer to live separately. These factors continue to create problems for the achievement of a peaceful coexistence between both ethno-regional groups, and do not encourage workers' solidarity.

land market quickly developed in those areas with important stranger concentrations (Meek 1957; Fisiy 1992). The resulting unprincipled access to land degenerated into numerous land disputes, especially in Victoria District where land shortages rapidly developed. Disputes arose because different villages sought to sell the same piece of land to strangers. Even strangers who had lived in an area for a long time could rent land to other strangers. A handful of local residents were gaining handsomely from this breakdown of customary tenure as they offered communal land to strangers for money.

Local chiefs and elders regularly protested to the British administration about the unscrupulous land-grabbing by strangers in their areas of jurisdiction but they did not usually obtain the expected support. The British authorities acknowledged the existing land problems but they did not bring about any structural change, not wanting to disturb the economic role of immigrants whose entrepreneurial spirit and hard work were said to compare favourably with the consumerist attitudes and laziness of the local population. In addition, the term 'native' was not clearly defined in the Native Lands and Rights Ordinance. In Section 2 a 'native' was defined as a person, one of whose parents was a member of any ethnic group indigenous to the British Mandate territory. The provision in Section 3 that "it shall not be lawful for any native holding a right of occupancy to sell, transfer possession, bequeath or otherwise alienate his title to a non-native except with the consent of the governor" therefore did not apply to any inhabitant of Anglophone Cameroon living in South West Province.

Land was not the only reason for the development of antagonistic relations between autochthons and strangers in local communities. The local population envied the settlers' success in agriculture, trade and other entrepreneurial activities. Moreover, they resented their frequent disrespect for local authority and customs, their regular seduction of local women and their alleged disinclination to invest in local development, preferring instead to transfer any accumulated capital to their region of origin (Ardener *et al.* 1960; Ardener 1962). It was generally believed that settlers were only interested in exploiting and dominating the local population, while continuing to be loyal to their own ethnic group, which was ultimately evidenced by their frequent desire either to return home at the end of their working life or to be buried in the land of their ancestors.

The simmering conflict between natives and strangers has sometimes exploded in the past, leading to various forms of ethnic cleansing. Strikingly, any violent conflict of this nature used to occur between autochthons and settlers originating from outside Anglophone Cameroon. As on the estates, the local population, often instigated by regional politicians (Kleis 1975; Amazee 1990), directed its anger after the Second World War at the eastern Nigerian settlers who had come to dominate the regional administration and trade. Particularly the Igbo became victims of verbal and physical attacks by frustrated local inhabitants and were often told to return home. Early in February 1948 the Bakweri Native Authority passed the following rules to control relations between natives and Igbo:

- Nobody is allowed to sell his or her house to an Igbo, neither may anybody give his or her house for rentage to an Igbo.
- No farmland may be sold to an Igbo or rented to an Igbo.

- Nobody may allow an Igbo to enter any native farm or forest for purpose of finding sticks for building or for any other purposes.
- Houses or farms already sold to an Igbo man shall be purchased by the Native Authority who will afterwards resell same to some suitable person.
- Nobody shall trade with Igbos for any thing of value or not.
- All landlords must ask their Igbo tenants to quit before 15 March 1948.
- No Cameroon woman is allowed to communicate with the Igbos in any form.[2]

An even more serious incident occurred in 1966 when a long-standing conflict between the local Bakossi and Bamileke immigrants in the Tombel area ended in a bloody confrontation. The Bamileke, inhabitants of the Francophone part of the Grassfields, are renowned in Cameroon for their mobility and entrepreneurial ethos (Warnier 1993; Tabapssi 1999). They had acquired a great deal of land in the Tombel area, often after having been employed as labourers on the CDC estates in the area and on the cocoa farms of the local peasantry (Levin 1980). After the 1950s, tensions developed between the local population and the Bamileke immigrants. The Bakossi had become jealous of seeing the Bamileke prosper on the land they had acquired in the area at low cost and land disputes erupted. Tensions increased further after the outbreak of the *Union des Populations du Cameroun* (UPC) rebellion in Francophone Cameroon in 1955 (Joseph 1977). The UPC received strong support in the Bamileke area and many Bamileke youths became UPC guerrilla fighters. UPC guerrilla warfare soon affected the Tombel area close to the border between Anglophone and Francophone Cameroon. UPC guerrillas started looting local farms and enterprises and kidnapping or killing any person unfortunate enough to cross their path. The Bakossi accused Bamileke farmers in the area of supporting and protecting their UPC brothers. In 1966, they began to hold meetings, in which Bakossi secret societies and medicine men played a significant role, in order to prepare themselves for an attack on the Bamileke settlers. When they heard on 31 December 1966 that UPC terrorists had killed five Bakossi, they immediately mobilised to take revenge. They, and particularly the Bakossi self-defence units that had been armed by the government to combat guerrilla attacks, went into action, killing no less than 236 Bamileke and setting fire to 181 Bamileke houses (Ngalame 1997; Ejedepang-Koge 1986).

No such incident has occurred since. The simmering conflict between autochthons and allochthons in the southwestern communities, however, continues to provide for explosive material that can easily be manipulated and used by political entrepreneurs.

The growing divide between the South-West and North-West elites in Anglophone Cameroon

In addition to the large-scale migration and settlement of North Westerners in South West Province, the growing divide between the South-West and North-West elites has contributed to the southwestern attack on northwestern strangers during current

---

[2] Letter from Bakweri Native Authority, Buea, to Senior Divisional Officer, Victoria, dated 21 February 1948, in BNA, File PC/h (1948) 1, Conditions of Settlement.

economic and political liberalisation. This divide within the Anglophone elite must be attributed to the South-West elite's perception of increasing political domination of the North-West elite at the regional and national level since the end of the 1950s.

During the nationalist struggle after the Second World War, the Anglophone elite initially demonstrated a large degree of unity. They strongly resented the administration of the Trust Territory of the Southern Cameroons as a mere appendage of Nigeria and eastern Nigerian domination of the Southern Cameroonian economy. They first demanded a larger representation in the Nigerian administration and later regional autonomy. Interestingly, in the late 1940s the question of reunification of Anglophone and Francophone Cameroon cropped up in the programmes of the various Southern Cameroonian political movements and parties, raising the possibility of an alternative political option for the Southern Cameroons to escape from its subordinate position in the British-Nigerian colonial system and Igbo domination (Johnson 1970; Konings 1999a and 1999b).

From the mid-1950s onwards, nationalist leaders in the Southern Cameroons became increasingly divided. Different points of view on the political trajectory of the area tended to be reinforced by personality differences between the major political leaders, Dr Emmanuel Endeley and John Ngu Foncha,[3] and ethno-regional differences within the trust territory.

Endeley, a medical doctor by training, was from the South West, being a son of the Bakweri Paramount Chief at Buea (Geschiere 1993; Konings 1999b). He was the leader of the then-ruling South West-based Kamerun National Convention (KNC) party. Following constitutional changes leading to a growing autonomy of the Southern Cameroons in the Nigerian Federation, Endeley became Leader of Government Business in 1954 and the first Prime Minister of the Southern Cameroons in 1958. He moved from an anti-Nigeria and pro-reunification stand towards a more positive view of Nigeria when the Southern Cameroons became a quasi-region within Nigeria in 1954. His new position was even strengthened when the Southern Cameroons achieved full regional status in 1958. From his perspective, regional status seemed an adequate answer to the problems of Nigerian domination, the lack of Southern Cameroonian participation in the Nigerian political system, and economic stagnation. With regional status, Southern Cameroonians could rule themselves, maintain their ties with the British colonial legacy, and avoid the violence and chaos of the civil war going on in Francophone Cameroon after 1955 when the UPC was banned by the French authorities. Endeley's increasing championship of Southern Cameroonian integration into Nigeria received the tacit approval of the British authorities.

Endeley's opponent, John Ngu Foncha, was a teacher by profession and hailed from the Anglophone part of the Grassfields, present-day North West Province. Foncha had been a leading figure in Endeley's KNC until 1955, when he broke away to form his own party, the North West-based Kamerun National Democratic Party (KNDP). Foncha and his supporters blamed Endeley for no longer adhering to the original KNC pro-gramme of evolutionary reunification of the two Cameroons and for his new pro-

---

[3] For a more detailed description of the lives and views of these outstanding early leaders in the Southern Cameroonian nationalist struggle, see Konings 1999b.

Nigerian stance. While Foncha's political views on the future of the Southern Came-roons were not always consistent, he seems to have mostly crusaded for secession from Nigeria and (eventual) reunification with Francophone Cameroon. Political dissension, however, was not the only reason for Foncha's break with Endeley's party. He also thought that a North West-based party was more likely to represent and defend north-western interests than a South West-based party. Ethnically different from the coastal forest peoples, the Grassfields had been socio-economically disadvantaged during the colonial period through the more extensive development of education, infrastructure, and agro-industrial and other enterprises in South West Province. Furthermore, South-West leaders had a louder voice in political affairs than those from the North West.

With the approaching independence of Nigeria and Francophone Cameroon in 1960, the 1959 elections became a relentless struggle for hegemony between the dominant parties and leaders in the Southern Cameroons. It was generally understood that the victor in these elections would be given a mandate to negotiate the political future of the territory. During the election campaign the KNDP used various strategies to defeat the KNC. First, it attempted to capitalise on the widespread 'Igbo scare' in the Southern Cameroons, an issue that the KNC apparently underestimated. KNDP leaders alleged that a vote for the KNC would mean the integration of the Southern Cameroons into Nigeria and the continuation of Igbo domination. Second, the KNDP attempted to present itself as a regional party, especially when campaigning in the more densely populated and less-developed North West (Ebune 1992).

By employing such strategies, the KNDP was able to win the 1959 elections. On the one hand, its victory was a political event with important consequences for South West-North West relations. While the South-West elite had dominated the political scene in the Southern Cameroons until the 1959 elections, the KNDP's victory signified the start of North-West hegemony in the territory, with Foncha becoming Prime Minister of the Southern Cameroons. Henceforth the North-West elite began to play a dominant politi-cal and economic role in the region. In pre-empting for themselves the choicest jobs and lands in South West Province, they provoked strong resentment among South Western-ers (Kofele-Kale 1981; Ngwane 1994). South-West sentiments have been intensified by the gradual success of entrepreneurial North Westerners in dominating most sectors of South West Province's economy, in particular trade, transport and housing (Rowlands 1993). On the other hand, the KNDP's victory was so narrow, winning 14 out of the 26 seats, that it did not provide Foncha with a clear mandate to start negotiating the politi-cal future of the Southern Cameroons at the United Nations. It was therefore agreed that Endeley should not be left out of these negotiations.

Since Foncha and Endeley proved incapable of resolving their differences on the political future of the Southern Cameroons, the UN General Assembly eventually decided to hold a plebiscite on the issue in the trust territory and more or less imposed the question to be asked. Do you want to achieve independence by joining Nigeria or by reuniting with the Republic of Cameroon (the new name of former French Cameroon after independence on 1 January 1960)?

The plebiscite was to be held on 11 February 1961. In the time preceding the plebiscite the KNDP and the Cameroon Peoples' National Congress (CPNC) – an alliance between Endeley's KNC and another South West-based party, N.N. Mbile's Kamerun Peoples' Party (KPP), with the obvious aim of forming a united front against the KNDP – used similar themes and tactics to win votes as during the 1959 elections. While the KNDP tried to win votes by capitalising on widespread anti-Nigerian feelings and vague sentiments of Cameroonian brotherhood, the CPNC singled out terrorism in the Republic of Cameroon to scare Southern Cameroonians from voting for reunification. The CPNC also tried to impress upon the electorate that reunification would mean a complete change of language, system of government and way of life (Welch 1966; Johnson 1970). Both parties also regularly appealed to ethno-regional sentiments and loyalties. The latter created a great deal of tension between the local population and the Grassfields settlers in South West Province and some southwestern politicians even threatening to expel Grassfielders by force (Chem-Langhëë 1976). CPNC leaders were often barred from campaigning in North West Province. In the end, the KNDP emerged victorious from the plebiscite: 233,571 Southern Cameroonians voted for reunification with the Republic of Cameroon while only 97,741 voted for integration into Nigeria. The ratio of votes for and against reunification with Francophone Cameroon was significantly higher in North West Province (3.5 to 1) than in South West Province (1.5 to 1) (Welch 1966). The results of the plebiscite reinforced the South West-North West divide. The South West elite insisted that the KNDP's victory in South West Province was due to the votes of northwestern workers and settlers there.

Following the plebiscite, a Bakweri cultural society, the Bakweri Molongo, claimed that 'native strangers' had voted for reunification because they wanted to continue dominating the Bakweri.

> Native strangers voted for reunification in the Victoria Division in order to seize the Bakweri lands, and in order to spite and over-run the Bakweri. We, the Bakweri, have voted for Nigeria because the Nigerian Constitution provides safeguards for the minorities which is what the Bakweri are (quoted in Chem-Langhëë 1976: 331).

The CPNC leaders strongly protested to the United Nations about the results that, to them, were very unsatisfactory. They held that ethnic sentiments had played a crucial role in influencing opinion during the plebiscite and called on the United Nations to interpret the results on an ethnic basis. When an ethnic group voted in favour of union with Nigeria or the Republic of Cameroon, it should be allowed to join the country of its choice. Their appeal was rejected, however, and the United Nations accepted the results as they stood.

The South West-North West divide manifested itself again when the Anglophone elite entered into negotiations with the Francophone elite about the creation of a federal state. Foncha headed the multi-party delegation to the constitutional talks held at Foumban from 17 to 21 July 1961 (Konings 1999a). The delegation included many KNDP ministers who were obviously inclined to limit the role of opposition politicians in the deliberations (Ngoh 1990 and 1996). The Anglophone elite proposed a loose form of federation with a large measure of autonomy for the two federated states, which, in their view, would provide for the equal partnership of both parties and the preservation of the cultural heritage and identity of each. The Francophone elite, on the contrary, proposed a highly centralised form of federation that they considered to be merely a transitory phase to the total integration of the Anglophone region into a strong, unitary state. Capitalising on its stronger bargaining position since Francophone Cameroon was much larger and more developed than Anglophone Cameroon and, more importantly, it was already an independent state, the Francophone delegation was able to impose upon the Anglophone delegation its own conception of the future federal state. The consequences of these constitutional arrangements have been dramatic for the Anglophone population. For the latter, nation-building in the post-colonial state has been driven by the firm determination of the Francophone political elite to dominate and exploit the Anglophone minority and to erase the cultural and institutional foundation of Anglophone identity (Mukong 1990; Konings & Nyamnjoh 1997; Eyoh 1998a).

At present, the South-West elite is inclined to indict the North-West elite as co-architects with the Francophone elite of the post-colonial order marked by the blatant recolonisation and marginalisation of the Anglophone territory by the Francophone-dominated state. They point out that northwestern politicians were in control of the Federated State of West Cameroon (the then-named Anglophone Cameroon) during the 1961-1972 period, when multi-partyism and federalism were abolished, accusing them of self-interested betrayal of West Cameroonian autonomy and identity. Eyoh (1998a) rightly observed that this South-West narrative was characterised by an impressive dose of historical amnesia, willed acts of selective remembrance of the past so as to discount the responsibility of the South-West elite in what was a collective elite project.

The South West-North West divide was actually one of the decisive factors preventing the Anglophone elite from forming a united front against President Ahidjo's attempts to weaken the federal structure and undermine the autonomy and identity of West Cameroon. The speed with which the entire Anglophone political elite embraced the single-party concept is clear evidence of their lust for power and influence within the changing power constellation in the federal state (Kofele-Kale 1987).

Contrary to current attempts by the South-West elite to make the North-West elite fully responsible for the Anglophone predicament, Dr Endeley was the first to be converted to Ahidjo's idea of a one-party state. As the leader of West Cameroon's minority party, Endeley saw Ahidjo's plans not only as an opportunity for him to play a role in national politics but also as a means of preventing his party from being dominated by the majority KNDP. Moreover, he was inclined to embrace the one-party state as a way of escape for the South West from northwestern domination (Ngwane 1994). Rivalry among the West Cameroonian leaders provided an excellent opportunity for Ahidjo to dissolve West Cameroon's parties and to create a single party in 1966. The gradual co-optation of the Anglophone political elite into the 'hegemonic alliance' (Bayart 1979) and the autocratic nature of the Ahidjo regime largely explain why they did not resist the abolition of the federation in 1972. To reduce any danger of united Anglophone action against Francophone domination, Ahidjo decided to divide the erstwhile Federated State of West Cameroon into two provinces. This decision, masterfully informed by the internal contradictions within the Anglophone territory between the coastal forest people (South West Province) and the Grassfields people (North West Province), would exacerbate these divisions that in future would serve as the Achilles' heel of most attempts at Anglophone identity and organisation.

The South-West elite's resentment at the continuing North-West domination in their region after the abolition of the federal state is reflected in their struggle for control over the CDC and Pamol. This struggle has often paralysed the CDC's administration and management (Konings 1996b and 1997). Since independence and reunification, the chairman of the CDC Board of Directors has usually been a South Westerner. Prominent South Westerners, like Chief Victor Mukete, Chief Sam Endeley, John Ebong Ngolle and Nerius Nomaso Mbile have all occupied this position. The daily management of the corporation, however, has become increasingly dominated by North Westerners. The appointment of a North Westerner, John Niba Ngu, as the first Cameroonian General Manager of the corporation in 1974 occurred on the advice of the CDC's external financiers but was strongly resented by the southwestern managerial and political elite. First, there were also some suitable southwestern candidates for the post, particularly Isaac Malafa, who used to be senior to Ngu in the corporation's hierarchy, having served as the Deputy General Manager for a couple of years. Second, the southwestern managerial elite feared that Ngu's appointment would reinforce northwestern domination over CDC management. Ngu's fourteen years in office (1974-1988) were marked by strong anti-North West feelings, he himself being regularly accused by the southwestern managerial elite of favouring his own countrymen. Ngu's severe conflicts with two of the southwestern chairmen of the CDC, Chief Victor Mukete and Chief Sam Endeley, have become almost legendary. Following considerable southwestern pressures, Ahidjo's successor to the presidency, Paul Biya, replaced Ngu in 1988 with Peter Mafany Musonge, a Bakweri. Ngu was then appointed Minister of Agriculture, a post that, incidentally, had meanwhile become Supervisory Minister of the CDC. In this capacity, Ngu continued to have influence in the CDC, thus denying his successor total freedom to carry out his duties. The southwestern managerial elite alleged that Ngu was using his brothers among the management staff to pester and remove Musonge. Together with other sections of the southwestern elite, they requested Musonge reduce North-West influence in the corporation.

An even more vehement conflict between the South-West and North-West elites developed in 1987 when Unilever decided to withdraw from plantation activities in Cameroon due to the government's refusal to support Pamol during the severe crisis facing the agro-industrial sector in the 1980s (Konings 1997 and 1998). Unilever then agreed to sell Pamol to a consortium of well-known northwestern businessmen with whom it had come into contact during mediation with the predominantly northwestern management staff. As soon as it became known that both parties had signed a contract, the South-West elite started agitating against the North-West takeover of Pamol, appealing to the state to intervene on their behalf. In a strongly worded petition, they declared categorically that they would never allow their ancestral lands, occupied by Unilever for decades, to be colonised and exploited by North Westerners. They claimed that a North-West takeover of Pamol would inevitably strengthen North-West domination over the South West. They therefore urgently appealed to the state to annul the contract between Unilever and the northwestern consortium and to support an eventual

South-West takeover of Pamol. The effective mobilisation of the regional elite was clearly a decisive factor in the ultimate success of the South-West political offensive. In the face of such a demonstration of unity and determination, the government did not dare to disappoint the South West, an area of vital importance to the national economy in terms of its oil, timber and agricultural resources (Ndzana 1987). When the government finally announced its decision to annul the contract between Unilever and the northwestern consortium, Unilever decided on 13 October 1987 to put the company into voluntary liquidation. Since then the South-West elite has made several attempts to buy Pamol.

Political liberalisation and the aggravation of the autochthony-allochthony issue in South West Province

Political liberalisation in the early 1990s fanned the rivalry between South-West and North-West elites in their struggle for power at the regional and national level. Out of fear of renewed North-West domination, the South-West elite, and especially the section that was closely connected with the regime in power, tried to stimulate South-West identity and organisation, even to the extent of inciting the autochthonous population in South West Province against the allegedly dominant and exploitative northwestern strangers or settlers.

The South-West elite became alarmed when the liberalisation of political space resulted in the rapid growth of both the North West-based opposition party, the Social Democratic Front (SDF), and several Anglophone movements which contested Francophone domination and demanded first a return to the federal state and later outright secession (Konings & Nyamnjoh 1997; Takougang & Krieger 1998). The growing popularity of these organisations immediately raised their suspicions of renewed North-West domination over the South West.

From a South-West point of view, such suspicions were not without foundation. The SDF was clearly a party organised and controlled by the North-West elite. Moreover, although the party, like the former KNDP, enjoyed less popularity among the autochthonous population in the South West than in the North West, it could nevertheless count on massive support from northwestern workers and settlers in the region. In addition, it soon became manifest that the SDF's frequent, and often violent, confrontations with the regime, turning the Anglophone region into a veritable hotbed of rebellion, had the paradoxical effect of advancing the political careers of northwestern politicians. The year 1992 witnessed first the appointment of a North Westerner, Simon Achidi Achu, as Prime Minister in an apparent attempt by the desperate regime to contain the enormous popularity of the SDF in the North West, and later the spectacular performance of the charismatic SDF chairman, John Fru Ndi, in the presidential elections.

Understandably, southwestern memories of northwestern domination in the Federated State of West Cameroon created resistance among the South-West elite against the Anglophone movements' advocacy of a return to a two-state (Anglophone/Francophone) federal arrangement. Furthermore, although South Westerners dominated the leadership of the most important Anglophone associations, the vast majority of its members appeared to be SDF members. Little wonder that the South-West elite was inclined to perceive Anglophone associations as auxiliary organisations of the SDF.

Given their repeated failure to form a party of the same standing as the SDF, the South-West elite started to create regional associations to represent and defend South-West interests. This gave rise to the emergence of the South West Elite Association (SWELA) and the South West Chiefs' Conference (SWCC) (Nyamnjoh & Rowlands 1998; Eyoh 1998b; Konings & Nyamnjoh 1997; Konings 1999b).

SWELA was an attempt to unite all the existing elite associations in the South West into one single organisation. Its leadership continually claimed that SWELA was a non-political pressure group, the main aim of which was to promote South West Province's socio-economic development and cultural revival. The South West was to be restored to its former glory after having been marginalised by the Francophone-dominated state and subjected to 'Grassfields imperialism'. Although the SWELA supported most of the Anglophone grievances about Francophone domination, it equally claimed that the South West had been more disadvantaged than the North West in the post-colonial state. Clearly, fear of renewed North-West domination was one of the underlying motives for its foundation. It came into existence after the launching of the SDF and the latter's subsequent expansion into South West Province. On several occasions, SWELA leaders, especially those closely allied with the ruling regime, issued public statements blaming the SDF for acts of violence and anti-government activities in the South West.

Strikingly, SWELA membership is restricted to citizens belonging to one of the region's autochthonous ethnic groups, a distinction which tended to exclude even second and third-generation immigrants from membership. This exclusion was based upon SWELA members' doubts about immigrants' loyalty to their region of settlement. After having been refused membership, Francophone immigrants subsequently formed an 'Eleventh Province' association. The name Eleventh Province is merely imaginary, as everybody knows that there are only ten provinces in Cameroon but by adopting the name Eleventh Province these immigrants expressed their marginalisation and their feelings of being recognised neither as Francophone nor as Anglophone citizens (Geschiere & Gugler 1998).

Following military brutalities in the South West during the government's 1993 anti-smuggling campaign, a split occurred in SWELA. On the one hand, there were those who maintained close links with the Biya regime and the ruling party, the Cameroon Peoples' Democratic Movement (CPDM), and who often displayed strong anti-north-western sentiments. This so-called Inkatha SWELA was usually viewed as a CPDM appendage and a resurrection of VIKUMA, the propagated Victoria-Kumba-Mamfe alliance in the 1960s to destroy Grassfields domination. They opposed the two-state federal system proposed by the Anglophone movements and championed a ten-state federal system based on the existing ten provinces in Cameroon, which would retain the present separation between South West and North West Provinces, and thus safeguard the former's autonomy. On the other hand there were those who were more critical of government policies and often offered their allegiance to the opposition parties like the

South West-based Liberal Democratic Alliance (LDA) and the North West-based SDF. They advocated closer cooperation between the South-West and North-West elites as a necessary precondition for an effective representation of Anglophone interests, and strongly supported the Anglophone movements' demand for a return to a two-state federal system.

Given the intensification of the power struggles between the South-West and North-West elites during the political liberalisation process, the Biya government found it increasingly lucrative and politically expedient to tempt the peaceful and conciliatory South-West elite away from Anglophone solidarity with strategic appointments and the idea that their real enemy was the unpatriotic, ungrateful and power-mongering North-West elite. The following example illustrates how successful this divide-and-rule tactic was. In September 1993, nine southwestern chiefs travelled to Yaounde to pledge their unalloyed allegiance to President Biya. They told him that they strongly condemned any attempt to partition Cameroon on the basis of Anglophone and Francophone cultures and that they were alarmed at the numerous demonstrations, blackmail, civil disobedience, rebellious attitudes and recurrent activities to destabilise the state and the government, which they particularly attributed to the SDF. They asked the Head of State to transform the present ten provinces into ten autonomous provinces, and drew his attention to the fact that, after reunification, South West Province had been discriminated against in the distribution of strategic posts.[4]

In response to South-West complaints of North-West domination, Biya began to appoint some South Westerners to key positions in their own provinces. For example, Dorothy Njeuma was appointed Vice-Chancellor of the newly created Anglophone University of Buea and Becky Ndive was transferred from Yaounde to head the Cameroon Radio and Television (CRTV) station in South West Province. Nevertheless, South Westerners still felt under-represented in the highest government offices and constantly requested that a South Westerner succeed the North Westerner, Simon Achidi Achu, as Prime Minister. So when, in September 1996, Biya appointed the CDC General Manager, Peter Mafany Musonge, as Prime Minister and maintained more South Westerners than North Westerners in key cabinet positions, "the people...went wild with excitement and jubilation and loudly praised the Head of State" for having at last listened to the cry of despair of South Westerners, who for over thirty-six years had been "confined to the periphery of national politics and socio-economic development". In the words of Musonge himself, this was "the first time in our history as a united nation that a South Westerner has been appointed prime minister", and South Westerners had "to come together to galvanise the second political awakening in South West Province" and "to strengthen our position and bargaining power".[5]

Government divide-and-rule tactics culminated in the 1996 constitution. While the previous (1972) constitution had emphasised national integration and equal rights of all citizens, including the right "to settle in any place and to move about freely", the new constitution promised special state protection for autochthonous minorities (Melone *et*

[4] See *The Herald*, 3-10 November 1993, pp. 1-3.
[5] See 'Significance of P.M. Musonge's Appointment' by a member of the South West, Kome Epule, in *The Star Headlines,* 20 November 1966, p. 5.

al. 1996; Konings & Nyamnjoh 2000). Significantly, it stretched the conventional notion of minorities to such ambiguous proportions that historical minorities like the Anglophones were themselves denied the status of minority, while any ethnic minority group that appeared to distance itself from the opposition could rely on government support. Not unexpectedly, the new constitution tended to boost South-West identity and fuel existing tensions between South Westerners and North Westerners.

The timing of its release was hardly accidental. It was promulgated only a few days before the 21 January 1996 municipal elections. The South-West pro-CPDM elite was shocked when the SDF won most key urban constituencies in their region. South West Province's Governor, Peter Oben Ashu, immediately blamed the settlers, who outnumbered the indigenes in most urban areas of the province, for the poor performance of the CPDM in the urban areas, and on several occasions he, and other members of the southwestern elite, ordered them to return home. Before the elections, Nfon Victor Mukete, the Bafaw Paramount Chief in Kumba, had used Bafaw vigilante groups to intimidate settlers in the Kumba municipal areas not to vote for the SDF. His action would be hailed subsequently by N.N. Mbile, one of the oldest political leaders in South West Province and at that time CDC chairman, at a joint conference of the South-West chiefs and elites in July 1999, and other traditional leaders were urged to emulate him.[6] The South-West elite immediately started demanding state protection for the autochthonous southwestern minority against the dominant and exploitative Grassfielders. Grassfields settlers were likened to scabies, a stubborn skin affliction commonly referred to in Pidgin English as *cam-no-go* (meaning an illness that cannot be cured or a visitor who would not leave). Appeals to the state for protection were often accompanied by threats of ethnic cleansing and the removal of strangers.

Straight after the elections, the government provided the required protection by appointing indigenous CPDM leaders as urban delegates in the municipalities won by the SDF. It is beyond any doubt that the Biya regime also rendered assistance after the municipal elections to the emergence of the so-called Grand Sawa movement,[7] an alignment of the ethnically-related coastal elite in South West Province and neighbouring Francophone Littoral Province on the basis of common feelings of exploitation by Francophone and Anglophone Grassfields settlers (Tatah Mentan 1996; Wang Sonné 1997; Yenshu 1998; Nyamnjoh & Rowlands 1998). This alignment came into being after the indigenous Sawa elite in Douala had staged government-condoned demonstrations against the Francophone Grassfielders, the Bamileke, who alone accounted for 70% of the Douala population, and who had provided for only one indigenous mayor out of the five councils in which they had won the municipal elections on an SDF ticket. The emergence of the Grand Sawa movement signified an important victory for the government in its divide-and-rule tactics. Evidently, it also had a devastating effect on

---

[6] See *The Herald,* 21 July 1999, pp. 1 and 3-4, for a detailed report on the conference held at the University of Buea on 17 July 1999.
[7] The term 'Sawa' was generally employed by natives of Douala who refer to themselves as coastal people. The term was subsequently extended to related coastal people in the Francophone Littoral Province and Anglophone South West Province. Of late, ethnic groups in Littoral and South West Provinces, living at a distance from the coast, have also come to identify themselves as such. See Yenshu 1998.

Anglophone identity and organisation, the Francophone-Anglophone divide becoming cross-cut by alliances that opposed the coastal people, the Grand Sawa, to the so-called Grand West, the alliance between the Anglophone and Francophone Grassfielders constituting the backbone of the major opposition party, the SDF.

To those who sought protection as minorities, the price to pay would increasingly be stated in no uncertain terms: Vote CPDM. This is exactly what the new Prime Minister, Peter Mafany Musonge, and other members of the southwestern elite were telling the people in the region. For example, on 21 March 1997, the Secretary-General of the SWCC, Chief Dr Atem Ebako, appealed to South Westerners to support the ruling party in the forthcoming parliamentary elections:

> Our communities, especially those in Fako and Meme Divisions, are swarmed by Cameroonians from other places and provinces...It is possible to have Cameroonians who are not indigenous to South West Province become representatives of South Western-ers...in local councils, parliament and government. This aspect of the evolution of the political life of South West Province, which became very obvious after the 21 January 1996 municipal elections, is most repulsive, resentful, indignant, and pre-occupying.
> Our choice is clear as we stated in the General Assembly meeting in Kumba on 8 March 1997. We called on all South Westerners and all their friends of voting age without exception to register and vote massively for the candidates of the CPDM party of President Paul Biya at the forthcoming parliamentary elections.[8]

The autochthony-allochthony discourse has not only become an important ploy for political entrepreneurs in their struggles for power. It appears also to have become part and parcel of the people's daily lives in South West Province.

During elections, the southwestern pro-CPDM elites became accustomed either to excluding northwestern settlers from voting in South West Province or to bringing pressure to bear upon them to vote for the CPDM. According to the Cameroon Electoral Code,[9] every citizen may vote in a locality where he has been resident for at least six months or where his name is on the income-tax assessment list for a fifth consecutive year. Despite such rules, northwestern settlers, especially those who were known to be SDF supporters, were frequently barred from voting in their residential area and requested to do so in their region of origin (to find out on arrival that they were supposed to vote in their region of residence). Some southwestern opposition leaders appear to have supported this form of exclusion. For example, the Chairman of the LDA, Njoh Litumbe, stated in 1997 that the Electoral Code should define somebody's home. Such a definition would help clarify where somebody was supposed to vote. In his view, a person's home was where he would be buried.[10] During a meeting of the South-West elite in Limbe in February 1997 it was decided that strangers had to obtain a residence certificate as a precondition for being registered to vote, a decision that settlers immediately condemned as intended to favour the party in power (Yenshu

---

[8] See 'South West Chiefs' Conference on the Plight of South West Province', in *The Pilot Magazine*, May 1997, p. 8.
[9] See Republic of Cameroon, *Cameroon Electoral Code, 1997 Revised Edition*, Yaounde: Les Editions de l'Imprimerie Nationale, 1997.
[10] *The Herald*, 31 March - 1 April 1997, p. 1.

1998). Although this rule was in clear contravention of the Electoral Code, pro-CPDM officials and chiefs, like Governor Peter Oben Ashu and Chief Mukete of Kumba, continued to insist on these permits. Since the appointment of the CDC General Manager, Peter Mafany Musonge, as Prime Minister in 1996, CDC and Pamol workers (the majority of whom are North Westerners and SDF supporters) have been subjected to persistent CPDM pressure to support the new prime minister by voting CPDM. CDC workers were even forced to make compulsory contributions to the CPDM. The CDC senior staff were equally called upon to ensure that their subordinates voted massively for the CPDM so as to maintain Musonge in power. Otherwise they would jeopardise their jobs in the corporation.[11] Traditional secret cults, like Mawu in the Mamfe area and the Nganya juju in the Bakweri area, were used to intimidate northwestern pro-SDF settlers during elections.[12]

The autochthony-allochthony issue is also the subject of continuous discussion in academic circles and in the press. The Anglophone private press, which initially encouraged Anglophone identity and solidarity, has become increasingly split along South West-North West lines. South-West papers, like *The Weekly Post, The Star Headlines* and *The Oracle* have been created to focus on regional issues of interest to South West Province and the SWELA, and to oppose the Grassfielders (both the settlers in South West Province and the autochthons in North West Province). Newer papers, like *The Beacon* and *Fako International,* have been created to attend more specifically to the political ambitions of the Sawa elite and to oppose Grassfields hegemony as a matter of policy. During election periods, the southwestern press sought, through the rhetoric of ethnic cleansing, to solve problems of political representation and to encourage a widespread antagonism of strangers as 'ruthless land grabbers', 'parasites' and 'traitors in the house'. North Westerners used the private press to fight back. In a similar manner, existing papers redefined their editorial focus, while new regional papers sprang up. The sheer volume of diatribes, commentaries, opinions and reports related to the autochthony-allochthony issue in northwestern papers, such as *The Post* and *The Herald,* are an indication of the recent obsession in the Anglophone area with this issue.

The autochthony-allochthony issue has also affected various institutions in South West Province. The Buea Anglophone University is headed by Bakweri who has used all means possible to maintain control over the predominantly northwestern students and lecturers. There is constant talk of Grassfields domination to the detriment of "sons and daughters of the soil".[13] Neither have the CDC and the Catholic Church escaped from the autochthony-allochthony phobia. When southwestern papers like *The Sketch* and *The Weekly Post*, both notorious for their anti-North West attitudes, informed the public that northwestern managers in the CDC had written a memo in which they accused the General Manager, Peter Mafany Musonge, of favouring his Bakweri kinsmen and victimising North Westerners, the Bakweri elite organised a march of shame in support of Musonge. Participants carried spears, machetes, guns and sticks, sang war songs and

---

[11] *Ibid.,* 19-20 March 1997, p. 1.
[12] *Ibid.,* 14-17 March 1996, p. 4.
[13] See, for instance, *The Post,* 18 September 1997, p. 7, referring to the 'Bakweri Mafia', dominating the University of Buea.

displayed placards like "Sack all these North-West managers", "CDC is our own", and so on.[14] The northwestern Catholic bishop of Buea Diocese, Pius Suh Awa, has been frequently charged in recent years with appointing more northwestern than southwestern priests in key positions in his diocese. The South-West Catholic population rebelled in 1996 when the bishop took action against a southwestern priest, Father Etienne Khumba, who had founded a healing church, the so-called Maranatha Movement, which attracted large numbers of Catholics but deviated, according to the bishop, from Catholic liturgical rites (Konings forthcoming). Following the priest's repeated refusal to obey orders, Bishop Awa excommunicated him and suspended his movement. In the 1996-1998 period, the South-West elite brought pressure to bear upon the bishop and regional authorities to leave Father Etienne and his movement alone and Father Etienne's followers regularly occupied the bishop's house and disrupted Catholic church services. After having been frequently warned by the South West Governor that he should obey his bishop's orders and stop his followers' actions, Father Etienne was eventually evicted from his house by security forces in 1998 and removed to North West Province where he was forced to stay in the house of a southwestern bishop.[15]

The autochthony-allochthony issue has exacerbated conflicts about land in local communities. It has even had an impact on marriages. Marriages between South Westerners and North Westerners are increasingly disapproved of, being seen as political and cultural aberrations.

Conclusion

The massive northwestern labour migration and the subsequent dominant northwestern position in the South West form the historical background for understanding the current regional obsession with autochthony and exclusion. Long-standing tensions between the autochthonous population and the northwestern settlers were exacerbated during political liberalisation in the 1990s when the regional pro-CPDM elite and the government began to champion various forms of ethnic cleansing. Obviously, such a strategy served the purpose of achieving or maintaining political power in a period when the Anglophone region was being transformed into a hotbed of opposition to the regime and newly emerging Anglophone organisations were demanding either a return to the federal state or outright secession.

The regional pro-CPDM elite has attempted not only to incite the autochthonous population against the northwestern settlers but also to amplify the differences between the two Anglophone provinces. They accuse the settlers of exploitation, land-grabbing and ingratitude to welcoming indigenes and hold them responsible for all political disturbances in South West Province, even going as far as insinuating that the poor performance at elections by the ruling CPDM and federalist/secessionist tendencies among Anglophones could be attributed wholly to settler opposition. Considering them-

---

[14] See *The Herald*, 21-24 July 1994, p. 3 and *The People's Voice*, May 1994, pp. 1 and 3-8.
[15] See, for instance, *The Oracle*, February-March 1998, pp. 32-35; and *The Herald*, 23-25 June 1998, pp. 1-2.

selves as having suffered greater disadvantage than North Westerners in the distribution of state power, they see more political capital in promoting southwestern identity and solidarity than Anglophone identity and solidarity. They are, therefore, inclined to construe the North-West elite as the greatest menace to the political fortunes of South West Province through a narrative of the post-colonial trajectory that indicts northwestern politicians as accomplices and beneficiaries of southwestern misfortunes.

The government in power has been actively involved in dividing the South-West and North-West elites, culminating in the promulgation of the 1996 constitution that promised state protection to autochthonous minorities. The regime has also encouraged the construction of new ethnic identities, in particular the Grand Sawa movement, an alignment of the ethnically-related coastal elite on the basis of common feelings of exploitation and domination by Grassfields settlers. While the autochthony-allochthony issue has increasingly become commonplace in both the public and private spaces of the South West, it has never been marked by such extreme forms of violence as in some other parts of Africa.

References

All Anglophone Conference 1993, *The Buea Declaration*, Limbe: Nooremac Press.

Amazee, V.B. 1990, 'The "Igbo Scare" in the British Cameroons, c. 1945-61', *Journal of African History* 31: 281-93.

Ardener, E. 1962, *Divorce and Fertility: An African Study*, London: Oxford University Press.

Ardener, E., S. Ardener & W.A. Warmington 1960, *Plantation and Village in the Cameroons*, London: Oxford University Press.

Barbier, J.-C., G. Courade & J. Tissandier 1980, *Complexes Agro-industriels au Cameroun*, Paris: ORSTOM.

Bayart, J.-F. 1979, *L'Etat au Cameroun*, Paris: Presses de la Fondation Nationale des Sciences Politiques.

Chem-Langhëë, B. 1976, 'The Kamerun Plebiscites 1959-1961: Perceptions and Strategies', PhD Thesis, University of British Columbia.

Chilver, E.M. 1971, 'Paramountcy and Protection in the Cameroons: The Bali and the Germans, 1889-1913', in P. Gifford & W.R. Louis (eds), *Britain and Germany in Africa: Imperial Rivalry and Colonial Rule*, New Haven: Yale University Press, pp. 479-511.

Clarence-Smith, W.G. 1989, 'From Plantation to Peasant Production in German Cameroon', in P. Geschiere & P. Konings (eds), *Proceedings/Contributions of the Conference on the Political Economy of Cameroon: Historical Perspectives*, Leiden: African Studies Centre, Research Report no. 35 (2 vols), pp. 483-502.

Courade, G. 1981/82, 'Marginalité Volontaire ou Imposée? Le Cas des Bakweri (Kpe) du Mont Cameroun', *Cahiers ORSTOM, sér.Sci.Hum* 18 (3): 357-88.

DeLancey, M.W. 1973, 'Changes in Social Attitudes and Political Knowledge among Migrants to Plantations in West Cameroon', PhD Thesis, Indiana University.

Ebune, J.B. 1992, *The Growth of Political Parties in Southern Cameroons 1916-1960*, Yaounde: CEPER.

Ejedepang-Koge, S.N. 1986, *The Tradition of a People: Bakossi*, Yaounde: SOPECAM.

Epale, S.J. 1985, *Plantations and Development in Western Cameroon, 1885-1975: A Study in Agrarian Capitalism*, New York: Vantage Press.

Eyoh, D. 1998a, 'Conflicting Narratives of Anglophone Protest and the Politics of Identity in Cameroon', *Journal of Contemporary African Studies* 16 (2): 249-76.

Eyoh, D. 1998b, 'Through the Prism of a Local Tragedy: Political Liberalisation, Regionalism and Elite Struggles for Power in Cameroon', *Africa* 68 (3): 338-59.

Fieldhouse, D.K. 1978, *Unilever Overseas: The Anatomy of a Multinational, 1895-1965*, London: Croom Helm.

Fieldhouse, D.K. 1994, *Merchant Capital and Economic Decolonization: The United Africa Company 1929-1989*, Oxford: Clarendon Press.

Fisiy, C.F. 1992, 'Power and Privilege in the Administration of Law: Land Law Reforms and Social Differentiation in Cameroon', PhD Thesis, University of Leiden.

Geschiere, P. 1993, 'Chiefs and Colonial Rule in Cameroon: Inventing Chieftaincy, French and British Style', *Africa* 63 (2): 151-75.

Geschiere, P. & J. Gugler 1998, 'The Urban-Rural Connection: Changing Issues of Belonging and Identification', *Africa* 68 (3): 309-19.

Geschiere, P. & F.B. Nyamnjoh, 2000, 'Capitalism and Autochthony: The Seesaw of Mobility and Belonging', *Public Culture* 12 (2): 423-25.

Gray, C.J. 1998, 'Cultivating Citizenship through Xenophobia in Gabon, 1960-1995', *Africa Today* 45 (3-4): 389-409.

Gwan, E.A. 1975, 'Types, Processes and Policy Implications of Various Migrations in West Cameroon', PhD Thesis, University of California.

Halldén, E. 1968, *The Culture Policy of the Basel Mission in the Cameroons 1886-1905*, Uppsala: University of Uppsala, Studia Ethnographica Uppsaliensia 31.

Heilman, B. 1998, 'Who Are the Indigenous Tanzanians? Competing Conceptions of Tanzanian Citizenship in the Business Community', *Africa Today* 45 (3-4): 369-87.

Johnson, W.R. 1970, *The Cameroon Federation: Political Integration in a Fragmentary Society*, Princeton: Princeton University Press.

Joseph, R.A. 1977, *Radical Nationalism in Cameroon: Social Origins of the U.P.C. Rebellion*, Oxford: Oxford University Press.

Kaptue, L. 1986, *Travail et Main-d'Oeuvre au Cameroun Sous Régime Français 1916-1952*, Paris: Ed. L'Harmattan.

Kleis, G.W. 1975, 'Network and Ethnicity in an Igbo Migrant Community', PhD Thesis, Michigan State University.

Kofele-Kale, N. 1981, *Tribesmen and Patriots: Political Culture in a Poly-ethnic African State*, Washington D.C.: University Press of America.

Kofele-Kale, N. 1987, 'Class, Status, and Power in Post-reunification Cameroon: The Rise of an Anglophone Bourgeoisie, 1961-1980', in I.L. Markovitz (ed.), *Studies in Power and Class in Africa*, New York/Oxford: Oxford University Press, pp. 135-169.

Konings, P. 1993, *Labour Resistance in Cameroon: Managerial Strategies and Labour Resistance in the Agro-industrial Plantations of the Cameroon Development Corporation*, London: James Currey / Heinemann.

Konings, P. 1996a, 'Le "Problème Anglophone" au Cameroun dans les Années 1990', *Politique Africaine* 62: 25-34.

Konings, P. 1996b, 'Privatisation of Agro-industrial Parastatals and Anglophone Opposition in Cameroon', *Journal of Commonwealth & Comparative Politics* 34 (3): 199-217.

Konings, P. 1997, 'Agro-industry and Regionalism in the South West Province of Cameroon during the National Economic and Political Crisis', in P.N. Nkwi & F.B. Nyamnjoh (eds), *Regional Balance and National Integration in Cameroon: Lessons Learned and the Uncertain Future*, Yaounde: ICASSRT, pp. 289-305.

Konings, P. 1998, *Unilever Estates in Crisis and the Power of Organisations in Cameroon*, Hamburg: LIT Verlag.

Konings, P. 1999a, 'The Anglophone Struggle for Federalism in Cameroon', in L.R. Basta & J. Ibrahim (eds), *Federalism and Decentralization in Africa*, Freiburg: Institut du Fédéralisme, pp. 289-325.

Konings, P. 1999b, 'The "Anglophone problem" and Chieftaincy in Anglophone Cameroon', in E.A.B. van Rouveroy van Nieuwaal & R. van Dijk (eds), *African Chieftaincy in a New Socio-political Landscape*, Hamburg: LIT Verlag, pp. 181-206.

Konings, P. (forthcoming), 'Religious Revival in the Roman Catholic Church and the Autochthony-Allochthony Issue in the South West Province of Cameroon'.

Konings, P. & F.B. Nyamnjoh 1997, 'The Anglophone Problem in Cameroon', *The Journal of Modern African Studies* 35 (2): 207-29.

Konings, P. & F.B. Nyamnjoh. 2000, 'Construction and Deconstruction: Anglophones or Autochtones?' *The African Anthropologist* 7 (1): 5-32.

Levin, M.D. 1980, 'Export Crops and Peasantization: The Bakosi of Cameroon', in M.A. Klein (ed.), *Peasants in Africa: Historical and Contemporary Perspectives*, Beverly Hills/London: Sage Publications, pp. 221-41.

Mamdani, M. 1996, *Citizen and Subject: Contemporary Africa and the Legacy of Late Colonialism*, Princeton: Princeton University Press.

Mathieu, P. & A.M. Tsongo 1998, 'Guerres Paysannes au Nord-Kivu (République Démocratique du Congo), 1937-1994', *Cahiers d'Etudes Africaines* XXXVIII, 150-152: 385-416.
Médard, C. 1996, 'Les "Conflits Ethniques" au Kenya: Une Question de Votes ou de Terres?' *Afrique Contemporaine* 180 (October-December 1996): 62-74.
Meek, C.K. 1957, *Land Tenure and Land Administration in Nigeria and the Cameroons*, London: HMSO.
Melone, S., A. Minkoa She & L. Sindjoun (eds) 1996, *La Réforme Constitutionnelle du 18 Janvier 1996 au Cameroun: Aspects Juridiques et Politiques*, Yaounde: Fondation Friedrich-Ebert/GRAP.
Molua, H.N. 1985, 'The Bakweri Land Problem 1884-1961: A Case Study', MA Thesis, University of Ibadan.
Mukong, A.W. (ed.) 1990, *The Case for the Southern Cameroons*, Uwani-Enugu: Chuka Printing Company Limited.
Mvondo, P.N. 1998, 'Le Régime Foncier Camerounais Face à l'Exigence Constitutionnelle de Préservation des Droits des Populations Autochtones', *Verfassung und Recht in Übersee* 31: 343-70.
Ndongko, W.A. 1975, *Planning for Economic Development in a Federal State: The Case of Cameroon, 1960-1971*, Munich: Weltforum Verlag.
Ndzana, V. Ombe 1987, *Agriculture, Pétrole et Politique au Cameroun: Sortir de la Crise?* Paris: Ed. L'Harmattan.
Ngalame, E.L. 1997, 'Bakossi and their Neighbours: A Study of Conflicts and Co-operation from Precolonial to 1976', Thèse de Doctorat de Troisième Cycle, University of Yaounde.
Ngend, J. 1982, 'Les Plantations de Cannes à Sucre de Mbandjock et Leur Influence Régionale', Thèse de Doctorat de Troisième Cycle, University of Bordeaux.
Ngoh, V.J. 1990, *Constitutional Developments in Southern Cameroons, 1946-1961: From Trusteeship to Independence*, Yaounde: CEPER.
Ngoh, V.J. 1996, *History of Cameroon since 1800*, Limbe: Presbook.
Ngwane, G. 1994, *The Anglophone File*. Limbe: Presbook.
Nyamnjoh, F.B. & M. Rowlands 1998, 'Elite Associations and the Politics of Belonging in Cameroon', *Africa* 68 (3): 320-37.
Ogachi, O. 1999, 'Economic Reform, Political Liberalisation and Economic Ethnic Conflict in Kenya'. *Africa Development* 24 (1-2): 83-107.
Pourtier, R. 1996, 'La Guerre au Kivu: Un Conflit Multidimensionnel', *Afrique Contemporaine* 180 (October-December 1996): 15-38.
Rowlands, M. 1993, 'Accumulation and the Cultural Politics of Identity in the Grassfields', in P. Geschiere & P. Konings (eds), *Itinéraires d'Accumulation au* Cameroun, Paris: Karthala, pp. 71-97.
Rudin, H.R. 1938, *Germans in the Cameroons 1884-1914: A Case Study in Modern Imperialism*, New Haven: Yale University Press.
Rüger, A. 1960, 'Die Entstehung und Lage der Arbeiterklasse unter dem deutschen Kolonialregime in Kamerun (1895-1905)', in H. Stoecker (ed.), *Kamerun unter Deutscher* Kolonialherrschaft, Berlin: Rütten and Loening, pp. 151-242.
Simo, J.A. Mope 1997, 'Land Disputes and the Impact on Disintegration in Contemporary Western Grassfields: Case Study of the Ndop Plain Chiefdoms', in P.N. Nkwi & F.B. Nyamnjoh (eds), *Regional Balance and National Integration in Cameroon: Lessons Learned and the Uncertain Future*, Yaounde: ICASSRT, pp. 225-241.
Socpa, A. 1999, 'L'Hégémonie Ethnique Cyclique au Nord Cameroun', *Africa Development* 24 (1-2): 57-81.
Tabapssi, F.T. 1999, 'Le Modèle Migratoire Bamiléké (Cameroun) et Sa Crise Actuelle: Perspectives Economiques et Culturelles', PhD Thesis, University of Leiden.
Takougang, J. & M. Krieger 1998, *African State and Society in the 1990s: Cameroon's Political Crossroads*, Boulder/Oxford: Westview Press.
Tatah Mentan, E. 1996, 'Constitutionalism, Press, and Factional Politics: Coverage of SAWA Minority Agitations in Cameroon', in S. Melone, A. Minkoa She & L. Sindjoun (eds), *La Réforme Constitutionnelle du 18 Janvier 1996 au Cameroun: Aspects Juridiques et Politiques*, Yaounde: Fondation Friedrich-Ebert/GRAP, pp. 182-98.
Wang Sonnè 1997, 'De la Dynamique de la Qualité d'Autochtone dans la Démocratisation au Cameroun: Cas de la Région de Douala', in D. Zognong & I. Mouiche (eds), *Démocratisation et Rivalités Ethniques au Cameroun*, Yaounde: CIREPE, pp. 179-99.
Warnier, J.-P. 1993, *L'Esprit d'Entreprise au Cameroun*, Paris: Karthala.
Welch, C.E. 1966, *Dream of Unity: Pan-Africanism and Political Unification in West Africa*, Ithaca, N.Y.: Cornell University Press.

Yenshu, E. 1998, 'The Discourse and Politics of Indigenous/Minority Peoples' Rights in Some Metropolitan Areas of Cameroon', *Journal of Applied Social Sciences* 1 (1): 59-76.

12

Population displacement
and the humanitarian aid regime:
The experience of refugees in East Africa

Patricia Daley

Displacement refers to the involuntary movement of people from their homelands often in times of political or environmental crises. This form of mobility has increased over time and space, and at the beginning of the twenty-first century, solutions appear intractable. This chapter traces historically the processes that have contributed to the displacement of people in Africa from the 1960s to the present. The increasingly precarious situation of contemporary refugees is examined through a discussion of the changing nature of the various responses to refugees, from the proliferation of international humanitarian agencies to the growing intolerance of African host societies. Forced migrants are defined and classified through international and national legislation into refugees and internally displaced peoples, and are labelled as problematic. Debates pertaining to notions of home, attachment to place and the construction of identity among displaced communities are explored. Empirical evidence drawn from the experience of Burundi refugees in Central and Eastern Africa is used to exemplify the interactions between global and national forces in shaping the African refugee problem and its solutions.

Introduction

In the latter half of the twentieth century, refugee migration became the dominant form of population mobility. Africa is often portrayed as the continent worse affected by refugees and in the past decade alone some 10 million people have been displaced internally or to neighbouring countries. Most have fled because of conflict-related social disturbance, which ranged from liberation struggles to inter-state and civil wars. While the former types of conflicts have largely ceased, intra-state conflicts have tended to be protracted and endemic, leading in some cases to the militarisation of African societies, state collapse and the existence of long-term refugee communities.

The pattern of distribution of refugees in Africa varies over time and space. Nevertheless, northeastern and central Africa have had a significant proportion of the continent's refugees since the 1960s. A recent feature of forced migration is the large number of people who have become displaced within their countries of origin. African refugees tend to move en masse and remain in the border regions of their countries of asylum. A small but significant group seek asylum further afield, such as in South Africa and Western Europe or are screened for resettlement in North America. Over the past four decades, some refugees have undergone multiple episodes of displacement, like the Angolan refugees who have been shunted back and forth across the border following successive peace agreements and fresh outbreaks of violence. For them, mobility and marginalisation are normative features of life.

This chapter traces historically the processes that have contributed to the displacement of people in Africa from the 1960s to the present. The increasingly precarious situation of contemporary refugees is examined through an exploration of the changing nature of the various responses to refugees, from the proliferation of international humanitarian agencies to the growing intolerance of African host societies. Empirical evidence drawn from the experience of Burundi refugees in central and eastern Africa is used to exemplify the interactions between global and national forces in shaping the African refugee problem and its solutions.

Defining forced migrants in Africa

The perception of population mobility as problematic is primarily a consequence of modernity, with its emphasis on the closed social and cultural entities associated with the territorial boundaries of the nation-state, in which identities are perceived as fixed and outsiders as problematic. While the mechanisms enabling faster and more complex patterns of mobility have increased, the fluidity of previous migrations is now constrained by state structures, be they geographical boundaries such as borders or legislation such as immigration controls and citizenship. In the midst of centrifugal and globalising forces, states persist in their attempts to contain, control and resist the fluidity of population movements. What is significant about contemporary refugee movements in Africa is that states are often powerless to hinder out-migration or influxes as the sheer force of numbers makes border controls irrelevant.

Forced migration is not a recent phenomenon in Africa. Its increasing visibility at the end of the twentieth century was primarily due to the evolution of the United Nations and its representation of refugees as an international humanitarian problem. Newly independent African states, fearful of internal divisions and strife, stressed national security and employed draconian measures to control both citizens and aliens. As hosting refugees was considered a humanitarian act and fostered international legitimacy, refugee-receiving states became the focus of benevolent international attention. Using both national and international legislation, many defined who were refugees and welcomed them. So far, the majority of those fleeing conflicts fall under the United Nations' (UN) and the Organisation of African Unity's (OAU) definition of refugees:

> ... any person who, owing to well-founded fear of being persecuted for reasons of race, religion, nationality, membership of a particular social group or political opinion, is outside the country of his nationality and is unable or, owing to such fear, is unwilling to avail himself of the protection of that country.[1]

Theoretically, this is a narrow definition that fails to take account of the differing forms of displacement producing refugee-like experiences. Although some of these factors were addressed by the 1969 OAU Convention in which the term 'refugee' was also applied to

> ... every person who, owing to external aggression, occupation, foreign domination or events seriously disturbing public order in either part or whole of his country of origin or nationality, is compelled to leave his place of habitual residence in order to seek refuge in another place outside his country of origin or nationality.[2]

At the end of 1999 Africa had an estimated four million refugees officially recognised by the 1951 UN Convention, those who had crossed an international border and there-fore were entitled to legal protection and humanitarian relief from the UNHCR. A further one-and-a-half million people were internally displaced within their countries of origin. Until the close of the twentieth century, the principle of non-interference in the internal affairs of member states, as enshrined in the OAU Charter, meant that those persons who had been internally displaced (IDPs) had little recourse to international protection and relief while remaining within their national territory. An attempt to rectify this legal discrepancy led the United Nations Commission on Human Rights to present, in 1998, its *Guiding Principles on Internal Displacement*, which defined the internally displaced as groups of people

> who have been forced or obliged to leave their homes or places of habitual residence in particular, as a result of, or in order to avoid the effects of, armed conflict, situations of generalised violence, violations of human rights or natural or human-made disasters, and who have not crossed an internationally recognised state border.[3]

These principles allowed for clarification of the category IDPs and for the provision of relief by UNHCR and other UN relief agencies. Theoretically, the differences between IDPs and refugees are purely semantic as they are subjected to similar experiences. International legislation and humanitarian action have combined to construct social categories whose defining features are mobility due to state failure. Such categories have acquired greater visibility and are global in that they transcend national boundaries and operate, through the focus of international aid agencies, in global spaces. Forced

---

[1] Article 1, Definition of the term 'refugee', *1951 Convention Relating to the Status of Refugees* and *1967 Protocol Relating to the Status of Refugees*, United Nations.

[2] Organisation of African Unity, *Convention Governing Specific Aspects of the Problem of Refugees in Africa*, Addis Ababa, 1969.

[3] United Nations (1998) *Guiding Principles on Internal Displacement*, E/CN.4/1998/53/Add.2.

migration thus links the global with the local and it is the interaction within and between these distinct spaces that poses a challenge to how mobility and its problematic are conceptualised in the twenty-first century.

The national policy framework and the practice of assistance

National security appears to be a key factor governing African states' response and treatment of refugees. As refugees often flee political conflict, their communities may include those who have participated in direct political action that was deemed threatening by their countries of origin, and as such are perceived as a security risk to their host states. It is not unusual for refugees to be pursued into exile by the governments of their countries of origin or to form political parties or guerrilla movements in exile. The OAU Charter included the principle of non-interference in the internal affairs of member states and those states hosting refugees have emphasised the humanitarian nature of asylum. The extent to which states have respected such rules depended on the political relationship between the host and the country of origin and on ideological differences or personal rivalry between the leaders.

Most African refugee legislation owes its origins to various colonial laws on the control of aliens. Cold War politics and liberation struggles from white minority regimes were crucial in the framing of the 1969 OAU Refugee Convention and in the degree of international involvement in Africa's refugee problem. Western governments and African states were keen to de-politicise refugees from friendly nations and support and/or arm those from hostile ones. African states enacted their own domestic refugee legislation that, invariably, has tended to be punitive, often confining refugees to designated areas. Border buffer zones were encouraged because camps and settlement schemes were often located over 50 miles from the border and considerable restrictions were imposed on the mobility of refugees. However, until the 1990s, African states were able to exercise control over refugee groups, fearing threats to their own internal security with the possibility of armies invading host countries in pursuit of refugees. States have had some difficulty reconciling the protection of refugees with national security and many states continue to lack the capacity to secure effectively their territories. Instead, they periodically round up individual refugees in urban centres or in particular regions and either forcedly repatriate them (*réfoulement* in international law), or confine them to settlements. *Réfoulement* has become the *de facto* solution to the problem of refugees.

While the legislation relating to refugees has not changed over time, its interpretation has been determined by global political and economic transformations. The UN Refugee Convention proposed three solutions to the refugee crisis: settlement in the first county of asylum, resettlement to a second country, and repatriation. During the Cold War, repatriation was not a solution propagated for refugees unless they were fighting colonial regimes. From the 1960s to the 1970s, settlement in the first country of asylum was the most attractive solution to the UNHCR and some regional governments. It fulfilled two goals. First, it allowed host states to exercise territorial control over refugee groups. Settlements were located in spatially-segregated sites away from the border and managed by the host government. Restrictions were imposed on mobility and access to resources outside settlement boundaries. Attempts were made to de-politicise and settle those refugees from states with no strategic or ideological impor-tance to the superpowers: the principal goal being one of containment in the host society. Indeed refugees were portrayed, on the one hand, as unwitting aid-dependent victims and on the other as a security risk. States pursued a policy of 'integration' in order to minimise the security threat.

Second, land settlement facilitated the promotion of productive, often agricultural activities that would, according to the rhetoric, enable the refugees to become self-sufficient. Conceptually, integrating refugees into the host communities meant that local people would share in the benefits accruing from the international aid investments, thus avoiding disparities in accessibility to material resources and minimising friction between the two groups. For the refugee, settlement and integration meant a shift from holding camps to permanent village communities established by international organisa-tions and run by the host government. Kibreab (1989), drawing on the experience of Eritrean refugees in Sudan, argued that, in practice, integration referred to economic and not political or social integration of refugees into host territories, as planned settlement promoted segregation and marginalisation of refugee communities. He noted a disjunc-ture between integration suggesting permanency and that of a temporary measure. It was assumed by humanitarian agencies that refugees needed only material comfort until they could repatriate voluntarily.

Furthermore, relief agencies had difficulty raising funds to initiate projects on integrated development due to their high capital outlay and the general reduction in humanitarian and development aid from western donors. In addition, UNHCR has often emphasised the 'non-operational' component of its statute, which excludes its direct involvement in development activities. But by the 1980s, it became apparent that self-reliance for refugees was an elusive goal in precarious African environments where the nationals were as susceptible as the refugees to the vagaries of climate, economic crises and political instability. The hand-over of the management of refugee settlements to the host state, where it did finally occur, marked a shift from international to non-existent local aid (Gasarasi 1994). Hand-over was characterised by a collapse of scheme-wide facilities as the local and national states were unable or unwilling to divert a significant portion of their budgets to assist alien refugees. UNHCR was often invited back to maintain the original level of service provision. Despite this, the rhetoric of integration pervaded policy documents till the late 1980s. At best, integration implied the removal of marginality and the extension of citizenship rights. However, under conditions of poverty where social exclusion is being experienced by the majority of citizens, the term integration is of limited value.

In the post-Cold War era, integration has become less fashionable and current strate-gies of containment are aimed at preventing people from crossing the border, as exem-plified in the creation of 'safe havens' and 'protected zones' within their countries of citizenship (Hyndman 1999). However, international and non-governmental organisa-tions (NGOs) find their involvement with IDPs fraught with difficulties as governments are often unwilling to sanction assistance to citizens who they perceive as a threat to the integrity of the state. Such displacement causes social disruption and a decline in productive activities and may lead to an intensification of health-related problems such as malnutrition and higher incidences of disease.

The post-Cold War restructuring of the global political economy led firstly to the reluctance of western governments to become directly involved in local conflicts. Their reaction to the Somalia debacle of 1992 was an emphasis on the training of African forces as regional peacekeepers. Secondly, cuts in aid budgets promoted the involvement of western governments in high-profile emergency aid rather than long-term developmental aid. UNCHR has found it increasingly difficult to meet its budgetary costs and has promoted repatriation as the only viable solution in the twenty-first century. The financial constraints on UNHCR have not prevented the proliferation of humanitarian relief organisations in line with the emergence of neo-liberalism and its anti-state philosophy. Two hundred NGOs were involved in the provision of relief to Rwandan refugees in Zaire (now the Democratic Republic of the Congo) between 1994 and 1996. The rapid increase in the number of NGOs from the 1980s onwards reflects, on the one hand, the undermining of the state in neo-liberal economic policies and, on the other, the limited resource capacity of economically marginal host states. In addition, the involvement of vast numbers of international humanitarian agencies seems to prolong the problems in countries of origin and prevent the search for viable political solutions (de Waal 1997). International agencies thus attempt to capture the politics of supposedly 'de-politicised' refugee communities and negotiate on their behalf. According to Ben Hammouda (2000: 32), "politics escapes the control of citizens and becomes the privileged area of action for the major international bodies". This is exemplified by the experience of displacement from and within Burundi.

Conflict and displacement from Burundi

Forced migration occurs when there is a collapse of the social order, usually during war, or in cases of persecution and marginalisation. Africa has experienced long and protracted wars of liberation as well as civil wars, the latter being the most dominant form of conflict in recent years. Adedeji (1999: 4) noted that at the end of the last millennium, "23% of Sub-Saharan African countries (11 countries) faced political crisis and turbulence while 38% (18 countries) were engaged in armed conflict or civil strife". Conflict in contemporary Africa is often explained as arising from competition for access to scarce resources. In some countries this is inter-penetrated by ethnicity, regionalism and religion. According to Allen (1995 and 1999), African politics in the early post-independence period was characterised by clientelism whereby access to state resources was determined by patronage, through which individuals were rewarded according to their party allegiance or membership of particular social/ethnic groups. Clientelist politics in Africa has been characterised by corruption and social exclusion of, usually, the ethnic or regional 'other'. When crisis ensues, as in the climate of economic depression of the 1980s, it becomes increasingly competitive and violent. Allen contended that such crises have been resolved through the emergence of a 'centralised bureaucratic' regime that transforms the nature of clientelism, as in Kenya. But where the crises remain unresolved, the consequence is often state collapse or 'spoils politics' characterised by "looting of the economy, lack of political mediation, erosion of authority, violent repression, communalism and endemic instability", as evident in countries such as Rwanda, Burundi, Sierra Leone and the Democratic Republic of Congo (Allen 1995: 308).

If 'spoils politics' is characterised by state collapse, the increasing scale of forced displacement points to its growing irrelevance in contemporary Africa as an institution for the protection of rights through citizenship. Displacement is also symptomatic of the failure of citizenship, defined as "a set of clearly defined social practices which dictates the relationship between the citizen and the state" (Ndegwa 1998). Citizenship accords members of a common society specific rights and obligations which should ensure their political, social and economic well-being. Rights are legitimised politically through citizenship. However, "citizenship...is never fixed; as a social process it is constantly changing and simultaneously being enacted, contested, revised and transformed" (Ndegwa 1998). This contestation is marked in societies such as those of Rwanda and Burundi where economic crises and clientelist politics have heightened social and political exclusion, and where the rights of citizenship are contested along ethnic and regional lines (Uvin 1998). Social groups that have been excluded from such societies tend to be the first to be subjected to oppression and forced to seek asylum in neighbouring countries.

Burundi is a landlocked central African country, with a predominantly subsistence economy and few perceptible economic resources. Its population of 6.2 million is divided into two main ethnic groups: an estimated 85% are Hutu and 14% Tutsi. Burundi's average population density of 240 per sq. km is one of the highest in Africa and with only 8% of the population living in urban areas, agriculture constitutes the primary subsistence activity for the majority. Burundi ranks relatively low on any index of human development. Its gross national product (GNP) per capita of US$140 is well below the Sub-Saharan African average of US$480. Its principal source of foreign-exchange earnings has come from the export of traditional crops such as coffee, tea and cotton. However, a decline in the value of export commodities on the world market, especially following the collapse of the International Coffee Agreement in 1992, has meant a reduction in foreign-exchange revenue. Efforts are being made by international financial institutions to diversify the country's economic base and promote the growth of horticultural exports to Europe. Burundi has relied heavily on external aid that peaked at US$312 million in 1992, the year before the second democratic elections in the country's history (World Bank 1999b). Throughout the 1980s, Burundi was the highest per capita recipient of low-interest loans from the IMF and the World Bank. Its international debt now stands at US$1.1 billion, constituting 123% of GDP. Debt servicing in 1998 amounted to US$30m or 58% of the earnings from export goods and services. In the last six years the Burundi economy has contracted by 25% and there has been an 80% increase in poverty in rural areas (World Bank 1999a).

The weakness of its economy and the scarcity of productive resources may partially explain the competitive nature of its politics. For more than 40 years, Burundi has been a theatre of ethnic violence and mass internal displacements as the struggle for power between the Hutu majority and the Tutsi minority became increasingly devastating, both in terms of loss of life and impact on productive activities.

Conflict in Burundi rests with the interconnections of ethnicity and state formation in periods of economic crisis. From the colonial period different interpretations of ethnicity and statehood have been used to justify policies of exclusion and inclusion and claims of legitimacy (Jefremovas 2000). Popular history recounts the Tutsi as traditional rulers who exploited and oppressed the Hutu masses, preventing their social and political advancement. German and later Belgian colonialism helped to accentuate the differences between the two as once-fluid social categories took on primordial meanings and rigid boundaries. Social inequalities were generated through the discriminatory state promotion of the Tutsi elite, be it in access to education, bureaucratic positions or in land-dispute settlements. Tutsi were promoted as colonial intermediaries and in many regions traditional Hutu leaders were replaced by Tutsi. The colonial policy of exclusion of the Hutu majority was given meaning by the promotion of a mythico-historical interpretation of the practice of clientelism in pre-colonial Burundi. In popular mythology, the patron was always Tutsi and the client Hutu. However, the political clientelism, which emerged in late colonial and post-colonial Burundi, excluded the Hutu from being beneficiaries of political patronage. By and large, Tutsi supported and promoted Tutsi, in education, civil service positions and in the military. Members of the Hutu intelligentsia have also been targeted in acts of violence (Reyntjens 1995; Lemarchand 1994). Citizenship rights became meaningful only to the hegemonic Tutsi ethnic group who constituted the modernised urban and political elite.

Since independence, besides a brief period in 1993, power in Burundi has remained in the control of the Tutsi minority. Their justification for holding power has been the fear of a Hutu-led genocide against them, with constant reference to the Rwandan crises of 1959 and 1994 and acts of violence against Tutsi in Burundi (Lemarchand 1995). However, history is contested and Hutu and Tutsi employ "competing and diametrically opposed interpretation of events" (Jefremovas 2000). Each Hutu uprising is interpreted by the Tutsi as an act of genocide and justifies near genocidal reprisals against the Hutu population. Hutu, who see themselves as the indigenous Bantu people, claim ownership of the land and promote a 'mythical history' that externalises the Tutsi by representing them as pastoralists from north-east Africa (Malkki 1995b). Similarly, successful Tutsi-dominated Burundi governments have used the Hutu threat to exclude the Hutu population from prominent roles in the political and economic spheres of the state. Besides the ethnic groups themselves, lack any form of internal cohesion and factionalism within both the Hutu and Tutsi political elites have aggravated conflicts (Prunier 1995a). Peace negotiations have been marred by the inability to bring all factions around the negotiating table (International Crisis Group 1999).

Within the country, the impact of modernisation has been socially and geographically unequal. In a situation of high population density, where agriculture is the main livelihood strategy of 90% of the population, land accessibility is of critical importance and a cause of intense conflict. Many commentators attribute the uprisings of Hutu peasants to conflicts over land or discriminatory coffee-pricing policies. It is not unusual to hear Hutu claims that the wealth generated by their labour is being used to support the non-productive urbanised Tutsi minority that controls the state. Whilst members of the political elite may manipulate conflicts along ethnic lines, the intensity of the violence, however, has profound roots in the economic marginalisation of the majority Hutu population.

Since 1966 Burundi has experienced periodic ethnic-related violence leading to persistent displacement and out-migration. The largest displacement took place in 1972 after near genocidal attacks against the Hutu causing the death of an estimated 200,000 people and the flight of an estimated 200,000 to neighbouring states. Renewed ethnic clashes led to a further exodus of some 60,000 refugees in 1988 and 40,000 more in 1991. On 21 October 1993, violence erupted following an army coup and the assassination of the first democratically elected Hutu president, Melchior Ndadaye, six months after he took up office. An estimated 700,000 refugees fled the country: 250,000 to Tanzania, 60,000 to Zaire and 400,000 to Rwanda. Since the mid-1990s Burundi has been subjected to continued political instability, activated by the death of Ndadaye's successor, Cyprien Ntaryamira, in a plane crash in Kigali on 6 April 1994 which also killed the Rwandan president, and a military coup in 1996 which put the Tutsi back in power. The civilian population has been subjected to a situation of low-intensity warfare waged by the exclusively Tutsi military and Hutu and Tutsi militias. Insurgency attacks by Hutu guerrilla movements and reprisals by the Tutsi military have created a climate of fear and impunity. Two hundred thousand people have been killed in conflicts since 1993, and a further 300,000 have fled to neighbouring countries (Amnesty International 1999).

Processes of exclusion have become more acute in Burundi where the state has begun to use forced displacement as a mechanism of control over potentially rebellious populations. Since 1996 the state has adopted a policy of forced relocation, sometimes known as villagisation or *regroupement*. An estimated 12% of the Hutu population, some 600,000 people, have been forcibly displaced into 312 camps under the supervision of the military. While the strategy may hinder collusion between the Hutu civilian population and the Hutu militias, it has done little to reduce the scale of insurgency. Instead it has contributed to economic collapse and violated the human rights of the Hutu population (Human Rights Watch 1998). Productive activities have declined and the economy has seen negative growth aggravated by a reduction in international aid and two years of sanctions by its East African neighbours. From the mid-1990s Burundi's population has been living under a siege situation, whilst general insecurity in the country has limited the provision of humanitarian assistance.

The refugee experience

Burundi refugees' experiences of exile vary considerable between host countries but are characterised by mistrust, geographical isolation, and social and political exclusion.

Map 12.1: Burundi refugee camps in Tanzania

They have experienced a vulnerable existence in camps and settlements due to the unwillingness of host societies to assimilate or integrate them. As a consequence, the long-term survival of their communities has been dependent on inputs from international aid organisations.

For the past twenty-nine years the Barundi have formed a major refugee community in East Africa, especially in Tanzania (see Map 12.1) where they now number around 400,000. The earliest arrivals relied on kinship ties in adjacent border regions for material support. A significant proportion of the 1972 cohort escaped registration by moving directly to live with relatives, especially those with some familiarity with the territory. An estimated 22,000 Barundi refugees settled throughout the border villages in Kigoma, Kasulu and Kibondo Districts (Lugusha 1980). Having similar cultural identities with the local Waha, the state and humanitarian agencies had difficulty distinguishing between them and the Tanzanian villagers.

However, the majority were drawn under the humanitarian umbrella and placed initially in transit camps. From 1973 to 1980 the dominant policy was to separate the refugees from their cause, and provide agricultural resources so that they could become self-sufficient in food. Whether for security or social and economic reasons, the result was the concentration of an estimated 82% of the 1972 cohort into eight settlement schemes. Between 1972 and 1985, the Tanzanian state was able to exercise considerable control over the Burundi refugees, and guerrilla incursions into Burundi were infrequent and largely contained by Tanzanian security. Refugees were not allowed to leave the settlement for any reason without the permission of the government authority. However, this did not prevent refugees from forming armed opposition groups like PALIPEHUTU.

The literature on refugee settlement schemes in East Africa has focused on the productivity of refugee communities and has dispelled the myth that refugees are necessarily a burden on their hosts. Daley (1993) has shown that the refugees in Rukwa region have made a significant contribution to the growth of the region as one of the major food-producing areas of Tanzania. Refugee schemes were relatively successful but in Tanzania their enormous size (the settlement of Mishamo is the size of the island of Zanzibar) created isolationism and resentment by locals because of the immense concentration of aid.

After 1985, changes in the political leadership in Tanzania and widespread economic crisis throughout the continent, coupled with financial pressure on UNHCR, contributed to a growing unwillingness of the state to accept refugee groups, and emerging xenophobia among the indigenous population. Consequently, the Burundi and Rwandan refugee cohorts of the 1990s found themselves confined to temporary holding camps. The 1998 Tanzanian Refugee Act empowered local authorities to force all refugees, even those long-settled in local villages, to relocate to camps. UNHCR, which has been reluctant to commit resources to the long-term maintenance of refugee populations, has promoted the most durable solution of repatriation.

This level of state control altered with the 1994 influx of genocidists and military personnel from Rwanda as part of the refugee population and the inability of the UN or the local state to administer the camps. Refugees from the Habyarimana's regime were able to move, with their weapons, into Zaire and Tanzania (*Tanzania Daily News* 1995;

Prunier 1995b). The Tanzanian state, weakened by political and economic liberalisation, lacked the resources to disarm the refugees and their plea to the international community for military assistance received only limited support. The Burundi state has been subjected to rebel attacks from within its territory and from bases in neighbouring Tanzania and the Democratic Republic of Congo. Tanzania has been accused of training and harbouring rebels, justifying the Burundi military's frequent cross-border raids in pursuit of them. The difficulty of policing the camps for the cohort of Rwandan and Burundi refugees has forced Tanzania to close its borders (as in March 1995), to forcedly repatriate refugees (as in December 1996) and to enact a refugee law with draconian controls over the movement of refugees. The closure of the border, however, appeared to have been a political gesture as refugees continued to cross unimpeded.

Internal displacement leaves refugee groups at the mercy of the state. In Burundi, the military has not been averse to raiding camps set up for displaced people, such as occurred at Mugano in 1996 when 15,000 fled to Tanzania (Prunier 1996). Displaced people have been subjected to forced labour and other forms of human rights violations by the Tutsi military (Human Rights Watch 1998).

The Rwandan and Burundi refugee crisis of the mid-1990s helped to transform the attitude of host states and the international humanitarian regime. States, particularly Tanzania, lost control of refugee populations in that they lacked the resources to disarm combatants and militias who fled with the refugee population into exile, and had to surrender control over the distribution of relief to some twenty or more international humanitarian organisations operating in the camps. This was partly due to the economic and political liberalisation that swept the continent. Host populations became more critical of the diversion of scarce resources to refugees and jealous of the vast inputs of international aid that accompanied each refugee community. Concerns were also expressed at the environmental and economic costs of hosting refugees. The emergence of competitive politics in Tanzania has led to contestations over citizenship and has also contributed to the use of refugees as scapegoats by political parties. Increasingly, repatriation is perceived as the only solution to the refugee problem in Tanzania.

Repatriation

Repatriation implies a return to one's homeland and former lifestyle. It is perceived as a durable solution and is encouraged by UNHCR as the most desirable outcome benefiting all parties, enabling them to rid themselves of the burden of refugees, and for the refugees themselves it is the chance to return home. In the past, refugees repatriated voluntarily, often after political change in their country of origin. But, in recent years, a transformation in politics has not been seen as a pre-condition for promoting repatriation, and the discourse now includes the more euphemistic term 'organised' repatriation which, in effect, is involuntary.

However, for many refugees, repatriation is often another form of displacement, as long-settled refugees become uprooted from the transitional place of the settlement, to which they may have developed some attachment and sense of belonging. Hammond

(1999) and Malkki (1995a) challenge the discourse of repatriation that sees a return to 'birthplace' as the natural order of things. Such views ignore the social and economic transformations that may have taken place in exile refugee communities as a consequence of having to adapt to new situations and the difficulty this may pose for reintegration into their homeland.

Many refugees have been uprooted from semi-permanent exile communities and returned to their homelands but not to their home. This has had implications for access to economic resources, in particular land and employment. While humanitarian agencies have attempted to address the difficult circumstances that returnees find themselves in, there is very little evidence to suggest that rehabilitation and reconstruction programmes have helped to integrate returning peasant communities successfully. Policies aimed at integrating returnees into their home societies tend to ignore the structural constraints that perpetuate marginalisation.

The current desirability of repatriation has led to rash programmes while the political situation remained fluid and unstable. The recent history of repatriation to Burundi in the 1980s and in 1992 prior to the democratic elections of 1993 and the proposed repatriation of 2000 suggest considerable disregard for the predicament of returnees (Amnesty International 2000). Throughout the 1990s, returnees to Burundi have been targeted by the security forces and their exile used as evidence of support for the opposition (Amnesty International 1996 and 2000). Reports of disappearances and summary executions of returnees have been widespread. Such dislocations could only intensify feelings of marginalisation.

While forced repatriation is discouraged by international humanitarian organisations such as UNHCR, they, nevertheless, appear powerless to prevent it and may even give tacit approval as in the case of the repatriation of Rwandans from Tanzania and Zaire in December 1996. Refugees are not empowered by the assistance given to them by international organisations, instead, aid serves to reinforce their marginality, constructing them as dependent and existing outside the norms of society (Zetter 1991).

Refugee identities in national and globalised spaces

Among refugee groups, identities are in a constant state of flux. Such migrants move, adopt and reassert specific identities according to historical moments and across space. Refugees, notably those in camps, are subjected to the essentialising policies of humanitarian aid providers who, in their own interests, often portray all refugees as victims: destitute and dependent. Such acts of labelling tend to result in identity construction as forced migrants imagine or perform prescriptive identities at critical moments, especially when under surveillance as in camp situations.

In camps and in popular discourse, refugees are an undifferentiated mass. Failure to acknowledge differences within refugee communities has resulted in aid agencies reinforcing gender subordination, while regional differences can lead to the misappropriation of resources and the collapse of the humanitarian mandate (Pottier 1996). Hyndman (1997) noted how the spaces of mobility among Somali refugees in Kenya in relation to access to food, medicine and the needs of citizenship were gendered, with women having the most difficulty negotiating these spaces. As research emphasises the heterogeneity of refugee groups and the implications of diversity for service provision, attempts have been made to unravel the multiplicity of identities that seemingly homogenous groups such as the Burundi Hutu refugees might possess. Apart from age and gender differences, refugees are differentiated according to class, regional origin, party and religious affiliation. For some refugee communities, displacement and camp life may result in the strengthening of particular identities. For the Burundi refugees, marginalisation in camps led to the reassertion of the Hutu ethnic identity and the formulation of forms of ethnic consciousness, ethnic politics and historical revisionism. Massey (1999) theorised people's connection to place by showing how the sense of place is created, manipulated and used to sustain individual and collective identities. Malkki (1995a), from her research among Burundi refugees in Tanzania, contended that the Hutu in camps had developed a mythical history which simplified Burundi's history and ethnic politics, and served to elevate their suffering and martyrdom. Those Hutu, who settled in villages, were less likely to interpret their situation along ethnic lines. Camps became sites of resistance, and the longer the refugees remained in them the more likely they were to develop separatist ideologies. Malkki's emphasis on a politicised ethnic identity ignores the other forms of identification that Hutu in camps employed. Religious identity, particularly Christian fundamentalism, transcended regional and gender differences to unite and divide the communities. Migration and settlement into new cultural settings can create spaces of social mobility and empower-ment for the formerly marginalised or subordinated, as Turner (1999: 9) found among young men in the Tanzanian camps, whose youth and adaptability enabled them to "grab hold of the liberating aspects of liminality rather then being paralysed by its dis-integrating side" thus challenging and overturning pre-migration authority structures. Similarly, the all-encompassing refugee identity was deployed at critical moments in aid provisioning.

The burgeoning literature on identity construction and refugee experience while asserting hybridity among refugees also questions the dominance of place-based identities in the discourse of conflict resolution, humanitarian interventions and refugee studies (Malkki 1992; Hammond 1999). Here the argument is that, in the era of global-isation, fixed identities should not be over-emphasised, as the process of mobility will lead to the eradication of difference. Kibreab (1999) challenged the assumptions of de-territorialised refugee communities, emphasising the continued attachment to place within a supposedly globalising world. Homeland and people's attachment to territory become significant in situations where, as in many African countries, democratic transi-tions and contested elections have led to the exclusion of alien communities and even of some citizens. At the same time that refugee problems are receiving global exposure and are being confronted by agents with universal agendas and prescriptions, refugees are re-emphasising the significance of territorially-based identities and are embarking on wars to return them to place. Territorial identities are critical in an economic and cultural context where, according to Kibreab (1999: 387), "rights of access to, and use of resources of livelihood are still apportioned on the basis of territorially anchored identity". For him, the significance of a territorialised identity has never been greater, as "there can be no de-territorialised identity in a territorialised space".

As the period of asylum becomes increasing extenuated, many refugee communities form trans-national communities and diaspora without losing links to place. While difference is increasingly emphasized in the academic discourse on refugees, the actions of progressive refugee groups still indicate that for conflict resolution to be meaningful within the existing boundaries of strife-torn states, collective identities which transcend ethnic, regional, class and gender differences have to be constructed. An interesting development with respect to this is the emergence of a transnational identity among the Burundi refugee diaspora that subscribes to the internet site *Burundinet*. Kadende-Kaiser and Kaiser (1998) noted the emergence of a citizenship that transcends the narrow sub-national ethnic politics of Burundi. *Burundinet*, they contend, provides a forum that allows feelings of regionalism, nationalism and transnationalism to surface in lieu of the exclusive emphasis on ethnicity that characterises Burundi's domestic politics. *Burundinet* recognises that people have multiple identities and its members promote national unity and national identity as opposed to difference. Here a perceived commonality is essential in defining citizenship and the rights and obligations normally associated with this status.

Conclusion

The plight of African refugees is bound up with transformations in economics and politics at the global and national scale. The beginning of the twenty-first century has witnessed a negation of the concept of asylum in Africa and elsewhere, particularly in the developed world. This is taking place at a time when the magnitude of the flow of refugees appears to be getting greater. Western donors have attached the label 'complex political emergencies' to conflicts in order to justify their intractability and irresolvability. The most common solution at present is political reform through multi-party elections and power sharing, which appears to exclude the masses from participating in the democratic process.

Displacement is closely associated with social exclusion as economic crises can reduce the capacity for patronage in clientelist politics leading to social collapse and conflict. Whether the permanent return of refugees is desirable or not, it is unlikely to succeed without programmes aimed at reconstruction and transformation in the economic structures of home countries. And they should be unlike the structural adjustment programmes of the 1980s, which have intensified the struggle over resources, aggravated social inequalities and exacerbated displacement. The example of Burundi refugees is used to illustrate the social disruption that can occur in a society whose existence is predicated on perpetual exclusion and displacement of a significant proportion of its population, whether at home or in exile. The practice of more inclusive politics, with clearly defined and protected rights of citizenship, would reduce the perceived security threat to ruling elites and states. In the post-Cold War global economy, western and African nations, rather than pandering to fears of xenophobia, should be more pro-active in promoting more inclusive politics. Certainly the growth in refugee migration and the intractability of associated political situations leave many refugees and displaced peoples in liminal or transitional spaces, where aspects of life may be suspended indefinitely (Mbembe 1999). Through this process of alienation, new communities are formed and new identities forged. It should, therefore, be of concern that the workings of the international humanitarian regime serve, inadvertently, to deny human agency to African refugee communities and contribute to an intensification and perpetuation of the refugee condition. As a consequence, 'refugeehood' serves to accentuate marginalisation and intensify politicised identities, thus raising the possibility of future conflict. Finally, a possible outcome of the current resurgence of effort towards greater regional cooperation in Africa would be the development of a more tolerant approach to population mobility and settlement.

References

Adedeji, A. 1999, *Comprehending and Mastering African Conflicts: The Search for Sustainable Peace and Good Governance*, London: Zed books Ltd.

Allen, C. 1995, 'Understanding African Politics', *Review of African Political Economy* 65: 301-20.

Allen, C. 1999, 'Ending Endemic Violence: Limits to Conflict Resolution in Africa', *Review of African Political Economy* 81: 317-22.

Amnesty International 1996, *Refugees Forced Back to Danger*, London: Amnesty International.

Amnesty International 1999, *Annual Report: Burundi*, London: Amnesty International.

Amnesty International 2000, *Great Lakes Region: Refugees Denied Protection*, London: Amnesty International.

Ben Hammouda, H. 2000, 'Perspectives on Globalisation and its Structure', *CODESRIA Bulletin* 1: 31-38.

Daily News (Tanzania), 25 October 1995, 'Tanzania Seeks to Separate Refugees'.

Daley, P. 1993, 'From the *Kipande* to the *Kibali*: The Incorporation of Refugees and Labour Migrants in Western Tanzania, 1900-1987', in R. Black & V. Robinson (eds), *Geography and Refugees: Patterns and Processes of Change*, London: Belhaven, pp. 17-32.

de Waal, A. 1997, *Famine Crimes: Politics and the Disaster Relief Industry*, Oxford: James Currey.

Gasarasi, C.P. 1994, *The Tripartite Approach to the Resettlement and Integration of Rural Refugees in Tanzania*, Uppsala: The Scandinavian Institute of African Studies, Research Report 71.

Government of Tanzania 1998, *Refugee Act, 1998*, Dar es Salaam: Government Printer.

Hammond, L. 1999, 'Examining the Discourse of Repatriation: Towards a More Pro-active Theory of Return Migration', in R. Black & K. Koser (eds), *The End of the Refugee Cycle: Refugee Repatriation and Reconstruction*, Oxford: Berghahn Books.

Human Rights Watch 1998, *Proxy Targets: Civilians in the War in Burundi*, New York: Human Rights Watch.

Hyndman, J. 1997, 'UN Assistance to Refugees and the Politics of Mobility', in J. Fairhurst, I. Booysen & P. Hattingh (eds), *Migration and Gender: Place, Times and People Specific*, Pretoria: University of Pretoria, Department of Geography & International Geographical Union, pp. 117-28.

Hyndman, J. 1999, 'A Post Cold-War Geography of Forced Migration in Kenya and Somalia', *Professional Geographer* 5 (1): 104-14.

International Crisis Group 1999, *Burundi: Internal and Regional Implications of the Suspension of Sanctions*, Brussels: International Crisis Group.

Jefremovas, V. 2000, 'Treacherous Waters: The Politics of History and Politics of Genocide in Rwanda and Burundi', *Africa* 20 (2): 298-308.

Kadende-Kaiser, R. & P.J. Kaiser 1998, 'Identity, Citizenship and Transnationalism: Ismailis in Tanzania and Burundians in the Diaspora', *Africa Today* 45 (3/4): 461-80.

Kibreab, G. 1989, 'Local Settlements in Africa: A Misconceived Option?', *Journal of Refugee Studies* 2 (4): 468-90.

Kibreab, G. 1999, 'Revisiting the Debate on People, Place, Identity and Displacement', *Journal of Refugee Studies* 12 (4): 384-410.

Lemarchand, R. 1994, *Burundi: Ethnocide as Discourse and Practice*, Cambridge: Woodrow Wilson Center Press & Cambridge University Press.

Lugusha, E. 1980, *A Preliminary Report of a Socio-economic Survey of Spontaneously Settled Refugees in Kigoma Region*, Dar es Salaam: University of Dar es Salaam, Department of Sociology.

Malkki, L.H. 1992, 'National Geographic: The Rooting of Peoples and the Territorialization of National Identity among Scholars and Refugees', *Cultural Anthropology* 7: 24-44.

Malkki, L.H. 1995a, 'Refugees and Exile: "Refugee Studies" to the National Order of Things', *Annual Revue of Anthropology* 24: 495-523.

Malkki, L.H. 1995b, *Purity and Exile: Violence, Memory, and the National Cosmology among Hutu Refugees in Tanzania*, Chicago: University of Chicago Press.

Massey, D. 1997, 'A Global Sense of Place', in T. Barnes & D. Gregory (eds), *Reading Human Geography: The Poetics and Politics of Inquiry*, London: Arnold, pp. 315-23.

Massey, D. 1999, 'Spaces of Politics', in D. Massey, J. Allen & P. Sarre (eds), *Human Geography Today*, London: Polity, pp. 279-94.

Mbembe, A. 1999, 'At the Edge of the World: Boundaries, Territoriality and Sovereignty in Africa', *CODESRIA Bulletin* 3-4: 4-16.

Ndegwa, S.N. 1998, 'Citizenship Amid Economic and Political Change in Kenya', *Africa Today* 45 (3-4): 351-68.

Pottier, J. 1996, 'Why Aid Agencies Need Better Understanding of the Communities They Assist: The Experience of Food Aid in Rwandan Refugee Camps', *Disasters* 20 (4): 324-37.

Prunier, G. 1995a, *Burundi: Descent into Chaos or Manageable Crisis*. http://www.unhcr.ch/refworld/refworld/country/writenet/menu.htm

Prunier, G. 1995b, *The Rwanda Crisis 1959-1994: History of a Genocide*, London: Hurst & Co.

Prunier, G. 1996, *Burundi: Update to Early February 1996*. http://www.unhcr.ch/refworld/refworld/country/writenet/menu.htm

Reyntjens, F. 1995, *Burundi: Breaking the Cycle of Violence*, London: Minority Rights Group.

Turner, S. 1999, 'Angry Young Men in Camps: Gender, Age and Class Relations among Burundian Refugees in Tanzania', Geneva: UNHCR, *New Issues in Refugee Research*, Working Paper No. 9.

Uvin, P. 1998, *Aiding Violence: The Development Enterprise in Rwanda*, West Hartford, Con.: Kumarian Press.

World Bank 1999a, *Burundi Country Profile*. http://www.worldbank.org/afr/bi2.htm

World Bank 1999b, *Entering the 21st Century: World Development Report 1999/2000*, Oxford: Oxford University Press.

Zetter, R. 1991, 'Labelling Refugees: Forming and Transforming a Bureaucratic Identity', *Journal of Refugee Studies* 4: 39-62.